The Economic Consequences
of Democracy

How small, of all that human hearts endure,
That part which laws or kings can cause or cure!
Still to ourselves in every place consigned,
Our own felicity we make or find.

Samuel Johnson, lines added to Goldsmith's Traveller

SAMUEL BRITTAN

The Economic Consequences of Democracy

Second Edition

WILDWOOD HOUSE

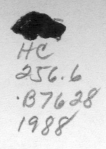
© Samuel Brittan 1977, 1988

First published in 1977 by
Maurice Temple Smith Ltd

Second edition published in 1988 by
Wildwood House Ltd
Gower House
Croft Road
Aldershot
Hants GU11 3HR
England

and distributed in the United States by
Gower Publishing Company
Old Post Road
Brookfield
Vermont 05036
USA

British Library Cataloguing in Publication Data
Brittan, Samuel
 The economic consequences of democracy
 —— 2nd ed.
 1. Great Britain —— Economic policy
 —— 1945 -
 I. Title
 330.941′0857   HC256.6

ISBN 0-7045-0570-3 Pbk

Printed and bound in Great Britain by
Biddles Limited, Guildford and King's Lynn

Contents

List of Figures

List of Tables

Preface to the Second Editon

The essays and shorter pieces in this book were mostly written in the early and middle 1970s; but basic issues do not change all that quickly, and there have been some requests for a new edition.

As the title suggests, the main theme is the economic strains that threaten the liberal democratic system. These arise from excessive expectations about the possibilities of political action and the disruptive effects of the interest groups and pressure groups, which liberal democracy must permit, but which undermine its effectiveness. These strains are at least as prevalent in dictatorships and totalitarian systems, but their expression and form are different; and their results are to be found in coups, concentration camps, cemeteries and interrogation cells. All known alternatives to liberal democracy are far worse; but, to preserve it, we will need to explore ideas regarded as politically impossible by exponents of the adversarial British system.

At the mundane level of economic management, too many critics of recent policies want to react against the errors of the 1980s by going back to the earlier errors of the 1970s. Part I may serve as a reminder of where that route leads. The automatic rules with which I desired to constrain policy-makers have proved more elusive than I had hoped. But the need to combine a long-term framework, with day-to-day discretion, remains; and further thoughts on the matter are to be found in the later, but companion, volume *The Role and Limits of Government*.

Part II deals with all too topical topics, such as the call for an 'industrial strategy' in which government and industry would combine to defeat foreign competition. This view of trade as a form of international warfare has its historical roots in Fascist thinking, even though the call often comes now from the middle of the political spectrum, or from supposedly non-ideological businessmen. Part III is an introduction to the roots of British unemployment in the malfunctioning of the labour market. The Thatcherite years have not dissipated wishful thinking on the role of monopolistic trade unions, or of muddled businessmen who boast about their small, but well-paid, labour forces.

The section of the book which has attracted most comment is however Part IV, *Economics and Democracy,* and especially Chapter 23, *The Politics of Excessive Expectations,* which is devoted to the economic strains on liberal democracy. I have therefore inserted in this new edition a follow-up essay, written not long afterwards, entitled *Inflation and Democracy.* Here I suggested that inflation would lose its power even as a temporary solvent for tension, but that this would make the underlying problems more visible and more difficult.

I would also like to draw attention to another essay in Part IV, *What's Wrong with Economics,* which discusses the disrepute into which the subject has fallen through its mistaken identification with 'the forecasting delusion'.

The suggestions for constitutional reform in Chapter 25 – including electoral reform – are now quite fashionable among parties out of office. But they are usually advanced for naively populist reasons, and I try to put forward more convincing arguments which treat majority voting as a convenient decision rule rather than as a fundamental principle of political morality.

The underlying political economy on which this and all my other recent books are based is to be found in a book originally entitled *Capitalism and the Permissive Society,* first published in 1973, now being reissued by Macmillan under the title *A Restatement of Economic Liberalism.*

Samuel Brittan, October 1987

Acknowledgements

Too many people have helped me with information and advice on subjects related to this book for it to be feasible to mention them all. But there is one person whose name I must single out specially. Without the editorial assistance of Peter Riddell, this book could not have appeared. It was he who first sorted out the mass of material in a form suitable for a single volume; and the grouping of subjects derives from his original suggestions. He largely compiled the Calendar of Events and, without any commitment to their content, helped edit a few of the sections of Part I.

The list of acknowledgements that follows serves the double purpose of thanking various journals for permission to republish and of indicating the original sources of the various chapters. Where no individual acknowledgement is given for a dated article, it can be assumed that it is entirely or mainly compiled from a contribution to the *Financial Times,* to the editor and management of which I am particularly grateful.

The citing of the date in a sub-heaing indicates that the passage that follows is taken directly from an article or articles published at that time. Sometimes a broad date span is given, e.g. 'March to June 1973'. This usually indicates that the section has been compiled from more than one article taken from the period in question. In the case of the longer journal articles, where there is normally a substantial lag before publication, the date of *composition* is given. In some cases extra passages in square brackets have been put in to explain the context. Undated sections were compiled specially for this volume, but sometimes incorporate and adapt earlier material. Many of the titles are retained from the original articles, but I have felt free to change them in the interests of clarity – or, more often, to take the title of one article for a chapter compiled out of several. The references given at the end of some chapters to other authors are not intended to be a complete bibliography; they cover words cited in the chapter in question, or which helped to spark it off.

The word 'billion' has been used in the sense of 'thousand million' throughout the text that follows.

Sources

Chapter 1, 'Some Governing Illusions', makes some use of material which originally appeared in *Management Today,* under the title 'Mismanaging the Economy' (May 1976).

Chapter 13, 'The Deceptive Attractions of the Corporate State', was originally given as one of the Stockton Lectures for 1975, published by the London Business School. A little extra material is included from the version published by the *CBI Review* (Winter 1975–6).

Chapters 14 and 16, on 'Choice and Competition' and 'Social Tokenism', draw on both *Financial Times* articles and on Part I of *Participation without Politics* Institute of Economic Affairs (1975).

Chapter 19, 'The Impact of the Strike Threat', draws on 'The Political Economy of Union Monopoly', *The Three Banks Review* (September 1976).

Chapter 20. The section on 'Job Rights', also draws on the above.

Chapter 21 draws on *The Rebirth of Political Economy,* Encounter (May 1973) as well as on *Participation without Politics.*

Chapter 23, 'The Politics of Excessive Expectations', was originally given as a paper entitled 'The Economic Contradictions of Democracy' to Section F of the British Association at its 1974 Annual Meeting. A revised and extended version appeared in *The British Journal of Political Science* (April 1975), which was reprinted in shortened form in *Why is Britain Becoming Harder to Govern?* (ed. A. King) (BBC, 1976).

Chapter 24 is based on my essay in *The Political Economy of Inflation,* (edited Hirsch and Goldthorpe), Martin Robertson, 1978.

Chapter 25 incorporates a few passages from 'The Best Way for the Country to Choose its Leaders', *The Director* (February 1976) and from 'Can Democracy Cope?' *Encounter* (May 1976).

PART I

Trying to Manage an Economy

1   Some Governing Illusions

The words 'economic management' should set off warning bells. They suggest that somewhere in the recesses of Whitehall is a Great Manager surrounded by computer terminals, buttons, charts and flashing lights. The Great Manager is nothing but an updated version of the Captain on the Bridge of the Ship of State, steering us through storm-tossed seas. If the captain–manager performs well, we are supposed to arrive safely wherever we are going. If he is incompetent, or his rule book is bad, or he is distracted by party politics, the ship will go aground on the rocks; or, in the modern form of the metaphor, the circuits will fuse and the machinery grind to a halt.

Of course the metaphor is all wrong. A modern economy is not much like a ship or a giant power station or an oil refinery. There are millions of individuals trying to achieve their own different ends in a myriad of different ways. They are held together by a mixture of benevolence, self-interest and force. The co-ordinating mechanisms have evolved over many years, and the vast majority of them are unknown to the actors or to observing social scientists. The mechanisms are perhaps most mysterious and least amenable to central control within the so-called public sector.

Certain activities are financed by taxes or government borrowing, rather than from the private purse. These activities give rise to a national budget which may be in surplus or deficit. Because the Government can borrow from the banking system, decide what kind of money is to be legal tender and use exchange controls to prevent other kinds of money from circulating, there is a close relationship between the conduct of public finance and the amount of national currency in citizens' possession.

There is a perfectly clear non-metaphorical reason why the more ambitious concept of economic management or demand management came to replace the old-fashioned terms 'public finance' and 'monetary' or 'credit' policy. This was because of the almost universal belief among the *cognoscenti* in the postwar period that changes in the budget deficit or surplus, or in the tightness of credit conditions, determined not merely the internal and external value of sterling but the number of people at work and the level of capacity untilisation. They did not merely believe that, by manipulating financial regulators, the Chancellor could help to iron out the fluctuations of boom and slump; they believed that demand management really determined the level of output and employment around which the fluctuations took place. The fiscal and monetary levers were therefore situated on the real commanding heights.

These fond beliefs have been discredited both by experience and by critical theory, which was formulated *before* the disillusioning experiences. The possibility of raising output and employment through injecting 'demand' into the economy depends in most circumstances on 'money illusion', i.e. on people continuing to believe that a pound is a pound in the face of its losing value. Once money illusion is punctured and people begin to think in terms of real purchasing power, injections of monetary demand mainly increase the inflation rate and depress the exchange rate. Such injections can no longer determine (if they ever could) the average unemployment percentage or rate of capacity utilisation around which cyclical fluctuations take place.

The illusion that real things can be controlled by money flows has now worn very thin. The demand managers ought long ago to have realised that, like Shakespeare's Prospero, their 'revels now are ended' and their spirits 'melted into thin air', and like the 'baseless fabric' of their vision 'shall dissolve' and their 'insubstantial pageant faded, leave not a rack behind'.

Prospero's Wisdom Lacking

Unfortunately, those who manage the affairs of nations have not had Prospero's wisdom; at no time was it more lacking than in Britain in most of the 1970s. Indeed, much of the history of the period can be seen as the persistence of the demand management illusion – which, with no originality, and drawing heavily on American economic writing, I had already exposed in the final edition of *Steering the Economy* published in January 1971, as well as in *Financial Times* articles throughout 1969 and 1970.

Allied to the demand management illusion was a second: the forecasting illusion, which is still very much with us. A history of the various crazes that have both entertained and afflicted humanity might start with the passion for apples in the Garden of Eden, say a little about the craze for tulips in the Netherlands in the seventeenth century and for South Sea investments in London in the eighteenth century; but the weirdest chapter of all would be the last one, which would have to be on the craze for economic forecasts which began in a small way in the United States even before the Second World War, then subsequently gathered strength and was raging at full force in London in the 1970s.

There was a time when a few Treasury economists sat around a table and did a few sums and discussed the outlook with each other. But this only showed how technologically out-of-date they were. The model had to be enlarged and computerised to a point where it contained six hundred equations and required two hundred exogenous assumptions and no single person could understand how it was all supposed to work. Not only did this official activity stimulate numerous competitive forecasts from academic institutes and firms of consultants; but many industrial organisations asked their economists to make their own models. Every self-respecting stockbroker sought to equip himself with his own forecast. For a suitable fee you could be given a guess of the GNP of any country in any year you liked.

The whole process reached its culmination in the degree of reverence with which the autumn official National Income Forecast (NIF) of 1976 was treated. In the middle of one of the worst sterling crises, and during a period of acute political demoralisation, the Treasury's assessment and advice to the Government on what to do was held up for nearly two months until the NIF was available. Both the arrival of an IMF mission and the negotiation of urgently needed financial standbys were postponed until the forecasts were ready.

Under the so-called 'Bray Amendment', the Treasury was committed to publishing the forecasts, in highly summarised form; but this did not stop a flourishing guessing game from developing beforehand; and large sums of money were paid to computer firms by private clients who fed in their own assumptions to produce a Treasury-type forecast. People playing this game had to sign an undertaking that they would not claim that a pretend-Treasury forecast was the genuine article.

The British Cargo Cults

Unfortunately, the Government itself was staking most on the NIF just when its actual value was at its least. To say 'garbage in, garbage out' would have been only a shade too harsh. The model could not help to answer major uncertainties on matters such as the course of world trade, the extent to which the pay limits would stick, how overseas holders of sterling would behave or whether British consumers would be in a saving mood. At most, a forecasting model could say whether the different assumptions were consistent with each other. But a consistent forecast can be even further from reality than an inconsistent one.

In the actual job of reporting and commenting on British economic policy I have been reminded irresistibly of the cargo cults that have developed in the South Seas. Those who saw the film *Mondo Cane* will remember the sad scene of natives dancing around the battered hull of an aircraft, praying that another bird would come down from the sky, full of wonders and signs and portents for the future. They danced and waited; and nothing came; while the camera gradually slid away.

A third illusion, additional to that of demand management and forecasting, was that of 'fine-tuning'. The term was coined by Professor Walter Heller, who was the first chairman of the Council of Economic Advisers in the Kennedy Administration. It meant a readiness to switch policy, and especially government spending, taxation and monetary policy, backwards and forwards to offset the ups and downs of the private economy. 'Fine-tuning' later became a term of abuse, and few of its practitioners admitted to believing in it.

The name is not in fact a particularly well chosen one. The real issue is that of discretionary intervention by politicians and officials versus guidelines, rules or automatic mechanisms. The question is not whether the Government is attempting to determine the level of aggregates such as output or exports to several places of decimals. The anti-fine-tuners doubt whether the actions of governments and central banks to offset booms and slumps or exchange rate fluctuations have really dampened them down at all, and suspect that they have made them worse. Perverse effects can be due not merely to forecasting difficulties *per se*, but to the time lags between diagnosis, action and the results of policy changes, which may take several years to have their full effects. For any given impact of government action, the net effect may be destabilising even if that impact is more frequently in the right than in the wrong direction. This can be seen by treating natural fluctuations and official intervention as two sets of random disturbances — which is another way of saying the Government guesses right half the time. The sum of the two sets of disturbances then fluctuates more widely than either set on its own. Thus the Government has to do considerably better than be right half the time if it is to dampen fluctuations; and it can intensify them even if the impact of its actions is less than the size of the disturbances it is trying to counter. Even more important are the distortions introduced by changing political objectives, and fashions and wishful thinking about the compatibility of different goals. In the British case the results have sometimes been almost deliberately destabilising internally, as action has been geared mainly to the state of the balance of payments at a particular exchange rate.

The three illusions of demand management, forecasting and finetuning interact in a fairly obvious way. If you believe in macroeconomic forecasts, you will be more inclined to try your hand at fine-tuning. If you believe that demand management can determine the long-term level of output and employment, you will be more insistent on forecasting and intervention than if all that is at stake are fluctuations around levels that are not determined by monetary flows at all. British economic management in the 1970s was for most of the time a long struggle to stay within these triple illusions by men who had been in the vanguard of one revolution – the Keynesian one – and were in no mood for a counter-revolution originating in alien climes and modes of thought.

The Balance of Payments Obsession

These illusions would have caused a great deal of trouble if they had dominated policy in a relatively self-sufficient economy such as the American one. (They have in fact caused harm in the United States, but policy there has never been quite so dominated by wishful thinking about demand management; and the limitations of executive power make fine-tuning more difficult to attempt.)

In the British case the illusions have been compounded by what can best be called the balance of payments obsession. Ever since I entered economic journalism in the late 1950s, sharp and unpopular changes of policy have been introduced for one reason only – fears about the sterling exchange ι ate; and improvements in the rate – or in the balance of payments when the rate has been pegged – have been the prelude to domestic relaxation. Over this period I have changed my mind about many things, and have switched from being a demand expansionist to being a believer in stable monetary and fiscal guidelines; but one aspect on which I have not changed my mind at all is that the balance of payments fixation has been a disaster.

The exchange rate has sometimes been fixed and sometimes been supposedly floating – but subject to much official intervention. But never have our rulers allowed it to be determined by market forces and followed stable long-term guidelines for internal policy. For most of the last few decades our affairs have been managed by people most of whom do not at heart believe that inflation is a monetary phenomenon, and nearly all of whom are preoccupied with flows across the exchanges – which would balance automatically if only we would let them and cease trying to 'manage' the sterling rate.

Worries over sterling and the current trading account have led to sudden and ill-timed monetary clamp-downs, followed by runaway excesses whenever the heat has been off the foreign exchange market. Yet the actual course of the balance of payments and the sterling rate has been so erratic as to call in question the value of these abrupt switches of course. The alternative to fine-tuning would be a clean float of the exchange rate, backed up by stable long-term rules for the money supply and public sector borrowing. This does not mean crude budget balancing. The government accounts would still move into automatic deficit in recession and surplus in boom, but politicians and officials would not be constantly meddling with the controls.

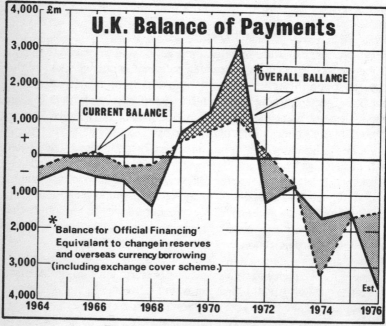

Fig 1. UK Balance of Payments

Examining the record is nearly always better than looking in the crystal ball. The Treasury was keen on the Roy Jenkins squeeze to prevent a second sterling devaluation soon after that of 1967. The 1967 devaluation eventually worked; the balance of payments went into record surplus (Figure 1); and in 1970 Mr Jenkins and his colleagues were thrown out for their pains.

Why did the Heath Government dissipate the heritage? Personalities aside, it was because the Treasury's main arguments against monetary and fiscal stimuli in 1970–1 were couched in balance of payments terms; and when sterling turned out for a time embarrassingly strong, the Treasury became discredited. The way was then open for the so-called 'Barber boom' (for which Mr Anthony – now Lord – Barber was less responsible than almost any other senior member of the then Cabinet. He contemplated resigning on one or two occasions over public expenditure. But he never went as far as drafting a letter of resignation, partly out of excessive loyalty to Mr. Heath and partly because he saw no advantage to the country in announcing to the world that his attitude to public expenditure was not shared by a majority of his colleagues).

One of the reasons why inflation was allowed to get out of control and eventually reach 25–30 per cent in 1975 was the official myth that rising prices mattered mainly because 'we would price ourselves out of world markets'. This balance of payments emphasis postponed for decades any examination of the domestic consequences of runaway inflation. As late as the winter of 1975–6, the official counter-inflation-leaflets relied for their appeal on fears about pricing ourselves out of work markets; which were nonsense if one believed what the British Treasury had publicly told the IMF that very same winter about allowing the exchange rate to move to maintain the competitive power of British goods. We pay a high price for so-called realists who will not 'tell it like it is'.

In the chapters that follow these and other themes will be illustrated by commentaries I wrote at various times in the 1970s. The aim is to present the issues with greater vividness than would be possible with a more continuous narration written with hindsight.

Reference

Friedman, M., 'The Effects of a Full-Employment Policy on Economic Stability: A Formal Analysis' in *Essays in Positive Economics* (University of Chicago Press, 1953).

2 The Start of the 1970s

[For a good many years it was generally thought that high unemployment and inflation were alternative dangers and that if a country had one it would not have the other. The problem of policy was regarded as that of devising means of keeping prices reasonably stable without having to suffer heavy unemployment as a consequence.

This turned out, however, to be much too optimistic a formulation. By the late 1960s inflation was much above the average levels hitherto prevailing in the postwar years, but unemployment was abnormally high as well. The combination of the two evils was known by ugly names such as 'stagflation'. The British problem was an especially acute case of a world problem; and before going into British policy, it might be helpful to begin with commentaries written in 1970 on the international setting, as it seemed at the time.]

The British Economy in a World Setting (March–June 1970).

A former president of the World Bank, Mr Eugene Black, had a pithy way of dealing with economists who argued that a little bit of inflation did not harm. 'A little bit of inflation is like a little bit of pregnancy,' he would remark, 'it grows.'

For a long time such forebodings seemed more witty than accurate, as for much of the 1950s and 1960s the major industrial countries managed to muddle along well enough with moderate, but non-accelerating, rates of inflation. Now, however, the long-predicted acceleration has come with a vengeance. This is brought out very clearly by the following figures for the twenty-two industrial countries that make up the OECD.

10

The Start of the 1970s

Average annual increase in consumer prices	
	%
1960—5	$2\frac{1}{2}$
1965–8	$3\frac{1}{2}$
1969	$4\frac{3}{4}$
[1970]	$[5\frac{1}{2}]$
[1971]	$[5\frac{3}{4}]$
[1972]	$[4\frac{3}{4}]$
[1973]	[8]
[1974]	$[13\frac{1}{2}]$
[1975]	$[11\frac{1}{4}]$
[1976]	[8]

The acceleration of prices is only partly a matter of the business cycle. The rate of inflation for the OECD as a whole was greater in 1969 than ever before in the organisation's history, and the most inflationary previous year was 1968. Ten years ago, as Mr van Lennep remarked, the normal annual rate of increase of US prices was little more than 1 per cent per annum. Now it is expected to be above 4 per cent even in a recession year. In no previous German boom has the rate of increase of consumer prices been as much as $4\frac{1}{2}$ per cent – usually it has been a good deal less. Now – despite revaluation – it is above 5 per cent and seems likely to rise further. As for the United Kingdom, the sad story is shown by the table below.

It is necessary here to distinguish between symptoms and underlying diseases. The symptoms are currency problems and payments difficulties; but the underlying problem is the difficulty that has emerged in keeping inflation under control in conditions of full employment. The distinction was well made by Dr Zijlstra, the Governor of the Netherlands Central Bank and president of the Bank for International Settlement (BIS), who warned that wage and price increases might make a recession inevitable. The danger to which he alludes is not the classic one of a recession spreading from the United States. The

Change in UK retail prices at annual rates	
	%
1955–65	3.0
Nov. 64–Nov. 67	3.6
Nov. 67–Feb. 68	5.4
Aug. 69–Feb. 70	6.7
[1970]	[6.5]
[1971]	[9.5]
[1972]	[6.9]
[1973]	[8.3]
[1974]	[16.0]
[1975]	[24.2]
[1976]	[16.5]

American recession cannot be far off bottom, and so far the rest of the world has held up extremely well, with each estimate of world trade above the previous one. The real danger is of a policy-induced recession coming about because countries can find no other way of tackling the inflationary threat. Dr Zijlstra sees recession arriving through the collision between rapidly rising wages and restrictive monetary policy. He sees this as encroaching on profit margins and thus leading to a decline in investment. Currency imbalances would be aggravated because in a highly inflationary world there are likely to be much bigger differences between cost trends in different countries than in a moderately inflationary world. But the root of the problem is internal to each country.

There would be a strong case for accepting some rate of inflation, even a fairly high one, as the price of full employment and business prosperity, provided that the rate of inflation was itself stable. This was the basis of the postwar compromise. In strict theory the pregnancy analogy was wrong as it would be possible to have a rapid but non-accelerating rate of inflation. But once the economic system is fully adapted to any given rate of inflation, there is no more benefit to employment, growth or anything else. Merely to prevent inflation from accelerating, the labour market has to be kept with the same amount of slack as would have been required before for a policy of rough price stability. To suppose anything different would be to argue that workers are suckers and can be bought off in a tight labour market by higher money wages without their taking the real value of their earnings into account.

It may be helpful to set out the general influences on money wages that seem to be at work in the modern world.

1. The higher the demand for labour, the more rapidly will money wages rise.

2. The more rapidly that prices are expected to increase, the faster money wages will grow in a given state of the labour market.

3. Workers, like other groups, are resistant not only to reductions in their absolute standard of living, but to reductions in the rate of increase to which they have been accustomed. If real incomes have been squeezed in the recent past, wage demands will be more aggressive than would otherwise have been expected in the same economic climate. This is very much what has happened in Britain, where disposable incomes, after allowing for price changes, did not grow at all between the middle of 1968 and the end of 1969, reflecting the need for a large shift in resources away from the home market in a short space of time.

4. Under fixed exchange rates, the general behaviour of world prices has a big influence on how much employers will concede. This is not the only influence, or exchange rates would never get out of line; but it is a large one in any particular country. It cannot, however, explain why the world rate of inflation is where it is.

5. Non-market forces such as political and social tensions, trade union attitudes or government policies can sometimes [but not permanently] swamp the other influences.

The real change that makes 1970 in some sense worse than 1964 is that economic behaviour is now governed by inflationary expectations. Both sides of industry are taking price expectations into account; and wage bargaining starts from the belief that in Britain, a 6 or 7 or 8 per cent increase is equal to zero in real terms because of rising prices. Thus, the worse inflationary expectations become, the greater the rise in unemployment that will be required to slow down the rise in wages and return to more normal conditions.

More rapidly rising wages are themselves associated with more rapidly rising prices. The result is that, if the demand for labour is above some 'natural' level, or unemployment below it, inflation tends to accelerate. While a few years ago this acceleration looked as if it would take several decades, it is now visibly gathering pace between one wage round and the next.

Money is too useful a social invention to be destroyed by ever-increasing inflation. The real crisis facing the West is that the 'natural' rate of unemployment consistent with any stable rate of price increase (which could be well above zero) now seems so very high.

There is therefore a great market for theories purporting to show that there is no relation between unemployment and wage inflation. Many of their authors fall into the trap of supposing that, because wage increases are affected by many factors other than the state of the labour market, the latter does not matter. Whatever other causes there may be pushing earnings up, a high demand for labour raises them still further. To deny this is a triumph of hope over all experience from the time of Diocletian onwards.

Of course the natural rate of unemployment is anything but 'natural'. It has been pushed as high as it is by the greater use that unions are making of their monopoly power. It is also swollen by regional imbalances and by archaic training arrangements and demarcation agreements, which prevent unemployed people from being trained to exercise skills that are in short supply.

No economist could guarantee that in this situation the 'natural' rate of unemployment would be a socially tolerable one. Even if there were a coalition government not worrying about an election, and advised on monetary policy by a triumvirate of Dr Zijlstra, Lord Cromer and Professor Milton Friedman, it is possible that the level of unemployment required to bring us back from where we are now to, say, a stable 4 or 5 per cent inflation rate might be so high that there would be a revolution first. The revolutionary government would then face the same situation.

Long before such a crunch is reached, fresh attempts will be made at a voluntary prices and incomes policy, both in the United Kingdom and in other countries. If an incomes policy were easy, it would have been achieved long ago. But as the OECD has pointed out, no country has operated one for very long without severe setbacks. The difficulty in getting the unions to keep to their part of the bargain is only part of it – although the longer such a policy is enforced the greater the temptation is for a breakaway union or group to strike out on its own.

An even greater obstacle is that of finding a *quid pro quo* on the other side. A policy of dividend limitation at company level ossifies the industrial structure and favours the inefficient and slow-growing firms. Universal price control involves rationing and black markets. One is back, therefore, with some form of regulation of corporate rates of return. But this too means that risky or unorthodox investment will be penalised, as the uncertainties will not be worth running.

Moreover, once the Government assumes a responsibility for company profitability, it also becomes irretrievably involved in shoring-up operations to keep insolvent enterprises in existence at the taxpayers' expense. Worst of all, it creates a society in which it is more important to keep in with the establishment of the moment than to observe known rules applicable to all.

One should in all fairness add that there is some much more positive thinking in TUC back rooms. This puts the emphasis on a faster rate of economic growth in return for wage restraint. But how is this faster growth to be achieved? If by more investment, this can be achieved only at the expense of a smaller increase in real wages here and now – jam tomorrow at the expense of jam today. If by increasing the yield from existing resources, this involves a greater readiness to break up uneconomic enterprises and to move jobs and retrain – the very opposite of the instinctive desire of trade unions to 'preserve' existing jobs.

One fears that by faster growth the TUC still means at heart a policy of boosting home demand. The political setbacks suffered by Mr Maudling and George Brown are eloquent testimony to the effects of believing the TUC on that one. The real *quid pro quo* for some restraint on incomes is not less unemployment but a smaller increase in unemployment than would otherwise be necessary. It is not that the next government, whatever its party, will callously increase the unemployment rate because of speculative theories; the increase in the number of jobless and the checks to business will come through apparent Acts of God, whether in the shape of sterling crises or as errors in the domestic forecasts.

The curtain is thus going up again on a drama with which one is all too familiar, but which this time is likely to reach its denouement a little faster. Indeed, one can well imagine the present world inflation leaving such nasty traces in the memory that, as in Europe in the 1920s and early 1930s, a resistance will develop even to the most reasonable of anti-recession and employment programmes. The Romans had a saying: 'If you want peace prepare for war.' The equivalent today would be: 'If you want full employment, fight inflation and fight it now.'

3 Dissipating an Inheritance

[The period of Labour government from the end of 1967 to the general election of 1970 represented on the whole an Indian summer for the British economy. For the first time for decades, the conditions were created for external and internal balance. The parity was right and internal monetary policy was sufficiently firm to prevent another inflationary explosion. Although Tony Benn was making speeches as minister of technology, and the engine contract that led to the subsequent bankruptcy of Rolls-Royce was negotiated, there was remarkably little of the misguided direct intervention that was to characterise the 1970s. Public expenditure may still have been too high, but it was under better control than at any time before 1977. Roy Jenkins as Chancellor did not remove all 'political' taxes; but he refrained on the whole from piling on taxes motivated by pure envy; and he was more mindful than his Conservative successors were to be of the delicate balance of incentives on which a mixed economy rests.

Of course, ministers were coming under attack from the 'Labour movement' for not being socialist enough; and the Conservatives were stridently denouncing the Government, mostly for the wrong reasons. These were all signs that we were in one of our rare periods of reasonable government. In the non-economic sphere, although there were plenty of traditional brutalities left, and the violent wing of the Left was beginning to show itself, society was more humane and free than at any time in British history. The two Labour Parliaments of 1964–70 did more to 'set the people free' and remove sources of needless misery, with the reforms of the abortion and homosexuality laws and in the administration of the Home Office, than all the attempts of Tory governments to liberalise in the economic field – which have floundered because of innate Conservative authoritarianism and distaste for analytical thinking. But men know not their good fortune. Labour politicians, as soon as they were out of office, began to apologise for their record; and the Conservatives, in their early Heath phase, were disdainful of the better parts of their own traditions and came to office in 1970 with a puerile optimism about the powers of government to transform society.

The successes of Roy Jenkins, who became Chancellor in November 1967 following a 14 per cent devaluation of the pound from $2.80 to $2.40, were the result of what he himself described as a 'long, hard slog'. Devaluation was at first slow to produce results. The slowness was attributed by conventional economists to the J—curve. This describes the initial effect of devaluation in worsening export proceeds as exporters cut dollar prices; according to this view, the benefits are delayed until export volume is stimulated by the lower prices. But a much more likely reason is that in the first year after devaluation a tight budgetary policy was accompanied by a lax money supply policy, which was not tightened until the autumn of 1968, partly under the prodding of the IMF. There then came four successive years of current payments surplus, 1969—72; but the result was never a foregone conclusion and there were many anxious months of waiting in 1968 and 1969 until the evidence of the payments turnround showed in the figures.

Mr Jenkins's first priority after he came to office was to limit the growth of public spending. The combined effect of the public spending curbs and tax measures that came in the 1968 and 1969 Budgets, as well as in an autumn package in between, was to eliminate the public sector borrowing requirement entirely. The current balance of payments moved into surplus in 1969 and stayed there for four continuous years until 1972.

Although originally trained as an economist, Mr Jenkins did not attempt to get bogged down in technical arguments. He could not wait several lifetimes while the controversies of this 'semi-science' were being resolved. He reduced the growth of the money supply because UK experience and that of other countries had shown that fiscal action on its own was not enough.

Of course, there were time bombs ticking away in the Indian summer of 1968—70. The failure of the Wilson attempt to reform trade union law, when the Prime Minister was forced to withdraw *In Place of Strife,* was a foretaste of the power that the union barons would subsequently claim. It is often forgotten that Mr Jenkins did preside over a temporary incomes policy, and carried the unions with him in it. He imposed a ceiling for wage and dividend increases in 1968. The policy was a holding operation to keep wage increases back to 6—7

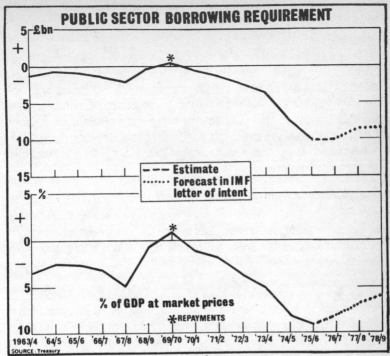

Fig 2. Public Sector Borrowing Requirement

per cent while other policies had a chance to work. Wage controls for all practical purposes disappeared by the end of 1969 as a result of union opposition. There followed a wage explosion in the winter of 1969–70, which economists attributed to the abolition of the controls, to the backlash from them, or to quite other factors, according to taste. The fact remains that the explosion was not expected by *any* school of economists; and monetarists are more impressive when they stress the uncertainty of time lags, and of the uncertain short-run response of wages and output to changes in monetary demand, than when they compete with the fine-tuners at their own game and attempt to provide single-value forecasts.

If Roy Jenkins had remained Chancellor in the 1970s, he would have had an unpleasant choice to make between abandoning his monetary guidelines, and standing back and allowing unemployment to gather force as unions priced their members out of the market. Nobody, not even Mr Jenkins himself, can know what he would have done. But it is worth noting that the guidelines were originally imposed primarily for balance of payments reasons; and for a brief period in the early 1970s the British balance of payments was almost embarrassingly strong.

It is against this background that the Conservatives, who confounded the opinion polls by winning the election of June 1970, took office. Near the end of the election campaign a statement was issued with Mr Heath's endorsement suggesting that prices could be reduced 'at a stroke', a statement that was to dog his government for its term of office and provide a permanent addition to the stock of journalistic catch-phrases. From here the story is taken up through *Financial Times* commentaries.]

After the Election (June to August 1970)

One of the few good features of the 1970 election was that rising prices emerged as an issue on its own. Despite all the talk about inflation and incomes policies in the past, politicians and officials had until then been concerned mainly with the effects of British costs on the balance of payments.

With world trade expanding at its recent rate and the benefit of a devalued currency and a severe squeeze at home, it would have been a miracle if we had not achieved a large surplus in 1969–70. But the Treasury's June Economic Assessment admits quite candidly that the calculation that our devaluation advantage is still intact is based on figures that only go up to the end of 1969. Since then British industrial earnings have been rising at roughly the rate of our competitors while productivity has been rising a good deal less. This is slowly but surely undermining the devaluation advantage.

The balance of payments is, however, a pseudo-problem, owing to rigid exchange rates between countries experiencing different rates of inflation and different movements in the other forces affecting the supply and demand for their currencies. The real harm is not done by revaluations or devaluations, which simply bring the external value of a country's currency into line with international value. It arises from the domestic, social and economic effects of rapid or accelerating inflation.

Economists have long been familiar with the 'dilemma' situation that arises when, under a fixed exchange rate, there is a conflict between internal and external requirements. We are now in a new kind of 'dilemma', of a purely internal kind. The state of the real economy — production, employment, investment, etc. — suggests at least to those who still believe in 'fine-tuning' that a stimulus is required. The behaviour of the nominal indicators – prices, costs, wages, etc. – points in the opposite direction. The new Government has the unenviable choice between abandoning the monetary guidelines inherited from Roy Jenkins and financing inflation, or keeping the monetary controls at the expense of slack growth and rising unemployment. The immediate question it has to face is: 'Did Roy Jenkins make a mistake in his last Budget?' Much conventional economic wisdom has been coming round to this opinion, which is incidentally shared by a number of Labour MPs and ex-Cabinet ministers.

There were two basic reasons for Mr Jenkins's cautious 1970 budget judgement. First was his extreme preoccupation with the balance of payments and the need to err on the side of safety for that reason. Secondly, Mr Jenkins was influenced by Treasury forecasts that output would grow this year by $3\frac{1}{2}$ per cent. This was slightly faster than the growth of productive capacity, and if correct would actually have reduced unemployment a little.

The real reason for backing Mr Jenkins's budget judgement and for adhering to it today, however, has little to do with the forecasts. It is quite simply that, with incomes and prices rising at an unprecedented rate, it would be folly to inject extra spending power into the economy. The distinction between demand and cost inflation is worth making for some purposes; but they are not entirely unconnected phenomena. If the demand for goods and labour is increased, wages and prices are likely to rise still further. To suppose otherwise would be a triumph of hope over experience.

There is, however, a vulnerable aspect that needs to be watched. Mr Jenkins came to acquire a strong personal commitment to controlling the money supply, even if this meant allowing large movements in gilt-edged prices. Because of the great strength of gilt-edged there is no immediate difficulty about the 5 per cent money supply target for 1970–1; but the strong ministerial commitment is missing. If the autumn economic forecasts were to come up with a continued low-growth prognosis, or if a great outcry is raised about investment and company liquidity, the temptation to ease the present monetary restraints could grow.

Indeed, such relaxation would be logical from the point of view of the fine-tuning philosophy still held by many official economic advisers. The idea of a fixed annual growth of the money supply cannot happily coexist with the traditional postwar philosophy of demand management, which looks at the economy entirely in real terms and is prepared to finance any rate of inflation that emerges from the wage and price-fixing process.

Some eyebrows have been raised that such a severe line is being taken by a commentator who criticised Mr Selwyn Lloyd for keeping the squeeze on for too long in 1962, and who was unhappy at mistimed deflationary measures in the past. It would be idle to deny that both recent experiences and theoretical writings have brought a shift of emphasis in my beliefs about the economic system.

But there is also a big difference between the situation today and the early 1960s. During the recession of 1962–3, the rate of inflation was about 3 per cent and not tending to accelerate. Today it is approaching 8 per cent, and is in danger of becoming self-perpetuating; for if people begin to think an 8 per cent rise in prices more or less normal, wage bargaining will start from this point, and 8 per cent will be taken off the nominal value of any settlement to allow for inflation – and perhaps a little bit more to allow for the increasing tax take as incomes rise.

Indeed, if the unions are able to use their monopoly power in an attempt to gain larger increases in real income than the productivity of the system will allow, the rate of inflation could accelerate further. In this unprecedented and dangerous situation the argument about the relative value of fiscal and monetary policy is peripheral. Both are technical means – best used in a mutually reinforcing way – of regulating demand.

The real argument is between the 'touch of the tiller' school of thought and those who believe in long-term guidelines. The new Conservative Government, like many new governments, has been influenced by the hope of finding an expansionist way through our dilemmas. The Treasury, on the other hand, fears that an injection of demand would only make the situation worse.

It is impossible to predict exactly where the balance will be struck. It is most unlikely that a small adjustment of purchase tax, SET or hire-purchase terms would make decisive differences one way or another. The advantage of adhering to at least some rough underlying target for the fiscal balance and the growth of the money supply is that it provides some inhibition on the indefinite financing of inflation.

If fiscal and monetary targets are even broadly observed while money incomes carry on rising rapidly, the result is likely to be some sort of crunch. For credit will be very scarce, interest rates high, production slack and unemployment rising. This interval of recession conditions is probably the price we shall have to pay for having allowed inflation to go so far.

Hotfoot from Selsdon (August 1970)

[A belief prevails in some Conservative and business circles that the Heath Government was working sensibly to establish a market economy in its first year or two, but was then deflected in 1972. This is self-delusion. Its main interest was not in market forces, as both friendly and hostile writers wrongly supposed, but in a series of *ad hoc* measures, such as trade union legislation, tax reform and new *machinery* for scrutinising public spending, which had been adopted as party policy in the mid-1960s. A suggestion by Mr Brendon Sewill, head of the Conservative Research Department, made just before the Government came to office to switch priorities to fighting inflation, was brushed aside.

The initial Conservative rejection of incomes policy was based not on any abandonment of traditional full-employment commitments, nor on any serious plan for tackling union monopoly (the authors of the Industrial Relations Act did not claim it to be that), nor on a policy of tolerating increasing inflation. There was no realisation by Mr Heath's Young Turks that, if they did not like postwar 'macroeconomic policy' or economic management, some set of monetary and fiscal rules would have to be put in its place. But the reaction of the economic establishment made one doubt if a more clear-sighted policy would have had a more favourable reception.]

The main impression that the Conservative Government has given in the economic sphere between mid-June and early August is one of respect for the proprieties. There have been no rushed decisions. Little has been forced over the dead bodies of civil servants; and Whitehall has been asked to review all the ideas of the incoming Ministers over the summer recess in the approved and respectable way. Compared with the present British Government, President Nixon's celebrated 'low profile' seems like a range of the Himalayas.

It is already apparent that economic policy, in the sense of demand management, the balance of payments and the problems of sterling, does not have much sex appeal for the present Government. The main interest of the Heath Government is in public expenditure, the tax structure and the machinery of government. In this there is a swing of emphasis not only from the Labour Government but from the previous Conservative administrations of the 1950s and 1960s.

There are now two teams of business advisers attempting to ginger up governmental procedure. There is the new team based on the Civil

Service Department and the old one originally established by Labour in the Department of Economic Affairs and now based on the Ministry of Technology. The old team was supposed to make government intervention more efficient; and the new is supposed to reduce the role of the State. But both seem to attract very similar jokes from the established regulars. There is, indeed, a danger that the idea of more systematic analysis of public expenditure programmes will be confused with the argument about businessmen in government. It is possible to have one without the other, and it does no good to present the two concepts in a single package.

The public expenditure review, in which so much political capital has been invested, has two aspects. There is the normal trimming back of expenditure plans necessary in most years after the forward projection of the Public Expenditure Survey Committee (PESC) in early summer. This has become embroiled with a search for additional economies to make possible cuts in direct taxes as soon as possible. The changes being considered are a mixture of Treasury hardy annuals and items from the Conservative election manifesto.

Examples of Conservative thinking, not all of them firm commitments, would including the following:

1 a shift from direct to indirect taxation, possibly by means of a value-added tax;
2 a shift from deficiency payments to import levies for farm support;
3 a reduction in investment subsidies and or aid to industry;
4 more selectivity in housing subsidies and possibly other social service payments.

With the exception of the agricultural change – which is a retrograde move to disguise the degree of farm protection – these suggested changes are in principle in the right direction. The effect in many cases will be that the citizen will pay for public services through prices in the shops rather than via PAYE.

But there is a time and place for everything. Even were the proposed reforms administratively viable within the next twelve months, which many of them are not, this would be a very bad time for any avoidable action to increase shop prices and add to inflationary expectations. The arguments for caution are reinforced by the possibility that membership of the EEC will, despite the transitional period, add a further twist to the price–wage spiral.

The search for economies that will really reduce government claims on resources, and not just be bookkeeping transactions, is proving far from easy. The October White Paper is bound to contain some unpopular items, such as dearer school meals or Health Service charges; and the political outcry is all too predictable.

It is probably safe to assume that some payments will be made to cushion the effects on lower-income families. Equally, there will be some transfer to the upper-middle-income groups from the mass of the population (and perhaps also from families to bachelors). A large number of changes for a large number of people will amount to self-cancelling shifts in tax rates, prices and charges for public services. It is a political illusion to believe that the tax burden has been reduced for somebody who pays £25 a year less in income tax and £25 more for Health Service or school meal charges. A charge can be regarded as a price in the economic sense if it is meant to influence the demand for the article in question. A rise in council house rents, offset by a negative income tax for the poor, would be a genuine move to a market economy based on freedom of choice. But an increase in the weekly insurance stamp, or even in the price of Health Service dentures and spectacles, for which the demand does not vary appreciably, is a tax in all but name.

No one expects these subtleties to be taken into account in the October review. The acid test in judging the Government's political philosophy will be Concorde, which absorbs nearly £100 million per annum of real resources. If this is left out of the proposed economies, it will be a sign that the economic liberals have lost the first round and the change of Government has done them little good. [It was left out, and the new Government turned out a disaster for proponents of the market economy.]

4   The Treasury Again Under the Tories

[The following articles are included for the light they shed both on Whitehall and on the Conservative Party, two institutions that are constantly changing, but in some ways remain very much the same.]

Mr Heath's Government and the Economic Establishment (21 January 1971)

There are occasions when subjects that are causing upset and excitement behind the scenes benefit from being given a public airing, instead of being shrouded in tactful obscurity. The unhappy state of relations between the Heath Government and the economic establishment has now reached the stage where a little frank discussion could do no harm.

The economic establishment, like the elephant, is easier to recognise than to describe. It comprises: officials in the central policy-making departments, Oxbridge economists interested in policy, and most of the economists likely to do time in bodies such as the Treasury, the National Institute of Economic and Social Research, NEDC, and the OECD in Paris, as well as sympathetic observers of their activities in other walks of life. Indeed it was Mr Heath's objection to some pointed comments by the OECD on Britain's anti-inflation policy that first allowed the general public to catch a whiff of this state of affairs.

A great many British economists do not, of course, belong to the establishment in question. A large number of academics in the redbrick universities and in London are most conspicuously not members of it. Indeed, an alternative focus is provided by the Institute of Economic Affairs (IEA), which has, with its propaganda for competitive markets, become a sort of anti-establishment. Almost the only people who turned up at the pre-Christmas party of both the National Institute and the IEA were a few journalists. But it is the establishment group that has been at the centre of affairs; and Conservative ministers are, with one or two exceptions, even less likely to know IEA-type economists than they are establishment ones.

Of course, if taken too literally this picture becomes a caricature. Many of the best academics cannot be clearly identified with either group; there are IEA-type economists who have worked in Whitehall; and there are some key officials in senior positions who are strong supporters of many of the Heath policies. Yet the element of truth remains. There is an economic establishment, however hard it is to define its boundaries, and many of its members are feeling pretty unhappy at the trend of events.

Considerations of lofty principle are not the only ones at stake. A government that is inclined to cut advisory bodies and reduce the number of economic posts can hardly expect to be popular among the victims of its axe. Obviously, this is not all there is to it. There is genuine dissatisfaction with the style of Conservative economic policy. As with all matters of nuance and atmosphere, one cannot easily pinpoint the precise issues. Perhaps the two most prominent ones are the cuts in public spending and the policy towards inflation.

Treasury officials and outsiders who comment on their actions have long been accustomed to public expenditure cuts and are not easily shocked by them. But past public expenditure packages have been introduced to release resources for the balance of payments or to curb domestic 'overheating'. The idea of introducing such a package not in response to any economic crisis, but simply out of a desire to cut taxes, seemed to the economic establishment a disturbing piece of frivolity.

The establishment is also extremely sceptical of the Government's policy of tackling inflation with no other economic weapons than a tough line on public sector wages together with (some still largely hypothetical) talk about bankruptcies, and the hope that these together will lead to a change in the public mood. The typical view would probably be that a policy of reducing demand and employment might work, although at a prohibitive cost, and so might a prices and incomes policy; but that the present approach is too much like faith-healing, or hiving off economic policy to Wilberforce.

One has yet to see who will have the last laugh here. It would be easier to be impressed by this kind of criticism if one thought that Whitehall officials and economists had in their top drawers a better anti-inflation strategy, if only ministers would let them implement it. There is, alas, no reason to suppose any such thing. One gets the impression that if a confidential poll could be taken of the Treasury there would be a large majority in favour of a 'prices and incomes policy'. But this is simply to pose the problem and not answer it.

It would also be other-worldly to ignore the political overtones. Most members of the economic establishment are light years removed in their views from the typical Labour member of Parliament. While Labour MPs instinctively want to keep all prices down, economic opinion is often worried that they are being held artificially low in relation to costs; and its main anxiety about profits is that they may be inadequate to finance a sufficient level of investment.

Yet on the whole the sympathies of the establishment are not with the Tories. This is due to a mixture of factors: traditional loyalties dating from the 1930s and 1940s, the fact that middle-class Labour ministers come from a similar background to dons and officials (while there are very few social contacts with the Tories), a belief by many of those concerned in equality at least as an ultimate aim, and an aesthetic distaste for both the feudal and the go-getting business type of Tory.

This kind of half-conscious Fabianism could happily coexist with the Conservatism of the early 1960s, with its indicative planning incomes policy, its round-table approach. It is alienated by the disengagement-prone, untalkative, stand-on-your-own-two-feet style of current Conservatism. The tension is aggravated by the fact that the top Conservatives closest to Mr Heath have little interest in, or feeling for, the 'macro' problems of demand management and the balance of payments, so close to the heart of the reigning British economic school.

The nanny-like view that 'there are faults on both sides' happens to be true of the tensions discussed here. Ministers do not help by their extreme sensitivity to open discussion of key issues such as the exchange rate or anti-inflation policy – whether by the OECD or even by commentators in the British press. They are prone to the fallacy that public discussion of such topics makes matters worse.

On actual policy, an extremely good case can be made for reducing some of the highest marginal tax rates, for returning to the individual many decisions now left to the public authorities, and for concentrating social service spending on those who need it most instead of spreading it thinly for everyone. But ministers only spoil their own case when they speak as if a modest reduction in the standard rate of income tax will cause a sudden upsurge of economic growth. Economists of all schools of thought, even anti-establishment, would regard this as unproven and improbable. Nor does it help when politicians speak as if a move from farm protection by subsidy to protection by levy were a way of making the consumer pay the true costs of food; which it manifestly is not.

Credibility is also not aided when government spokesmen emphasise that they have rejected the OECD advice to reduce demand and employment, but proclaim the importance of a restrictive monetary policy. One wonders, then, how monetary policy is supposed to act; and there are voices not slow to whisper that the money supply is regarded by Conservative politicians – even if, not after his latest speech, by Mr Barber – as a form of black magic which will act directly on wages without restricting output or employment.

The economic establishment tends, in its turn, to be too negative in its response. The Treasury might have used the change of government as an opportunity for re-examining the sacred cows among public spending programmes (and also among official restrictions and controls). Instead, the tendency has been to come out with traditional packages of cuts; and the implicit reply to any criticism of their side effects is 'After all, this is a Tory Government.'

The ministerial desire for quick announcements plays up to this mood, but does not excuse it completely. Mainstream British economic advice has been concerned too exclusively with the effects of public expenditure (and other policies) on total demand. The rational allocation of resources, involving the comparison of returns against costs in alternative uses, is the heart of economics, even though the run of crises has obscured this truth.

Even on the central issue of prices and incomes, the establishment view is vulnerable. The operational part of a prices and incomes policy is not statements by ministers, or public declarations by representative bodies, or paper guidance on 'norms'. It is not even legislative controls, which would be atrophied by economic forces in the course of time. The area where government action (other than demand management) can make a difference is (a) in public sector settlements and (b) in the way ministers use, or fail to use, their conciliation services and personal influences in disputes of all kinds.

A stiffer attitude here can reduce the amount of unemployment otherwise required to prevent runaway inflation. Ministers may exaggerate what they can achieve in this way, and a tighter rein on demand may yet be needed (or may occur half-wittingly). Yet incomes policy enthusiasts should forget the verbiage and realise that the present approach is achieving all that can be hoped for, short of a full-scale wage or price freeze.

There is a moral for both sides. Mr Heath has let us all know that his favourite opera is *Fidelio*, because it treats so movingly of human freedom. It is easy to sympathise. But he would do well to realise that he sometimes appears to people not as Don Fernando the liberating minister, but as Don Pizarro the prison governor. (Pizarro, in his famous aria 'Ha!Welch ein Augenblick!' exclaims that he was 'nearly in the dust, a prey to open mockery', but that now it is his turn to twist the steel in his adversary's wound, crying 'Triumph! Victory is mine'.)

For its part, the economic establishment might reflect that there are all kinds of opportunities for making use of market forces and the price mechanism that were not there before; and however hostile an economist may be to doctrinaire *laissez-faire*, the role of price and markets is his main professional expertise. The rest is statistically of dubious meaning without this foundation.

It is wrong to identify a Conservative government, even a 'radical, right-wing' one, with either the market economy or the use of prices and markets as a policy instrument. The mainsprings of Conservative policy are very different. But there is an area of overlap. Economic officials, advisers and commentators would be much more profitably engaged in exploiting this area of overlap than in digging in for a long, hard winter, which is what they are too inclined to do.

'Open Government': the Unfulfilled Pledge (5 August 1971)

One of the most interesting pledges in the manifesto on which the Conservatives fought the last election was that there would be 'more open' government. Of course, oppositions tend to think that governments are too secretive, while ministers in office can always find a million and one reasons for not publishing the documents on their desk. Nevertheless, the natural feelings of the then Opposition did go so far as a specific pledge; and this is rather important for a government that has set such exceptional importance on fulfilling the letter of its election promises.

The exact text of the pledge is: 'We will eliminate unnecessary secrecy concerning the workings of the Government, and we will review the operation of the Official Secrets Act so that government is more open and more accountable to the public.' It must straightaway be said that a committee has been set up under Lord Franks to review the Official Secrets Act; and one must wait to see what that will bring. But this is only one half of the pledge. The decisions about what to publish and what to conceal are taken by ministers (with a great deal of official advice) in the course of their normal duties. It does not need any change in the Official Secrets Act for them to publish more of the information and analysis that lies behind their decisions. The Act only comes in if, despite a decision not to publish, the information – or some version of it – nevertheless finds its way into print. There is then usually a 'leak inquiry' (unless the leak comes from ex-prime ministers or ministers, in which case it becomes a literary event).

But as far as official disclosures by ministers are concerned, the direction of movement has been backwards. In subjects with which I have been professionally concerned as an economic commentator, information policy can be divided into two categories. There are areas in which ministers have accepted the Labour Government's decisions about what to publish as the last word in wisdom and have refused to budge a millimetre. There are other areas in which they have moved backwards and are now actually publishing a great deal less.

The best-known area of backward movement concerns the EEC White Papers. The recent White Paper is a much flimsier document than its 1970 predecessor. To take just one instance, the 1970 White Paper made some estimates of the eventual impact of the EEC budgetary and agricultural policy in transfers across the exchanges: the present White Paper limits itself to the transitional period ending in 1977.

The stock response to this criticism – that the eventual impact is unforeseeable – simply will not do. The value of a professional analysis, here as in other areas, is not in the final answer, but in the systematic setting out of the factors on which the answer depends. What is lacking in the present White Paper is a 'do-it-yourself' kit. If this had been provided, it would have been possible to work out the net cost of payments to Brussels on varying assumptions about the yield of levies, the size of the Community's budgetary expenditure, the return flow of funds to this country, the yield of customs duties and other key variables. Even if the Government hopes to alter the result once inside, the analysis would still have been of interest.

Perhaps the first indication of the secrecy-mindedness of the present regime came with the publication of the Public Expenditure White Paper last winter. So far from developing and improving the previous presentation, the last White Paper made a giant leap backwards by withdrawing all revenue projections. This was accompanied by a whole host of explanations of why, in contrast to all business organisations in Britain and to most governments in most parts of the world, it was right for the British Government to estimate its outgoings without any mention of its incomings. The explanations did not even convince the Government's own back-benchers interested in the subject.

Needless to say, there has been no suggestion of publishing the medium-term economic assessment, which would be required to make full sense of the Government's expenditure programme. Even under the Labour Government, the assessment was published only on two or three occasions – late, and in bowdlerised form. So one could hardly expect anything other than complete silence now. This would be understandable if a Conservative Chancellor had discovered an entirely new way of regulating public expenditure and the medium-term assessment had been abolished. But no such intellectually interesting development has occurred. As far as one can tell, the assessment plays exactly the same role under the present Chancellor as it did under all his predecessors.

Or, to take a related area, the Select Committee on Procedure went out of its way to formulate a compromise between those who wanted a full parliamentary committee on economic affairs and the Treasury, which did not, by suggesting a carefully circumscribed sub-committee on taxation and finance which would itself by merely a branch of the already established Expenditure Committee. The aim was to proceed gradually, circumspectly and in co-operation with the Treasury. Nevertheless, it came as no surprise when the Treasury Chief Secretary turned down the whole idea in the Budget Debate in an avuncular fashion which suggested that MPs were children who would have to be disappointed of this particular treat.

Perhaps the most revealing experience of all is to sit in the gallery when the Chancellor is examined on questions of current economic policy. A major shift has just been announced here of greater importance than the Budget itself. But every question relating to the underlying Treasury analysis is parried by the Chancellor by some remark such as 'It is not the custom to give this information except at the time of the Budget.' When MPs wonder, as well they may, about the effects of the new spending spree on the borrowing requirement and the money supply, they are told that Mr Jenkins would not have given this information in his (Mr Barber's) place (an assertion that some philosophers would label a 'counterfactual').

Defenders of the Government's attitude might point out that the examples I have given relate to forecasts and projections; and Conservative ministers may legitimately be more sceptical of such exercises. After all, 'thinking of a number' and 'taking away the number you first thought of' would hardly have given worse results than some recent balance of payments forecasts. But it is, unfortunately, at just this point that Conservative ministers make a profound logical error. *The fact that a forecast, or other piece of Whitehall analysis, is dubious and unreliable makes it all the more desirable to disclose as much as possible of the reasoning behind it so that it can be subjected to the widest possible outside scrutiny.* To conceal speculative pieces of Whitehall arithmetic is only to increase their potential for harm.

Ministerial attitudes would be justified only on the assumption that policy decisions were not influenced by Whitehall numerical predictions and projections. In fact, they are just as heavily influenced by them as was the case under the Labour Government; and the present regime has not shown the slightest interest in those approaches to economic management that would be less dependent on forecasts or in recruiting economists interested in developing such approaches.

A franker approach might reveal that – for all the rage worked up by some Labour and trade union leaders – the reasoning behind Whitehall advice has hardly changed from what it was under Labour. The analysis is carried out by the same people, too. For one of the striking features of the 'irregulars' that the present Government brought into Whitehall is that they are nearly all business executives concerned with machinery and execution rather than advisers on policy. Even the Central Policy Review Staff (CPRS) under Lord Rothschild is largely staffed by civil servants or near-civil servants and firmly embedded in the Cabinet Office.

Admittedly, one of our curses is the pathetic credence that becomes attached to any statement that has a number attached to it – and still more to any statistical exercise that has gone through a computer. But concealment will aggravate rather than cure the disease and only leave the field open for peddlars of figures uninhibited by Whitehall's conscientious scruples.

While Conservative propaganda tends to mock 'the man in Whitehall', Conservative ministers tend to be very dependent on official Civil Service advice. This does not imply that they always take it, but that they are not aware of any intellectually respectable alternative. This is all tied up with the case-by-case approach and the disinclination of the present Conservative leadership to put up any positive philosophy of a market economy in place of the interventionist consensus. In behaving like this ministers get the worst of both worlds. They are bitterly accused of 'following classical economics' and being devoted to market forces. Yet at the same time they are deriving none of the advantages that could be derived from doing just this. Action without words is liable to be just as unsatisfactory as words used as a substitute for action.

5 When the Cheering Has to Stop

[Mr Anthony Barber was made Chancellor suddenly after the unexpected death of Iain Macleod in the summer of 1970. After a shaky start, he surprised his critics by a well-presented Budget Speech which introduced tax reforms and gave a moderate 'stimulus'. Unfortunately, there was reason to worry about the underlying economic stategy and the trend of political discussion. Most of Mr Barber's critics, both in his own party and in the Labour Party, were urging radically misguided courses on him, bad advice to which – with the aid of much prodding from the Prime Minister – he eventually succumbed.

Some of the tax reforms introduced by the new Chancellor were basically sound, but killed by lack of imagination. The failure to tie the new starting points for the basic and higher rates of personal tax to an index of the value of money meant (as I warned in a passage not reproduced here) that they would soon be eroded by inflation. Thus the worst of all worlds was achieved; trade unionists and the media were led to believe that large sums of tax relief had been received by the rich, while the supposed beneficiaries knew that the combination of inflation and progressive taxation was crushing them in a trap which would have been there even without the subsequent Labour measures.]

The Capacity for Self-Delusion (8 April 1971)

This year's Budget Debate in the House of Commons has been a fine example of the national capacity for self-delusion and wishful thinking. Of course, the Budget was well received. Which of us could not have produced a popular Budget with £546 million of taxation to remit in 1971–2 and £680 million in a full year, especially when there are no countervailing cuts in government spending and the funds are obtained by going into deficit?

Labour criticism official strategy was based on the irresponsible suggestion – repeated in nearly every opposition speech – that the

Chancellor should have handed out even more than he did. Even the minority of Conservatives who called for stricter control of the money supply played to the gallery by claiming that inflation had nothing to do with wage settlements and that monetary policy was a near painless cure.

I hate to spoil the fun, but last week's Budget reminded me more than anything else of the one introduced by Mr Selwyn Lloyd exactly ten years ago. The parallels are uncanny. Mr Lloyd, like Mr Barber, had been previously criticised as an economic lightweight, placed in No. 11 by the then Prime Minister, Harold Macmillan. Mr Lloyd, like Mr Barber, then proceeded to turn the tables on his critics with a crisp, well-written Budget Speech containing several reforms. Of course, the reforms were not identical; Mr Lloyd introduced the 'regulator', while Mr Barber promised reforms in the tax structure. Both Chancellors, however, introduced long-overdue reliefs in the absurdly high marginal rates of tax on larger incomes.

Mr Lloyd in his 1961 speech stressed the danger 'that the cost inflationary process will speed up further. That, I feel, is the principal menace at present and one which it is impossible to exaggerate.' Mr Barber said: 'It is right that I should end with this warning. All our hopes for the future will be but dust in our mouths if we do not repel the assault upon the value of our money.' Both chancellors, having made obeisance to the problem, then proceeded to pass by on the other side.

To add to the ominous parallels, the 1961 Budget, like its successor of a decade later, was introduced against a background of speculation in favour of the German mark, which was met by a series of palliatives by central bankers. We know that in July 1961 Mr Selwyn Lloyd had to announce a wage freeze, and that many of those who had cheered him uncritically in the spring became bitter and unreasoning opponents in the summer.

The novelty this year is the contradiction between the policies ministers say they are following in those speeches that are not scripted by Whitehall and the doctrines of the Budget Speech. In their political speaking ministers warn that if wage claims are pressed too far they will lead to bankruptcies, redundancies and unemployment. Although controversial, this embodies one possible approach to wage inflation. It is, however, in complete contradiction to the Budget Speech, which forecast an increase in unemployment if nothing were done and then undertook to increase purchasing power to prevent this happening. The release of spending power was in no way conditional on what happened to wage settlements. Demand is, according to the Budget doctrine, to be increased to make sure that people are not priced out of a job. To make sure that there was no misunderstanding, the Chancellor explained in his Speech and reiterated when winding up this Monday that if 'a further stimulus is needed, then the usual instruments are always available and I would not hesitate to use them'.

There is something to be said for the Treasury doctrine of keeping up real output and employment and tackling inflation by some (unnamed) other means; there is something to be said for the present Heath doctrine of refusing to bail out firms and workers who push up wages and prices too rapidly. But the two doctrines are mutually contradictory, and cannot both be enforced simultaneously.

Even if it were right to prevent unemployment from going much higher, it would still be wrong to do so by stimulating *home demand* alone. A policy based on a 2 per cent increase in export volume (including 'invisibles') and a 6 per cent increase in imports, as forecast in the Financial Statement, is not viable for very long. The right way to have stimulated demand would have been by acting on the profitability of exports and imports by the only non-subsidy, non-protectionist method available – that is, acting on the exchange rate, whether by floating or some system of small and regular adjustments. Even if the rate did not move very much at first, the simple assurance that overseas profitability would be maintained in the face of adverse cost trends would be a powerful stimulus to both exports and investment.

If such a move is for the time being ruled out, what should be the verdict on the Chancellor's Budget judgement? It is the usual case of 'to much too late'. The total true adverse wing is around £1.2 billion in the public sector requirement. But although the total stimulus will probably be too big in its eventual effect, it will also be slow-acting and long delayed. None of the fiscal measures will even begin to come into effect until July. All will take a long time to have their full effect. The main stimulus, the halving of SET, is both extremely uncertain in its total effects and likely to take a long time to work through the economy. Thus we could well have the worst of both worlds: an unnecessary increase in the unemployment trend over the next few months, leading to pressure to pump still more money into the economy.

Yet by 1972, the extra £1.2 billion of funds already provided is likely to be giving home demand an embarrassingly large boost. A better recipe for fresh stop–go and a payments crisis would be difficult to find. A smaller stimulus with an immediate impact, such as purchase tax reductions, would have been far preferable from a demand management point of view, and would also have had a bigger impact on the cost of living.

In short, I think the total Budget give-away was too large and the choice of stimulus misguided. We have no policy for inflation, and only the greatest good luck will prevent a fresh balance of payments crisis within the next couple of years when we ought, instead, to be preserving a substantial surplus to meet the costs of EEC membership.

Too Much, Too Late Again (20 July 1971)

[The Budget measures did not prevent a continued rise in unemployment, and in July of the same year the Chancellor came back with a fresh package of stimulants, mostly in the form of reductions in consumer taxes.]

The writer of Ecclesiastes observed 'there is no new thing under the sun'. There is nothing more familiar to connoisseurs of chancellors' statements than a change of economic direction. Yesterday's summer Budget marked a change from a relatively cautious demand management policy to one of expansion. We had precisely the same change of direction under Lord Butler in the early 1950s and under Mr Maudling in the early 1960s. An equally familiar observation is that changes of direction never last for long; and neither an expansionist philosophy nor one of maintaining a margin of slack is ever adhered to long enough to be given a chance to work. The net effect of such changes of fashion is to increase the fluctuations in the economy beyond what would otherwise be necessary.

Previous experiments in demand expansion came to grief for two reasons. First, it was merely home demand that was expanded. Because these experiments were, like the present one, undertaken when the balance of payments was relatively secure, adequate thought was not given to ways of protecting the balance of payments in later phases of the expansion. Secondly, and more fundamentally, such experiments increased the pressure on the labour market and stoked up inflationary pressures, which could then be curbed only by a freeze and a squeeze.

The extent of the change in direction can be seen by looking at the so-called 'arithmetic' of the package. It is worth doing this, not out of any belief in Treasury forecasts, but for the light they throw on official assumptions. The new summer forecast predicted a growth rate of just over 3 per cent in the coming twelve months. The package is expected to jerk up this growth rate to $4\frac{1}{2}$ per cent. This means, after taking account of indirect and second-round effects, an increase in demand of £500m.–£600m. over and above the large, but excessively delayed, stimulus announced in the Budget.

This cannot be explained by any new economic diagnosis. If the Chancellor had simply tried to compensate for the fact that the economy was starting from a lower base line than he thought at the time of the Budget, the required injection of demand would only have been about $\frac{1}{2}$ per cent, or £200 million. If the official calculations work out as intended, demand will now grow about $1\frac{1}{2}$ per cent faster than the growth of productive capacity, and unemployment should fall by just over 100,000 in the next year or so.

This massive boost is being given at a time when money earnings are $12\frac{1}{2}$ per cent above a year ago (despite some industrial evidence of a further slowdown), and when even the Chancellor was not willing to say any more than that this inflationary trend had 'levelled off'. The April Budget was expected to lead to a £1 billion deterioration in the government borrowing requirement. Quite apart from the tax reliefs announced yesterday, the enforced squeeze on nationalised industry prices will swing their accounts into deficit by an extra £300 million or so, all of which will have to be met by additional government borrowing.

The change of direction marks a clear defeat for the official Treasury line and a victory for the Prime Minister's camp. But before cheering too loudly, one should remember that a change can be for the worse, and that, although the Treasury is often wrong, its critics are even more frequently so.

In a sense, however, the Treasury deserved its fate. The reason that it has come unstuck is that it has presented its advice far too much in terms of short-term forecasts and not nearly enough in terms of basic economic analysis. This made it very easy for the young Turks around the Prime Minister to point out (a) that for the last year and a half the Treasury had overestimated the pressure of home demand and (b) that the forecast deterioration in the balance of payments had not so far taken place.

Forecasting errors are not in one direction only. If one disregards the precise arithmetic of 3 and $4\frac{1}{2}$ per cent, there are all too many reasons for fearing that the package is yet another example of 'too much too late'. Just as world trade is beginning to accelerate and export volume to pick up, just as the main Budget measures are beginning to come into effect, and when unfilled vacancies are beginning to rise and the increase in unemployment to level off, political forces have decreed another stimulus.

Some might suggest that the CBI attempt to put a ceiling of 5 per cent on price increases by its members creates an entirely new situation. The sectors covered by the CBI (not just the two hundred main concerns) and the nationalised industries together account for about a third of the retail price index. Giving the CBI all the benefit of the doubt, the price index will rise by nearly 1 per cent less than it otherwise would. On top of this, the Chancellor expects the purchase tax cuts to take $\frac{3}{4}$ per cent off the index. The net effect will be not price stability, but a rate of inflation of $1\frac{1}{2}$ per cent to 2 per cent less than would otherwise be expected.

For some time, the new 'at-a-stroke' policies will no doubt work in the direction intended. This is quite irrespective of whether or not the TUC makes the noises expected of it. For the next few months wages will continue to be influenced by current unemployment levels, which will take time to decline. On top of this the slight reduction in inflationary expectations should make workers value a given money wage increase more highly and employers take a more sober view of how much they can pass on.

But those who believe that a virtuous circle will now ensue are likely to be disappointed eventually. As time goes on, the pressures in the labour market will build up; and unless trade union monopoly power is tackled, this will lead to a re-acceleration of wage increases from a level that will still be very high. It is a fallacy to suppose that, because long-term effects are more difficult to predict, they do not matter. Moreover, it is quite naive to suppose that the man in Whitehall has the knowledge to push up the growth rate to $4\frac{1}{2}$ per cent and then shade it down to 3 per cent or 2 per cent if demand has overshot the mark. This is the fine-tuning fallacy supposedly characteristic of left-wing governments.

The most disappointing feature of the present regime at the Treasury is that, while there has been fundamental rethinking of other aspects of government policy, such as housing and social security, economic strategy remains frozen in the Butskellite mould. Instead of looking for long-term guidelines, policy here is still dominated by the myths of short-term demand management and the mirage of a voluntary incomes policy. One sensed in some of the Labour questioning a surprise at the abandonment of all pretence of a new economic philosophy and some incredulity that the Chancellor had gone so far on the basis of so little concrete delivery from the TUC. In the short term the Cassandras and those who care for principle may seem wrong; but in the longer run it could be a very different story.

6 Spending Ourselves into Prosperity

Bad Advice from High Places (9 March 1972)

It has been obvious since the end of last autumn that the Government has been planning yet another much larger, fresh fiscal stimulus. The National Institute of Economic and Social Research has caused a stir by advocating a much larger sum than the Chancellor is likely to remit – no less than £2.5 billion – on the assumption that these reliefs are all of a kind that immediately affect consumers' expenditure.

The value of the National Institute on such occasions is that it comes out with such a high figure that whatever the Chancellor does in the end seems modest in comparison. High officials will be able to tell bodies such as the OECD's 'Working Party Three', and the Chancellor will be able to assure visiting Finance Ministers, that he has been very cautious and conservative by comparison with what he had been advised to do by responsible outside experts.

It is important to avoid misunderstanding. The National Institute's forecasts and recommendations are honest calculations made on the data available and with the aid of theories which it sincerely holds. The ritual element is built into the situation and is a typical product of human action but not of human design.

It will not however do for an outsider simply to recoil from the £2.5 billion figure because it seems very large. As the Institute points out, owing to inflation and real growth the orders of magnitude have increased very much over the last few years. The Institute's forecasting record has been no worse than that of other bodies attempting similar projections, and in the last couple of years it has been somewhat better than the Treasury's. If the underlying assumptions of the whole approach are accepted, then the National Institute's figure is as good as any other. If it is to be queried, it can only be by querying those assumptions.

The four crucial controversial assumptions seem to me the following:

1 There are no built-in automatic forces that will tend to bring unemployment down towards the minimum level. This is held to be so despite the recent increase in the money supply at an annual rate of about 20 per cent and the prospect that the authorities will do all they can to make sure that an inadequate growth of the monetary stock is not a source of 'deflationary' pressure.

2 It is nevertheless possible to reduce unemployment to some pre-ordained level considered desirable – in this case $2\frac{1}{4}$ per cent – simply by reinforcing monetary expansion with enough deficit finance; in other words, to spend ourselves into 'full employment'.

3 Economic forecasts are sufficiently reliable in a rough-and-ready way to enable one to inject confidently a very large sum of purchasing power into the economy, the full effects of which will be subject to long and uncertain time lags. (The alternative to relying so heavily on the forecasts is to make smaller, and if necessary more frequent, adjustments in accordance with the current situation, or to proceed by some long-term budgetary rules, or evolve some compromise between the two.)

4 Not only is it possible to move to a much higher level of output and employment, but it is safe to do so very quickly. This is implied by the target of a 5 per cent increase in output between now and the first half of 1973. A growth rate of this kind would be of record dimensions and nearly 2 per cent above the Institute's own estimate of the underlying growth of capacity.

Most of those who will be denouncing the Institute for lack of moderation will themselves share these assumptions (with the possible exception of the fourth), which have governed economic policy since the war and are based on what is sometimes called the 'naive Keynesian' model. The reason why I would not endorse the Institute's recommendations is that I believe these assumptions to be no longer plausible.

It will be noted that there was no reference to the balance of payments in the dubious assumptions listed. The former is mainly a matter of the exchange rate and can be averted by a sufficiently prompt and gradual downward adjustment of the sterling parity if and when the threatened deterioration appears. This might involve reversing some of the tax cuts, whose place would be taken by an export stimulus; but to criticise the Institute on these grounds would be to fall into the trap of basing policy on forecasts about the most unpredictable item of all — the overseas balance.

The key objections to the National Institute philosophy of demand management relate to prices. Personally, I would settle for a high but steady rate of inflation if by this means one could secure a lower level of unemployment; and so probably would the electorate. But unfortunately, the benefits to employment of pumping more and more money into the system, regardless of what is happening to prices, depends on inflation not being anticipated. As people come to realise what is happening, the monetary pump needs to be turned faster and faster, and prices allowed to rise more and more rapidly, to secure any given benefit to employment; and while the social and economic system can adjust to a high rate of inflation, it cannot adjust to an accelerating or explosive rate.

If for any reason the natural rate of employment required simply to hold the rate of inflation stable is too high for the political system to tolerate, we come across the tiger-by-the-tail dilemma (an analogy due to Hayek). Suppose we start from a situation where unemployment may seem in all conscience high enough, but is still below the natural rate; then prices will be rising at an increasing rate, and we will be on the tail of an inflationary tiger.

Either we hang on to the tail and are pulled along at ever-increasing speed until business calculations become impossible, something else is used for money and all possible benefit to employment is lost, or else we let go of the tiger and are eaten by him — which translated out of metaphor means an intolerable increase in the amount of unemployment we need *over the average of a cycle* to prevent this inflationary explosion.

The fact that it has taken twenty-five years for this impasse to be reached rather than the fifteen that Hayek originally expected does not affect the issue. The National Institute's recommendation is to hang on to the tail of the inflationary tiger while it gathers speed — in the hope, no doubt, that at some stage in its run it will swallow a magic potion known as 'Incomes Policy' which will change it into a slower and nicer animal.

What, then, should someone recommend who believes that high unemployment basically reflects union monopoly power and structural maladjustments of supply to demand, which are in the long run made worse by the Conservative policy of propping up lame ducks? The answer has already been given implicitly above. Even with existing union monopoly power, one may hope that the minimum rate of un-employment is below rather than above a million. As Keynesian policies still have some moderate short-term potency, a stimulus of, say not more than £400 million might be recommended on the grounds that the hard evidence to date suggests that unemployment has at best levelled off and may not have even done that. Tax reliefs of this order would also fit in with the goal of a moderate and fairly steady overall budget deficit calculated on a 'constant employment' basis.

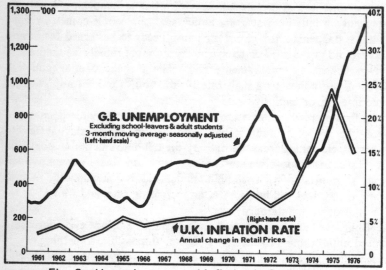

Fig 3. Unemployment and Inflation in Great Britain

The much larger reliefs the Chancellor will probably give will no doubt stimulate output and even have a beneficial effect on inflation for a temporary period; and the tiger may appear to be a phantom after all. But the long run is becoming even shorter; and once the Government and the country realise that it can no longer escape the dilemma of explosive inflation or intolerable unemployment, the present collective bargaining system will not be able to survive. But to describe the changes that will either occur or be needed as 'Incomes Policy' is to use a euphemism to obscure what will either occur or be needed.

The Dash for Growth (3 March 1972)

With a 21 March Budget deadline to meet, the Chancellor could not wait for all uncertainties to be resolved and had to make a judgement.

The decision he took was to give priority to getting output up and unemployment down. The size of the Budget stimulus was larger than
might appear from the £1.2 billion cost of the tax reliefs in the present
financial year. The aim was to add 2 per cent to the annual growth of
output over and above what might otherwise have been expected. The
growth rate that the Treasury is hoping to achieve for the period up to
the middle of 1973 is 5 per cent per annum. It is starting from so high
a level of unemployment that the normal backroom calculations would
indicate that even this rate of growth would still lead to a peak in total
registered unemployed of 800,000–900,000 next winter. But when so
many predictions have gone astray it is quite likely that the figure will
be outside this range. If a boom really gets going, unemployment
might fall even faster. But there is also the nagging fear that unemployment will, despite everything, remain obstinately high. The
Chancellor is in principle quite prepared to give another stimulus
should that prove necessary.

Behind all the detailed arithmetic, the broad hope is clear. It is to
give British industry the confidence to invest ahead of EEC

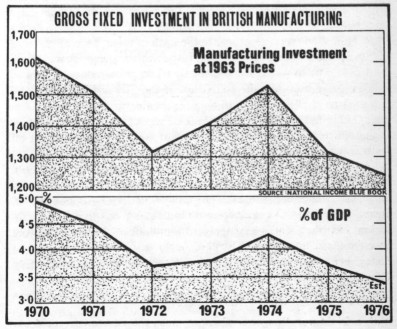

Fig 4.   Gross Fixed Investment in British Manufacturing

membership and to remove the fear that any future growth would soon come to an end as a result of another economic 'stop'. The Chancellor has tried to achieve this by giving his main stimulus to home consumer demand by means of an increase in the personal allowances which is meant to be as unprovocative as possible to the unions. Secondly, he has done his best to stimulate investment. 'Free depreciation', which is the stimulus most popular with industrialists, has been granted; and extra investment incentives on top of this are available in the high-unemployment areas. But the third and revolutionary departure has been an explicit undertaking that expansion will not be brought to a halt by measures taken to defend the exchange rate. Ministers are satisfied in their own minds that if it came to a choice between sacrificing 5 per cent growth and changing the exchange rate, it is the exchange rate that would go.

Mr Barber's exact words were that 'it is neither necessary nor desirable to distort domestic economies to an unacceptable extent in order to retain unrealistic exchange rates, whether they are too high, or too low.' There was no reason for 'this country, or any other, to be frustrated on this score in its determination to sustain sound economic growth and reduce unemployment'. Ten years ago one would have said that the shift of exchange rate strategy would be enough to do the trick. Now, however, the anxiety at the back of many people's minds is that the present unemployment may be due either to deep-seated structural causes or to wage-push caused by trade union monopoly power. It is for this reason that there are those in the City and elsewhere who fear that the public sector borrowing requirement of well over £3 billion might either have a disappointing lack of impact on unemployment, or – alternatively – relieve unemployment at the expense of starting off another wage explosion within a couple of years.

Thus, if the real obstacle to growth and full employment has been the exchange rate constraint and the effect this has had on the long-term industrial confidence, then one can be moderately optimistic. If, on the other hand, the underlying difficulties are due to cost-push inflation and trade union monopoly, the outlook is a good deal more problematical. Even this, however, does not exclude a period of reasonably rapid growth while union bargaining power is still being affected by high unemployment, and union expectations are being favourably influenced by the recent deceleration of price increases and tax concessions. But on this diagnosis, the period of rapid growth will be shorter – or will need new policies to sustain it – than would be the case if the main limitations were on the balance of payments front.

Sterling Floated — A Decade Too Late (June 1972)

The roots of the decision to float the pound go back to the change in orthodox thinking among central banks and Finance Ministries in the past few years. The general consensus is that the world should go back to what is supposed to have been the original intention of Bretton Woods. This was that exchange rates should normally be fixed, but that countries should be prepared to change them promptly if it became clear that they were unrealistic and could only be shored up by controls or by distortions of domestic policy.

The new and more flexible attitude to the parity was forcefully stated by Mr Anthony Barber in his Budget Speech. The Chancellor's object was, of course, to persuade businessmen — who were fearful that expansion would be brought to an end by a sterling crisis and another round of stop–go – that they could safely invest without such fear.

In the realm of high principle, the Government was then – and still is – opposed to floating rates as a normal method of keeping overseas payments in balance. Mr Heath has always personally disliked the idea; and so has the Bank of England. The favourite targets of politicians looking for an easy scapegoat have again been 'speculators'. Whether it is the price of accommodation, or changes in currency parities, it is easier to put the blame on men who move bits of paper about for supposedly sinister purposes than to seek out the fundamental forces at work.

The fact that speculators can do good as well as harm is conveniently forgotten in political speeches. Speculation can often moderate the more extreme fluctuations in exchange rates, as well as in other prices; and speculators who destabilise prices are likely to make overall losses, even though the smarter ones may gain at the expense of their brethren.

An enterprise system based on markets cannot function without professional speculation (and the same seems to be true of Soviet-type economies). Unfortunately, politicians theoretically pledged to free enterprise succumb to the temptations to blame others for the failure of their own policies, just as much as their left-wing opponents. Not only has Mr Wilson persisted in blaming speculators for the 1967 British devaluation, but President Nixon did the same for the US devaluation of last year, and now Mr Heath is taking the same attitude to the present British downward-floating rate of exchange. In fact, most of the forces that topple currency parities derive not from speculation but from precautionary actions by individuals and companies who wish to avoid making losses. International companies would be irrational if they did not move funds away from currencies that were expected to depreciate, or to cover contracts that had become subject to an exchange risk.

Mr Heath contends that the floating of the mark in 1971 and of sterling now — which he regards as threats to 'the whole international monetary order' — are due to the existence of 'vast masses' of highly mobile funds. He is, however, mistaking what is at most a magnifying factor for the root cause. The best antidote to unjustified speculation is not controls but a freer market. The massive movement of funds about which Mr Heath complains is the result of fixed, but distrusted, parities. Anyone taking a view on sterling last week, or the mark in early 1971, knew that there was only one way the rate could go. Neither a floating rate nor controls can prevent a devaluation that is justified by the fundamental facts of a country's competitive position. The real surprise was not that sterling should have weakened, but that it should have held up as long as it did in the face of a gloomy payments outlook.

A 'fixed' rate, known to be liable to change, encourages a short-sighted attitude on the part of the foreign exchange market; for traders have little incentive to think about the long-run trend and act accordingly, but are mainly concerned with whether the Government will be able to hold the parity in the next three months or so. This is why sterling remained so embarrisingly strong early in the year and sentiment changed so dramatically within the last couple of weeks. The selling was triggered off by the rail settlement, which suggested that the coal miners were not such a special case after all, and by the threat of serious industrial unrest arising from conflicts between unions and the Industrial Relations Court. With reserves and automatic drawing rights of over £3 billion, the British authorities could have held out a little longer; but there was no point in allowing the loss of reserves to gather momentum when the Government's own advisers shared the market's belief that a parity change was probable.

If the market had not forced its hand, the Government would almost certainly have preferred to devalue to another fixed rate at a time of its choosing. But once the pressure built up in the foreign exchange markets, the Chancellor emerged as a strong advocate of floating and won the day against some conflicting advice from the Bank of England. One attraction of floating for Mr Barber was that he could present the move as a way of defeating speculators and preventing a

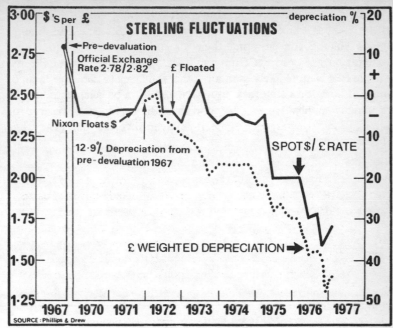

Fig 5. Sterling Fluctuations

reserve drain, which in fact it is.

In retrospect, the foreign exchange crisis may turn out to have proved a blessing in disguise. For it has nudged the Government into an exchange rate depreciation at a time when there is still slack in the economy and exports can be stimulated without the need for domestic restrictive measures. The rapid fall in unemployment despite the stagnation of exports showed that a potentially dangerous, purely home-market, expansion was developing. If this had been allowed to go further, and an exchange rate postponed until the autumn, domestic restraints might have been unavoidable. They may still be necessary, if only to curb domestic inflation; but they will be less severe and sudden than if the Chancellor had allowed the payments situation to worsen without taking action. [Domestic restraints *were* necessary, but were avoided altogether in the pursuit of incomes policy.]

The threat of a fall in the exchange rate is more likely to make the Government change its mind over wages and prices than any amount of verbal argument. At the moment, it is scarcely credible that not only ministers, who can hardly be expected to learn from the mistakes of their political opponents, but even official advisers who were involved in the Labour Government's entirely abortive 'Statement of Intent', should still be concentrating their efforts on an attempt to obtain voluntary wage restraint from the TUC. The movement of the exchange rate is more likely than any other influence to convince them of the need both for a statutory approach and for a parallel restriction of the money supply. There is no point in holding weapons in reserve for an inflationary emergency once it is clear that the emergency has already arrived.

7 A Wrong Assessment

[False judgements can in retrospect be informative about the period in which they are made. It is perhaps typical of the period that my worst assessments were my most optimistic ones. In the New Year of 1972 the Heath Government was worried about recession and unemployment, but inflation appeared to be receding. By the middle of February however the Government had been defeated by the 1972 miners' strike, the one with the flying pickets; the vast bulk of economic opinion assumed that the anti-inflation policy had already been defeated, an assumption that I shared too uncritically. The shift to incomes policy was largely a result of this prevailing interpretation of the miners' victory. I welcomed the initial stage of this incomes policy, the three-months' freeze. The article that follows is probably the most misguided I ever wrote.]

Why Mr Heath's Policy is right at last (9 November 1972)

It is not normally the economic commentator's job to act as a cheerleader for government policy. He should be the detached critic and not the leader of a claque. But there are exceptions to most rules; and when a government has adopted policies that one has been advocating oneself for several years, it is only honest to come out in support of them.

The fact that these policies have been adopted as a last resort, and against the extremely strong initial convictions of Mr Heath and those closest to him, is all the more reason for applauding this change of direction – just as it was right to support Mr Wilson when he devalued sterling and reversed his East of Suez policies, again in opposition to his most firmly held earlier convictions.

It is true that these reversals make for cynicism about politicians. But what is it that is really wrong? It is after all better that Prime Ministers should adopt the right policies, however belatedly, than that

51

they should stick to their earlier mistakes for the sake of consistency. What *should* cause justified cynicism is the habit of each Prime Minister – whether Mr Wilson in 1964 or Mr Heath in 1970 – of claiming that he can avoid the measures that most past governments in this country and others have had to adopt in the very difficult task of running a mixed economy. The real fault of the post-Macmillan party leaders is the hubris that enables them not merely to oppose the predictable responses of the other side to events (Oppositions are not there to give support); it is rather that they convince themselves that they have found the philosophers' stone – which will enable them to dispense with such measures themselves.

Ever since the wage–price explosion of the winter of 1969–70, it has been clear that any tolerably successful economic strategy would have to have three main elements: a temporary statutory wage–price freeze; a firm control over the money supply; and what may be called in shorthand a 'realistic' policy towards the exchange rate. These are not panaceas; and they cannot by themselves resolve the major economic tensions of modern society, in particular those produced by trade union monopoly power. But they are the main devices so far evolved for keeping the system running without an explosion.

Mr Heath has not only at long last introduced a wage–price freeze; in contrast to Mr Selwyn Lloyd and Mr Macmillan's freezes, his has been preceded by a floating of the pound before a severe payments deficit has had time to develop. The present \$2.35 rate amounts to an $8\frac{1}{2}$ per cent effective depreciation of sterling compared with the early spring of 1971 before the German mark floated and before the events leading to the Smithsonian agreement to devalue the dollar.

The United Kingdom is now embarking on a period of expansion, and is facing the payments burden of EEC membership with a margin of spare capacity, some statutory control over costs and a competitive exchange rate. If one had predicted this combination to a worried official or economist a couple of years ago, one would have been dismissed as wildly optimistic and lacking in all political realism. Yet not only do we now have all three together; but there are some signs that the gains will not be frittered away by a thoughtless expansion of the money supply as happened after earlier freezes. Mr Barber's speech in Tuesday's debate still seems to me to have the relative roles of incomes and monetary policy the wrong way round. He spoke of the consequences in terms of lost output and unemployment of relying exclusively on monetary regulation (when trade unions and perhaps other monopoly groups have the power to push up the per capita

money incomes of their members). *Unfortunately, some of his advisers
have not yet taken on board the high probability that this loss of output
and employment cannot in the long run be avoided by pushing up the
money supply and the budget deficit, except at the expense of an ever-
accelerating inflation which will itself cause the system to break down*
[Italics added.]

What is true is that any attempt to slow down the growth of the
money supply, or even to prevent it accelerating, is likely to cause
extra unemployment over and above that made inevitable by
monopolistic elements in the economy, simply because expectations
are geared to rapid and increasing rates of inflation. A monetary slowdown, unaccompanied by other policies, will have its main effect on
jobs long before it begins to affect prices and wages. Such an increase
might in some technical sense be temporary, but a temporary period
could last a decade or more, as in the 1920s when the United Kingdom
was attempting to use monetary policy alone to force down its internal
price level and suffered from heavy unemployment while the rest of the

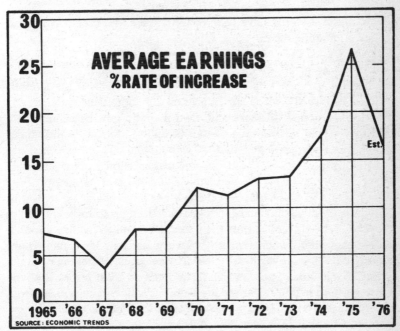

Fig 6.　Rate of Increase of Average Earnings

world was booming. The case for floating exchange rates is entirely dependent on taking seriously the adverse 'temporary' effects of relying on money supply control alone to bring us into balance with the rest of the world.

The role of the freeze and the subsequent Phase II is to reduce the level of inflationary expectation so that the expansion of the money supply can safely be slowed down. Without the wage–price freeze, unemployment would have to rise to unnecessary heights; but without control of the money supply no amount of incomes intervention will prevent the extra cash from finding its way into the price level as it has done throughout recorded history. Fortunately, however, it is not these subtleties that are for the moment politically important. The statistics reiterated by the Chancellor do show some sign of a monetary slowdown, and Mr Barber gave a fresh hint about the use of special deposits. *As a political animal, he is well aware that the behaviour of the British money supply is going to be watched eagle-eyed by EEC partners (an advantage of British membership for which Mr Powell ought to be grateful), the Bank of England and, above all, those of his own back-benchers whose support will be indispensable in future prices and incomes legislation.* [Italics added.]

Of course it would have been better if there had been a combined policy of floating the exchange rate, controlling the money supply and freezing wages and prices two years ago. As early as 5 June 1970, a warning was given in this column that the inflationary explosion created the greatest single threat to full employment. If the Conservatives had really made an attack on inflation their number one priority, the period of freeze and control would now be behind them and they would be in a much better position to introduce their other changes – both good and bad – without the embarrassments into which they have now run. But the practical question is not whether the Government should have acted sooner, but whether its measures are now too late to be of use; and there is not any convincing reason to think this. Both sterling and gilt-edged have held up remarkably well to the TUC refusal to talk while the freeze is on and to the fine imposed on the engineering union. Indeed, the very fact that Mr Heath so obviously did not have his heart either in the floating of sterling or in the present wage–price freeze, which he adopted as a last resort, is all the more reason for those who are more enthusiastic to give a cheer from the sidelines. To the Government the breakdown of the attempted concordat with the TUC and the CBI, and the need to resort to a statutory freeze, was a bitter blow. But from some points of view, so far from being a tragedy, this may have been the best thing that could have happened.

There are at least three reasons for believing this. The first is the very simple one that, while statutory freezes can work for a while and need not be followed by explosions, the TUC does not have the power to deliver voluntary wage restraint from its constituent members. Secondly, wage–price controls are supported by different people for different reasons. Adherents of the market economy find the occasional short sharp shock, which is equally unfair to everyone, a lesser evil than the attempted permanent control of wages and prices, which has never worked even in a partially free society, but the attempted enforcement of which can do a great deal of damage. The Federal Reserve Bank of Richmond (Virginia) put it very well in its October journal by saying that wage–price policies should be 'temporary and episodic' and that 'the Phase II machinery should be maintained just long enough to eliminate inflationary expectations and to improve the wage–price performance of the economy'. The third reason why the breakdown of the CBI–TUC discussions may not be the tragedy so widely assumed is that responsibility for any intervention that may be necessary with market forces has been thrown back on the elected government and Parliament where it belongs, and that plans to manage the economy by a consortium of Whitehall officials and producer interest groups have received a setback.

Anyone who believes that fears of a corporate state concern only ivory tower ideologues should read in *Hansard* the Prime Minister's answers to Harold Wilson on Monday. Mr Heath reported to the CBI and the TUC that matters such as EEC entry, the Industrial Relations and the Fair Rents Acts were political matters not to be decided in tripartite talks. Similarly, the Chancellor explained that, although he could listen to representations on subjects such as the VAT rate or subsidies for sensitive foodstuffs, such budgetary topics were up to him to decide. These were admirable sentiments. But are they really consistent with Mr Heath's own widely praised offer in his Conservative Conference oration 'to employers and unions to share fully with the Government the benefits and obligations in running the national economy'? If these sentiments are taken seriously, the trade union leaders who wanted to bring taxes, rent legislation, EEC policy and all the rest into a wage–price deal were being perfectly reasonable. If the responsibilities of government are to be shared with union leaders in this way, there can be no permanently excluded subjects, and, if the experiment had got off the ground, sooner or later every major act of policy would have had to be cleared with the TUC and the CBI first; and the leaders of these bodies would have powers of initiative greater than Cabinet ministers. If all this seems to be going much too far, perhaps the concept of partnership needs to be shelved in favour of the more traditional idea of government responsibility tempered by consultations and persuasion.

There are still many battles ahead. Although it has suffered a reverse, the corporate state is far from dead. The pressure will have to be kept up on the money supply; and although by a mixture of good luck and good contingency planning in the Treasury sterling is now at the best possible rate for EEC entry, circumstances could change and it would still be a mistake to peg the rate too early. There is thus very little danger that one will run dry of food for criticism in the months to come. There is a whole range of policies, from regional developments to the nationalised industries and support for aerospace, where there is nothing to retract of previous criticisms. The fact remains that, of all the possible scenarios that one might have sketched last spring for broad economic strategy, it is the best one that has been enacted.

[This article was indefensible even on the evidence available at the time it was written. The main sources of error are in the passages italicised in this (completely uncut) reprint. There was no warrant for believing that the authorities would either treat pay and price controls as a short and temporary affair, or that they would accompany them by the right monetary policies. Subsequent events showed the futility of expecting the EEC, the Bank of England or back-bench pressure to force the Government onto the right lines. The one part of the article to be vindicated was the pessimistic foreboding at the end on the union price for a 'voluntary' policy.]

References

Brittan, Samuel and Lilley, Peter, *The Delusion of Incomes Policy* (Maurice Temple Smith, 1977).

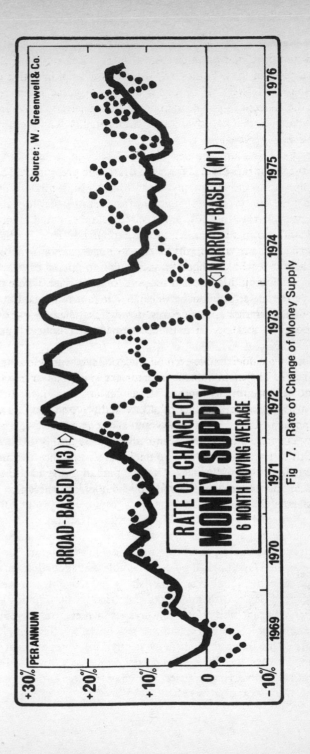

Fig 7. Rate of Change of Money Supply

8   Flat Out to the Next Stop

[*March – June 1973*]

Some readers have asked why, when I supported the original wage freeze last November, I should have become so critical of more recent government policy. My most prominent reaction last November was relief that the tripartite talks between the Government and the two so-called 'sides' of industry had broken down. This reaction was every bit as patriotic as that of the most committed government loyalists or middle-of-the-road Whitehall advisers.

For we were faced towards the end of last year with the strong possibility of a 'solemn and binding' declaration on pay and price restraint. If an agreement had been reached we would not only have been faced with the long-term shadow of the corporate state; there would have been a pressing and immediate danger that a sheet of paper with no more practical effect than Lord George Brown's ill-fated 1964 'Statement of Intent' would have been accepted as an excuse for ministerial inaction in the face of runaway inflation. At least the freeze, and the announcement of Phase II and III controls, showed a belated recognition that it was the Government's responsibility, and not that of producer interest groups, to take the required action.

But these negative reasons were not of course adequate in themselves. The main reason for my short-lived support for official policy was the view (backed by considerable evidence) that emergency wage–price controls can be surprisingly effective for a period of months. They are worth undertaking if used as an adjunct to more fundamental fiscal and monetary policies, which are thereby given more time in which to work, and are less likely to affect employment adversely in the interval. If history has anything to teach us at all, it is that controls soon lose their effect if kept on for very long; and without the right accompanying policies the gains of the early months are frittered away and even reversed.

It was of course obvious even last November that this was not how ministers and their most influential advisers regarded wage and price restraint. But 'hope springs eternal in the human breast', and I half expected that the pressure of events, and national and international central banking opinion, would push the Government into reducing the Budget deficit and limiting the money supply. This is indeed likely to happen, but much too late, and as a result of a crisis. Moreover, as a result of waiting so long the brakes will have to be slammed down more abruptly, and with more of a screech, than if action had been taken in time. Meanwhile, every mistake in the rule book has been made. So far from the prices and incomes controls being an adjunct to other measures, they have become the sole weapons of policy. Both the Budget deficit and the money supply have been soaring; and this has now affected not merely monetary indicators but the real economy, with shortages of labour and key materials increasing every day.

Leading ministers do not regard the present wage and price controls as emergency measures designed to produce lower and more realistic expectations about the most probable course of wages and prices. Instead, they see them as but the beginning of a permanent system of regulation. They have resurrected the medieval concept of a just price and a fair wage – concepts that are quite unworkable without the underlying theological agreement on status and hierarchy that made the medieval system possible.

It is true that in the long run monetary and fiscal policies may not be sufficient to prevent the cruel choice between runaway inflation and high unemployment, because of the existence and increased use of union monopoly power. But instead of tackling this issue – which would have involved examining the costs and benefits to individual workers of strike action – the Government chose to pick a battle with the TUC over the entirely secondary issue of the Industrial Relations Act.

One of the most distinguished economic forecasters in England, with long experience of government service, remarked to me the other day, in parody of the usual scholastic caution, that the outlook 'is more than usually easy to forecast'. He had the current balance of payments primarily in mind. I would see this as a symptom and put my main emphasis on the internal pressures. But for practical purposes the two kinds of analysis lead to very similar conclusions. With delivery dates lengthening and labour bottlenecks appearing, it is difficult to see how we can avoid sucking in imports at an even greater rate. Despite the favourable outlook for trade, and domestic price controls, it is difficult to believe that the buoyant home market will not divert some goods from exports.

If responsible monetary and fiscal policies were being followed, I would have considerable confidence that the depreciation of sterling that has already occurred would, with no more than gradual and moderate further adjustments in the rate, be sufficient to secure balance of payments equilibrium. In these circumstances it would be reasonable to resort to overseas borrowing – which would occur automatically because of interest rate pulls – to cover any temporary import bulge. But as these fundamental conditions do not exist, a severe change of course may well be necessary to control the interlinked depreciation of the external and internal value of the pound.

A little of the present embarrassment could have been avoided if the Government had not rushed into a decision to have an early Budget (nearly always a mistake) before the full extent of the tightening of the labour market was realised. If unemployment continues to fall as fast as it has done since last September, the seasonally adjusted UK total will be down to 450,000, or about 2 per cent, by very early autumn. This is slightly below the Treasury's working definition of reasonable full employment. Recent trends are, however, seen most clearly in the movement of vacancies, shown in Figure 8, which have proved a more reliable guide to the labour market over the last decade or so. These have doubled over the last year and do not have much further to go before they reach the highest recorded level, which was seen in the overheated labour market before the Wilson freeze and squeeze of 1966.

The more one thinks about it, the more our problems seem to date back to the over-hasty and ill-thought-out reactions to the unemployment of the 1971–2 winter, when taxes were slashed, public expenditure freed from restraints and an invitation card handed to every lame duck to call on the Department of Trade and Industry (DTI). It would clearly have been better if the Government had reflated earlier and less. This is obvious advice, ignored in every recession for political and institutional reasons. Even so, if the Treasury had been left to 'do its own thing', reflating and deflating too late, and then overcorrecting, the damage would have been limited. For this is the cycle we have been through again and again and again, and with which businessmen should be able to cope. The really serious damage was done by Mr Heath and his personal advisers, who thought that conventional demand management could not cope with the structural

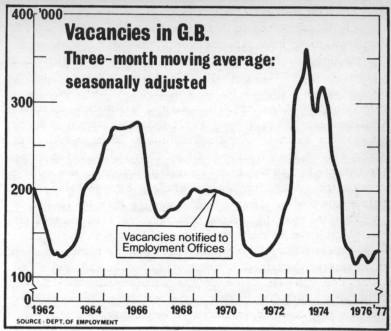

Fig 8. Vacancies in Great Britain

nature of our unemployment problems, and who therefore insisted on adding to the effects of a Budget stimulus a long-term increase in public spending and a long series of rescue operations for every ailing industry and firm.

Meanwhile, students of modern British economic history might find it helpful to remember two useful rules of thumb. One is that, whenever governments talk of faster growth, they usually mean printing more money, and that their detailed policy actions are usually calculated to hold growth back, for example by slowing down the movement of workers from declining to expanding firms and industries. The second is that, when one hears that 'stop–go' has been abandoned in favour of steady expansion, a major 'stop' is on the horizon.

The Denial of Overheating

Talk about a breakthrough is, of course, mainly political. At a more technical level, there are two arguments relevant to the domestic economy. The first concerns the degree of overheating that exists at present. The second concerns the likely future course of events.

The Treasury is apparently forecasting a slowdown from the present growth of 6 per cent to $3\frac{1}{2}$ per cent in the course of this year, without the need for fresh measures. It is relying on rising prices combined with pay restraint to hold back consumer spending, as well as on a slowing down in restocking and in the growth of government spending. The lack of weight that the Government attaches to the money supply, and its unwillingness to allow interest rates to take their own course, do not encourage great expectations. Moreover even recent rates of monetary expansion (annual rates of 20 per cent for 'M3' and 10 per cent for 'M1' up to summer 1973) are still very high by comparison with any period except 1972. Even on the most favourable assumptions, the time lags are so long that the economy will still be influenced by past monetary injections for a long time to come.

But more important than crystal-gazing about the future is the overheating that already exists and is apparent to anyone who tries to get the simplest job done in almost any part of the country. The overload on the building industry is hardly news. Hoover has had to ration washing machines to retailers. More recently, shortages of reinforced concrete, steel and timber have been reported in the *Financial Times*; and for some small electrical motors, delivery delays extend up to twelve months. Similar phenomena are reported in parts of the textile, chemical and aluminium industries. Yet, even though vacancies are at a record low, the Treasury indignantly denies that there is demand inflation; and the National Institute in its May 1973 issue denied the existence of 'overheating', which it condemned as 'an expression which has gate-crashed the literature of the day, avoiding payment of the entrance fee of a definition'. The NIESR went on to reassure readers of the 'robust structure' of the Heath incomes policy.

But perhaps the most serious implications are for wages and prices. The very sharp rise in earnings in April could conceivably have been a once-for-all reaction to the end of the Phase I freeze, but this is unlikely. With so many kinds of labour in such short supply, earnings are likely to rise very fast through shop floor drift, whatever national agreements are negotiated and whatever the Pay Board may do. Even if trade unions did not exist, wages would be tending to rise rapidly in the present situation.

More important than any quibble about the exact sustainable rate of growth is the patent fact that the present 6–7 per cent expansion rate is well above it. Any deceleration to a lower rate must take time; and meanwhile the degree of overheating is increasing. The Americans, who have experienced this difficulty already, have christened it the 're-entry' problem.

The case now is stronger for some demand restraint than the case against. It is surely better for confidence and long-term growth to take some risks on the side of restraint now than to risk a complete halt later, at a time when the world economy is likely to be much less buoyant and when it would be much more difficult for industry to pick up any slack in export markets.

It is reasonable at this stage to ask what I think should be done. The answer is not original. It is that the Budget deficit and the growth of the money supply should be reduced. This would unfortunately probably require an increase in the standard rate of tax – part of which should be used to finance an increase in family allowances (limited by 'clawback') and part retained to reduce government borrowing. There should also be a further blitz on government expenditure. Prestige projects such as Concorde, Maplin and the Channel Tunnel should not escape consideration for the axe. Even if the initial saving is limited, these sacrifices would convince opinion, as nothing else would, that the cuts are for real. In addition to these budgetary moves, the authorities should abandon the attempt to hold down nominal interest rates. On the contrary, consideration should be given to using the Bank of England's reserve power to raise the 'minimum lending rate', in Bank Rate fashion, to above the normal relation with Treasury bill rate.

Most ministers would now reject such a programme out of hand in the belief that it would mark a return to stop–go. It would not. But it will when they, or a post-election government, belatedly introduce it.

[Ministers who had previously been passionately opposed to a floating exchange rate treated it as the panacea which they had wrongly accused its advocates of believing it to be. In particular, they attempted to use it to prolong the government-induced 1972–3 boom long after it was clear to others that it was getting out of hand. But it is doubtful if they could have got away with this approach even as long as they did if they had adopted a clean float, or confined intervention to smoothing out short-term fluctuations.

Unfortunately, the British floating rate has been one in name only. All that it has meant is that the Government has not announced in advance the level or range at which it has been trying to maintain the rate and has left itself the option of changing the support points at any time. In 1973, the first year after the decision to float, the Conservative Government borrowed nearly £1 billion in the eurodollar market

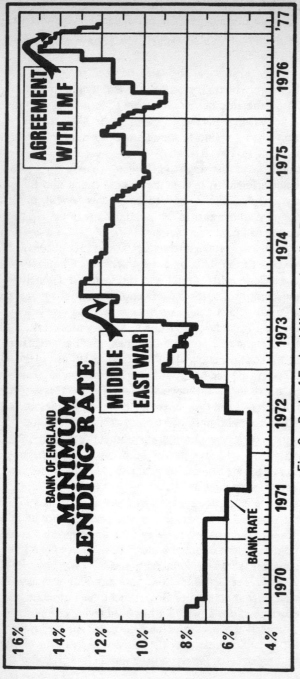

Fig 9. Bank of England Minimum Lending Rate

through the intermediary of the nationalised industries (who were guaranteed against foreign exchange losses). This was known as the exchange cover scheme.]

9 Overdoing the Doom Forecasts

[The euphoria in government circles survived a run on sterling in July 1973, which led to a crisis increase in the Bank of England's minimum lending rate (MLR) in two stages from $7\frac{1}{2}$ to $11\frac{1}{2}$ per cent (Figure 9). It survived even the outbreak of the Arab–Israeli 'Yom Kippur' War on 6 October. But the temporary and politically inspired cutdown of Arab oil supplies to the West at the end of October and beginning of November abruptly punctured this mood. The oil crisis coincided with the Government's wage struggle with the National Union of Mineworkers, the first stage of which was the overtime ban announced on 8 November. The acute crisis stage was reached on 13 November with a panic increase of MLR to 13 per cent.

The international energy crisis was merely the occasion for the abrupt end of the boom. It is the essence of such high-risk strategy that it is vulnerable to any piece of external misfortune, which can be relied upon to turn up sooner or later. The rapid boom which jerked so suddenly to a halt was, of course, a world-wide phenomenon. The sharp rise in commodity prices, on which the world inflation of 1972–3 and subsequent slump is frequently blamed, was not an accident. It was an inevitable reaction to the inflationary policies of the industrialised countries; and those that inflated most and whose exchange rates depreciated relative to the average had the largest rise in import prices. Even the oil price increase was to an appreciable extent a delayed reaction to many years of inflation in the oil-buying countries. The subsequent world slump was the inescapable result of the reduction in the inflation rate from the high levels it had reached. Even so, an atmosphere of grossly exaggerated despondency prevailed during 1974; and indeed, some of those who had been the most euphoric about the earlier dash for growth were now among the foremost prophets of national and international disaster.]

The Oil Crisis (January 1974)

The Arab increase in oil prices, together with the production cutbacks, has precipitated a change in the world financial balance of power, which the oil industry had long seen coming but had not originally expected until the middle 1970s. The suddenness of the change is due to the coincidence of a change in the world balance of supply and demand for oil (itself largely due to the big jump in the imports of the United States) and the effective organisation by oil producers of a functioning cartel.

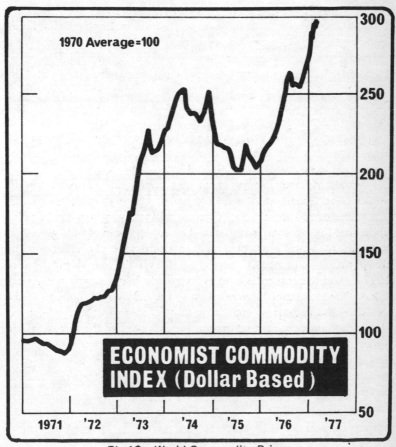

Fig 10. World Commodity Prices

As recently as the late 1960s, the oil producers were in a buyers' market; and OPEC first became an effective force when the oil companies tried to reduce the posted price of Middle Eastern crude. In 1970 the 'take per barrel' of the Arab countries was $0.88 and the total oil revenue of the countries concerned was a mere $8 billion. In 1973 the price was, of course, increasing throughout the second half of the year, and the total revenues are estimated at about $27 billion. But as a result of the three price increases recently announced – two in October and one at the turn of the year – oil revenue in 1974 may amount to more than $100 billion, most of which will accrue to the Arab countries who have the smallest capacity to absorb extra imports of goods and services.

This combination of enormous earnings with relatively small desire to spend them could, for a period, make the Arab oil producers, if they can maintain some semblance of unity, the greatest financial power the world has yet seen. There are obvious dangers in this position being occupied by countries for whom the marginal utility of money may be very low and that of political and military power rather high – self-restraint on the part of either Western or Soviet bloc countries in selling them arms is unfortunately too much to hope for.

Nevertheless, nothing has happened to justify the extreme gloom about the prospects for the industrial West that has become so fashionable, or the talk of 'ecodoom' for the British economy. In the first place, even with a Gulf price of over $11 per barrel, the economic argument for keeping oil in the ground has lost most of its force. This is well above the price at which it is economic to develop substitutes or alternative sources of oil itself. Therefore, the knowledge that the present level of oil prices (relative to that of other commodities) cannot last is a powerful incentive to sell as much as possible while the going is good – and to find the most profitable way to invest the proceeds. It was not surprising that the news of the latest rise in the oil price was followed by announcements of relaxation of some of the quantity restrictions.

Of course, one cannot be confident that short-sightedness, brinkmanship or the desire to put further indirect pressure on Israel will not lead to re-intensification of supply restrictions. But if one wants to bring political considerations fully into the argument it is worth mentioning, first, the dependence of certain Arab regimes on Western support for their survival and, second, the risk, to put it no higher, of military intervention if the Arab countries do try to bring European economies to a halt. Nor is it likely that the Soviet Union

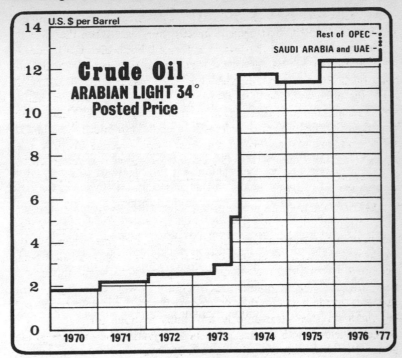

Fig 11.   Crude Oil Posted Price

would wish to jeopardise all its gains from *detente* by encouraging over-extremist courses.

One of the difficulties of the situation is that the normal forces that lead to the breakdown of cartels are exceptionally weak in the case of oil. Although the development both of substitute forms of energy and of methods of economising on energy itself will eventually put a check to the powers of the oil producers, this will not be for some years. It is worth mentioning that present oil prices are seventy times the unit cost of the cheapest oil, such as that found in Saudi Arabia and Libya, and seven times that of the highest-cost suppliers.

It is perhaps some consolation to the United Kingdom, although hardly a solution to the world problem, that there could well be a period, from the late 1970s, before the development of effective substitutes, when North Sea oil may allow this country to participate in the kind of riches now confined to the Middle Eastern potentates. Even in the period immediately ahead the United Kingdom could be much better placed than would be apparent from a simple look at the current balance of payments. If we assume that, for the time being, oil producers have no alternative but either to hold short-term currency assets or to export capital in more long-term form, the position of each importing country will depend on two main factors: its dependence on imported oil, and the portfolio preferences of the producer countries.

Meanwhile it would be foolhardy and self-defeating to attempt to close the 'oil gap' in the balance of payments of Britain or any other country. The best way to see this point is to look at it in terms of goods rather than money. We have the good fortune to be running up a deficit with countries that do not want anything like the equivalent of goods in exchange, but only claims on future goods to be acquired over a period of many years. In this situation, borrowing is the right and proper policy (and more sensible than forcing arms on the Arab states). As the OECD put it in its December *Economic Outlook*, about half of all oil imports come from countries 'which are sparsely populated' and 'are normally regarded as having low absorptive capacity'. The proportion of the United Kingdom's suppliers in this condition is probably a good deal higher.

Arab states with no immediate use for purchases to make with their oil revenues will, by definition, remain in current surplus. Ultimately, they will want to move into income-earning assets, including equities and property. In the meanwhile, however, they will have no alternative but to hold Western currencies, or fixed-interest securities. Thus, their current surplus will be offset automatically by a capital outflow. There is no guarantee, of course, that the outflow and the surplus will match up with all industrial countries taken separately. But so long as the latter stand together and rechannel any resulting currency flows, they cannot as a group be in payments trouble.

There are basically three main types of problems or dangers facing the oil-importing countries. The first is that they may base their policies on their current balance of payments alone, without taking into account offsetting capital inflows. It is now well appreciated in economic circles that any attempt to do this could only lead to competitive devaluations, trade restrictions or internal restraints, which might bring on a world recession but would not eliminate the inevitable 'oil deficit' of the importing countries. The main point now is to bring this intellectual reality home practically to the ministers and top officials who formulate policy. The general futility of competitive devaluation, deflation or trade restriction is realised in most OECD countries; but agreement on precise steps is another and urgent matter. Even more important than the mechanics will be to determine what a genuine 'oil deficit' is for each country, so that the oil situation cannot be used as an excuse for any nation living beyond its means as the United Kingdom was in 1973.

The other two problems are real ones. One is the danger of sudden switches in Arab capital funds from one country to another. In the present highly sensitive mood such dangers could be touched off by some chance unintentional remark by a politician or other public figure that gave offence. No state could, however, be brought to its knees in this way if a network of central bank swaps and IMF standby credits – the principles of which were established long ago – is in operation on a sufficiently massive scale. In this situation, however, it is very important to stick to floating rates (however 'dirty'), so that the oil-producing countries do not have genuine fears of sudden parity changes as a further motive for switching funds.

The third and most difficult problem of all is that of the countries that will be genuine losers. They are the ones whose oil payments will not be offset by capital inflows. Some continental EEC countries come into this category. The worst sufferer among the developed countries is Japan; but the biggest blow of all is being suffered by the less developed countries, of which India is the most notable example. Is one to regard this as simply part of the luck of international trade, to which they must adjust by reduced domestic spending and exchange rate changes? Or should they be completely cushioned by treating the oil deficit of the non-Communist world as a single whole? The practical answer will clearly be somewhere between the two. But a very large cushioning element is desirable, especially at the beginning, to sustain world trade and activity. There are limits to the speed with which resources can be moved from the home to the overseas market, and home consumption held down, in a short period of time.

Nothing that has been said above should lead anyone to expect that 1974 will be a buoyant and prosperous year in the United Kingdom. The instinctive feeling that living standards will not rise, and may actually fall, is probably justified – but for less cataclysmic reasons than sometimes given. The first drain on living standards will be the need to eliminate gradually that part of the current deficit that has nothing to do with oil at all. Even though British costs and prices are competitive at current exchange rates, and we may receive some help on the terms of trade, this will still mean a large switch of goods from the home market.

Secondly, before the present crisis, output was probably too high in relation to capacity. Too many companies were without any reserves of plant, manpower or materials, and many components were unobtainable. This degree of pressure on resources cannot be maintained for long without a runaway (or dangerously suppressed) inflation; and it will take a period of slow or zero growth simply to get back to a sustainable level of operations.

Thirdly, even if there are no horrendous cutbacks in oil supplies, it will take time to adjust to a radically new pattern in which both oil in particular and energy in general are much scarcer and dearer relative to other goods than in the recent past. The process of adaptation will take time, and will be impeded by an official prices policy that makes little allowance for relative scarcities. None of this, however, is any warrant for such forecasts as three years of zero growth, which are apparently being taken seriously in high places.

[Any danger of the UK trying to eliminate its share of the oil deficit evaporated pretty soon; and the Labour Government that took office in March 1974 was borrowing from abroad (as its Conservative predecessor was preparing to do) to finance an overseas deficit much larger than could be explained by the oil price explosion. The policy of spending ourselves out of the inflationary recession proved unsuccessful; and the United Kingdom did have the three years of zero growth, the probability of which I had decried. Whether prompter action would have enabled growth to be resumed more quickly is an interesting hypothetical question. But it was not long before the Labour Government started berating countries such as the United States and Germany (which were already running large budget deficits) for not doing more to spend their way out of the slump.]

Talk About a World Depression (21 November 1974)

There is a grave risk that we shall once again be plunged into a depression on a scale as great as we encountered over 40 years ago.

This warning, near the beginning of Mr Denis Healey's Budget Speech last week, would have had a greater impact if one had not heard such sentiments so frequently before. How often in the past few years have I been telephoned by broadcasting producers asking if I was prepared to predict 'another 1929', and if I was not, to give the name of someone who would be.

In the strict sense of a Stock Exchange collapse, we have already had in the United Kingdom a greater fall in share prices than in 1929. Between 1928 and the bottom of the bear market in 1932, the London

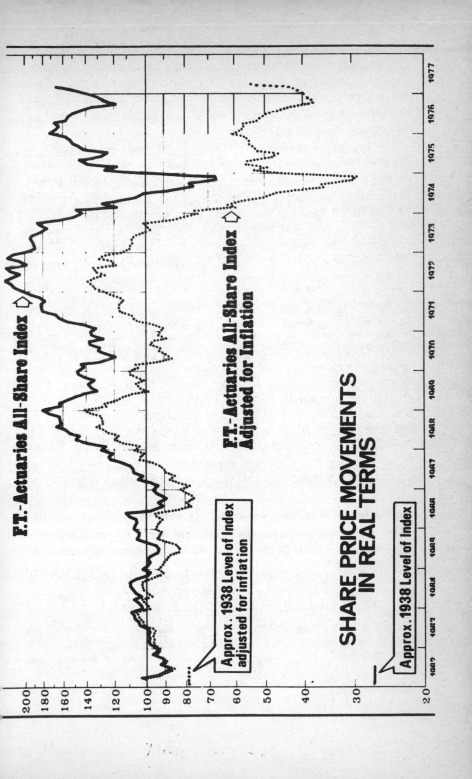

F.T. - Actuaries All-Share Index

F.T. - Actuaries All-Share Index Adjusted for Inflation

Approx. 1938 Level of Index adjusted for inflation

Approx. 1938 Level of Index

SHARE PRICE MOVEMENTS IN REAL TERMS

200
180
160
140
120
100
90
80
70
60
50
40
30
20

1942 1943 1944 1945 1946 1947 1948 1969 1970 1971 1972 1973 1974 1975 1976 1977

and Cambridge Index fell by just under 40 per cent. By contrast, the fall in the *Financial Times* Industrial Ordinary Index from its early 1972 peak has now reached over 65 per cent, or over 75 per cent if allowance is made for the fall in the value of money. Indeed, the drop in the real value of UK shares is not all that far short of what took place in Wall Street between 1929 and 1932. There is a danger signal here which economists would be foolish to ignore.

But what people really mean when they talk about 'another 1929' is not a stock market plunge in the United Kingdom but a world depression on the scale of the 1930s, when world industrial production fell by one-third, and a quarter of the US labour force was unemployed. The history of the postwar period is largely one of false alarms about depression when the real problem was excess demand, and the end result has been the present two-digit rate of world inflation.

There is always the danger that, having cried wolf so often, the prophets of slump will not be believed when they are right. After the experience of President Hoover and the well-known American economist Irving Fisher, who issued reassuring statements in 1929, I will not be so foolish as to rule out the possibility of another such depression. What I would say is that, if it comes, it is more likely to be as a reaction to a runaway inflation than for any other reason; and the most important way of minimising the threat is to give priority to the struggle against inflation, as the US, French and German governments are doing, much to the annoyance of the United Kingdom.

The world is already in a recession. So far it is all pretty modest. All the same, it would be foolish to pretend that the present recession will be just like any other postwar setback. Apart from the fact that it is taking place at a time of record inflation (hence such dreadful neologisms as 'stagflation' and 'slumpflation'), it also coincides with the fivefold rise in oil prices and the consequent vast surpluses for the producer countries.

There are two very different ways of analysing the petro-dollar problem. At the extreme there is what might be called – to insult the memory of a great man – the Keynesian method. This focuses on the danger that consumer countries will restrict domestic demand in a vain attempt to eliminate their quite inevitable current account deficits with the oil producers. To avert this danger governments are urged to reverse all tight money policies and give priority to boosting output and employment.

At the other extreme there is the more classical method of analysis, which has almost disappeared from the world of financial statesmen. According to this approach there is no reason why a fivefold increase in oil prices should either set off a runaway inflation or cause mass unemployment; and if either of these things happens, their roots lie elsewhere. If oil prices go up, the argument runs, consumers will have less to spend on other commodities, the price of which must come down. If the oil producers earn more than they wish to spend, they will invest the difference in the world's capital markets. Any potential surplus of saving over investment opportunities will be eliminated by a fall in another price, namely the rate of interest.

Both extreme views are in this case absurd and the truth lies somewhere in between. But the weaknesses of the first 'Keynesian' view are the more often overlooked. So long as currencies are inconvertible into gold or any other ultimate reserve asset, oil producers have no alternative but to hold financial and other assets of the main industrial countries; and the latter taken together cannot have an overall payments deficit.

Talk about such deficits only arises from taking too seriously the statistician's conventional division between the capital and current account. If governments had really taken seriously their current account targets in all the many postwar years in which they were incompatible, we would already have had several depressions. Again, however, there is the familiar point about not knowing when the cry of wolf proves justified. On the other hand, the element of long-run validity in the 'classical' view is in danger of being overlooked. It still remains true that, over a period of years, if the price of one commodity rises particularly quickly the prices of others will have to rise more slowly if any kind of control at all is to be maintained over the domestic and international money supply.

Moreover, there is one aspect of the classical adjustment mechanism that works much better than it ever did. Before the war, one reason why it was difficult to bring attempted savings into line with investment opportunities was that interest rates could not decline to negative levels. In an inflationary age they can and do. Three months' eurodollar rates have fallen from 14 per cent in August to around 10 per cent. This can be compared with an increase of 12 per cent in US consumer prices in the last twelve months. [In 1975 the US inflation rate turned out to be 9 per cent. Thus real eurodollar interest rates were approximately in the range between minus 2 and plus 1 per cent, depending on whether the market projected past US inflation rates or correctly anticipated the future drop.]

It seems to me that the industrial countries have been tough on the wrong subjects. There is no reason why they should not give some kind of real value guarantee of the currency assets of Arab and other oil producers. There is no technical reason why this guarantee should not be in such a form that leaves them with a negative rate of interest, if that is the market rate. It would still pay to export oil provided that the expected long-term rate of fall in oil prices relative to other commodities, as substitutes develop, is greater than the amount by which the interest rate is negative. The real gain of the oil producers is that they would not have to take a gamble on the world rate of inflation, and on whether this is likely to become explosive.

On the other hand, tne West has not been nearly tough enough on the question of the oil cartel itself. On present trends the OPEC countries would accumulate hundreds of billions of dollars worth of external assets by the early 1980s. It is difficult to believe that they would hold them in confidence without fear of sequestration. It is equally difficult to be sure that they will not try to convert their financial power into a political and military form. It would surely be better to have a concerted discussion of these problems fairly soon than to wait for a dangerous showdown later. If there is to be a great fall in trade and output it is much more likely to come as a result of a rupture of oil supplies following a Middle Eastern war or other conflicts than through a financial collapse.

10 From Heath to Healey

[Inside the United Kingdom the Conservative Government's attempt to hold down money incomes came to a dramatic end with the miners' strike of February 1974. Mr Heath had in fact strenuously sought to avoid a confrontation with the miners and the Phase III guidelines were deliberately drawn up to be acceptable to their union. But the Prime Minister was characteristically misinformed about the balance of power on the NUM executive, and in particular overestimated the influence of the 'moderate' president, Joe Gormley. The issue of union power on which Mr Heath went to the country was one that the country will have to face. But it was wrongly posed in an incomes policy context, and the Prime Minister went to the country unwillingly, with his heart still in a 'social contract' approach.

The Labour election victory did not lead to any large change of economic philosophy. Denis Healey, who became Chancellor in March 1974, took over in all essentials Mr Heath's corporatist and incomes policy approach. There were personal similarities between the two men in their abrasiveness and intolerance of criticism. But there was also a great deal in common in their vision of society. Both favoured a form of state-managed capitalism with taxpayers' money available on concessionary terms to approved firms.

Both were immensely self-confident about the ability of themselves and their advisers to choose the 'winners' in industry. Both saw an incomes policy not merely as an economic weapon, but as a concordat between the major power groups, such as government, TUC and the CBI, which together should run society. These matters should be stressed if only because Mr Healey always attached more importance to them than to the narrow aspects of public finance. He was not, however, able to achieve any part of his objective during a disastrous year and a half covering the second 1974 election and the period until just after the Common Market Referendum of June 1975.

Indeed, the biggest mistake of the incoming Labour Government was to give the impression that, irrespective of wage claims or restrictive practices, union leaders would be saved by government cash if they priced their members out of jobs. The pretence was dropped only after the EEC referendum and the movement of Tony Benn away from the Department of Industry; and even this did not prevent major rescue operations such as that for British Leyland and Chrysler.

The new Government also wasted valuable time, first making the business community fear that profits were under attack, then reassuring the industrialists that profits were after all welcome. The Treasury inadvertently contributed to the collapse of business confidence in the March 1974 Budget by increasing corporate taxation when corporate cash flow was already under severe pressure and many firms were on the edge of bankruptcy. This policy was reversed by the allowances for inflationary stock appreciation in the emergency Budget of November 1974; and following Mr Benn's departure from the Department of Industry the Chancellor lost no time in promulgating an industrial rhetoric about the need to encourage profitable investment.

Even then, when the high road of Heath–Healeyism had been regained, profits were regarded mainly as a source of finance, subject to tripartite negotiation. Their more important role in rewarding risk-taking and as a signalling system for the wants of the home and overseas consumer had still to be rediscovered; and the value of corporate cash flow incentives was vastly overstressed compared with cash in the pockets of the individuals making the efforts and running the risks. As far as the Chancellor's steering of the economy was concerned, the major change of direction had taken place during the closing months of the Heath–Barber regime. The move towards a more contractionary policy took place in the autumn and winter of 1973–4 when the increase in the Minimum Lending Rate (MLR) was followed by an announcement of severe and wide-reaching spending cuts. These were not implemented, partly because of the Government's desire to win the second 1974 election at all costs, and partly because of the new Chancellor's intial lack of curiosity about public spending. The large Budget deficits of 1974–6 were financed until mid-1976 without resort to the printing press from the very large increase in savings both by overseas oil producers and by the UK private sector.

While in the past tight fiscal policy was undermined by lax monetary policy, under Mr Healey, who took office as chancellor after Labour's return to office in March 1974, it was the opposite. In 1974–5 nearly £1.5 billion was borrowed under the exchange cover scheme, in addition to over £1 billion raised directly for the Government overseas by the clearing banks in a special operation. Some increase in borrowing both at home and overseas was an inevitable result of the oil price explosion. But we had rather too much of a good thing. Indeed, Mr Healey actually reduced consumer taxes without curbing spending in a mini-Budget in July 1974 between the two elections of that year. It was this that enabled him to claim that inflation had been reduced to '8½ per cent' in the three months before the second election in 1974, which Labour won with a bare majority in the House of Commons.]

The Cost of Delayed Adjustment (31 October 1974 and 6 March 1975)

The public sector borrowing requirement was running at £4.5 billion in the Conservatives' last year of office, 1973–4. Anthony Barber hoped his public spending cuts would bring this down to £3.5 billion in the present 1974–5 financial year; and Denis Healey initially aimed to cut it further to £2.7 billion with his tax increases.

This would have been too sudden a swing towards restriction at a time when the oil price increase was exerting a strong contractionary influence. But I need not have worried about any excessive overall contraction. Well before the October election, it was clear that the turnround would not take place because of large public sector pay increases, help for building societies, the July tax relaxations and many other factors; and the very necessary reliefs for companies in November added to it further. By November 1974 the estimate for the 1974–5 borrowing requirement had been raised to £6.3 billion. [In the end it turned out to be £7.9 billion.]

The sharp rise in public sector borrowing has been mainly due to government spending. The latest White Paper shows that public expenditure will have risen by 25 per cent over the three years between 1972–3 and 1975–6, then calculating in real terms and excluding financial transactions. [The biggest increase turned out to be in 1974–5, when public spending was £5 billion above the original estimate reckoning in prices of that year. Partly because of the change of government, it was almost impossible to allocate this extra spending between policy changes, estimating changes and control failure.]

There is no cut-and-dried answer to the permissible amount of public sector borrowing. The behaviour of the money supply is, in fact, the best available guide, worth more than yards of computer calculations, to questions such as: 'Can we borrow more because of the oil deficit; or for transactions such as nationalisation payments, which involve an exchange of paper title deeds?' If borrowing for these purposes does not push up the money supply unduly, it is probably safe. If it does, either the borrowing requirement must be cut back, or very unpopular offsetting measures must be taken in the monetary field. But there is reason to worry because so much of both the Budget and the balance of payments deficit is being financed by government-to-government loans (such as the Iranian one) or government-guaranteed public sector Euro-dollar borrowing, and not by the normal attraction of petro-dollar funds in the market; and this is the element that puts the whole policy at risk. Even if we disregarded this unstable prop, the public sector deficit is already without 'reflation' as high as, or higher than, the oil situation could justify.

The real counterpart to this is that home consumer spending has stayed up, despite all the talk of the need for a cut in living standards; and, alone of the major industrial countries, the United Kingdom has been running in the last few months even a non-oil current deficit. This has been financed by official borrowing under various guises; and it is this inflow that has held down the money supply and kept up the exchange rate.

The vulnerability of the situation is obvious, as is the need to stop propping up the exchange rate artificially and to embark on a phased reduction of public sector borrowing. But how have we got here? One reason is that far too much is being staked on future North Sea oil. The responsibility here goes beyond Labour Ministers to a large part of the economic establishment.

Mr Healey has deliberately tried to maintain employment at a time of accelerating inflation by raising home demand. His pre-election cut in consumer taxes in July [1974] never received the critical censure it deserved. He may have succeeded for a time in keeping the British unemployment percentage below that of other countries, but at the expense of greater and more prolonged unemployment in the period still ahead of us. A fiscal stimulus can sometimes act for a short time to sustain demand, although it will eventually peter out if not backed by a corresponding expansion of the money supply.

The Politics of Envy

Far more important than the technical mistakes has been the general atmosphere created for the ordinary conduct of personal and business decisions throughout the country by the new Government. People are more demoralised, gloomy, uncertain and dejected than can be explained by the business cycle, inflation, the price of oil or any other external or inescapable factor.

It should be said that little blame attaches to the Government for the combination of unemployment, slump and 20 per cent inflation we have had so far. A similar combination of misfortunes would have taken place whoever had been in power; it is not possible to do much about the overall state of the economy within a twelve-month period. [Indeed, the wage explosion was aggravated by the threshold payments payable under the wage agreements from the Heath period, which provided compensation for increases in prices above 7 per cent. This was a travesty of sensible wage indexation and attempted to guarantee real wages to workers irrespective of what was happening to the terms of trade and other external forces. Such guarantees were possible for a temporary period only, at the expense of sharper falls in living standards and employment in 1975–7].

One can see what has gone wrong by a comparison with the 1964–70 Labour Government. The social and libertarian reforms enacted in that period should prove an enduring monument; and whatever one might think of individual decisions, at least the aim of that Government's economic measures was sustained growth without inflation. By contrast, the present Labour Government is guided by two main aims: 'redistribution' and the furtherance of trade union objectives. Yet what I find most worrying is not these objectives, but the assumption that every whim of a government elected by a minority must be instantly obeyed.

There is no God-given right of even 51 per cent (which Labour has not got) to impose its will on 49 per cent. Wise governments proceed carefully and do not steamroll their way over even minority opposition. Countries with the good fortune to have a written constitution place obstacles to what can be achieved by a temporary majority – whether of the Left or the Right. But in this country the views and feelings of unorganised, or diffuse, groups that have so far not been able or willing to exercise threat power have been dismissed with utter contempt.

I am afraid one of the worst offenders has been the Chancellor. There was the attempt by Mr Healey and his team to railroad through Parliament an ill-prepared Capital Transfer Tax – an object lesson on how not to change the tax system – and there have been previous examples. The tragedy of such tactics is that they coarsen the level of the whole debate. There is a genuine case to be made against a system of estate duties, which were nominally high but often unavoidable. There is a case for treating wealth as a suitable basis for taxation. The right way to have tackled these questions would have been for the Select Committee on the Wealth Tax to have considered the whole basis for the taxation of capital and investment income.

But who is going to make such a case when we have a Chancellor who picks up with impatience every levy on wealth and its transmission of which he can think, piles it on top of income tax rates going up to 83 and 98 per cent on earned and investment incomes and on top of the capriciously severe redistributive effects inherent in a non-indexed tax system in an age of rapid inflation?

Many people, I am sure, would be prepared to pay considerable sums in redistributive taxation – perhaps even more than at the moment – if the claims were clear and definite, which means indexed. They would know where they stood and could make plans on that basis. It is the open-ended nature of the present taxes and penalties that is the real discouragement to personal or business enterprise. At the other end of the scale, measures such as the rent freeze and the introduction of food subsidies are the most inefficient methods of redistribution imaginable and create fresh problems of their own. Mr Healey has thus achieved the maximum of disincentive for the minimum of genuine redistributive effect – an extremely inefficient performance by the most rigid of social democratic criteria.

The Chancellor has ample advice from Old Cambridge, New Cambridge and mainstream forecasters. But is there anyone in his entourage with a feeling for markets and prices? It will not be long before he will be unable to obtain such economists even if he tries, in view of the rate at which (quite apart from the well-known cases) they are leaving this country.

11 The Return of the Incomes Policy Delusion [3 July 1975]

Julian the Apostate, the last pagan Roman emperor, realising that his efforts to turn back the tide of Christianity had failed, is supposed to have remarked on his deathbed: 'Pale Galilean, thou hast won.' It is doubtful if he ever said this. Nevertheless, that deathbed scene, however mythical, has long been my private metaphor for the unavailing efforts of Prime Ministers and Chancellors to hold back the tide of establishment advice in favour of a statutory or semi-statutory pay policy. But it would be better not to say which official adviser I picture in the role of the Galilean.

Individuals in the Treasury had hankered after 'an incomes policy' at various times in the 1950s. But the main departmental conversion came early in 1961 at about the time when the OEEC (the predecessor organisation of the OECD) published its report, *The Problem of Rising Prices*. By July 1961 we had the Selwyn Lloyd pay pause which was enforced by government and private employers, but without formal legislation.

Harold Wilson's first Labour Government, which came to power in October 1964, temporised for twenty-one months with the 'Statement of Intent' and an 'early warning system'. But by July 1966 it had been forced into a statutory freeze; and there were further statutory restraints imposed in 1968 after devaluation. Edward Heath, who came to office in June 1970, characteristically held out for a longer period. He imposed statutory controls after twenty-nine months.

The second Wilson Government was determined not to be forced down the pay control road again. Its resolve lasted precisely sixteen months. All this was broadly predictable. But one cannot help remarking on Mr Wilson's unending capacity to be surprised and 'blown off course' by entirely foreseeable sterling crises, and by the accompanying dire warnings from Treasury and Bank.

What effect have these incomes policies had? No scientific answer is possible because we do not know what would have happened without them. Historical observation suggests that a total freeze has a marked initial effect, but is eventually challenged and followed by an explosion. Indeed, the recent settlements of 25–30 per cent can be classified as part of the explosion following the Heath controls.

Something a good deal more definite can be said about the countries – the United States, Germany, France, Italy and Japan – that have cut their rate of inflation to a half or a third of our own. Not one of them has done it with an incomes policy. All have achieved it by conventional demand restraint; and this applies to most of the smaller countries not separately listed. Denis Healey no doubt would point out that other countries have had a worse recession. Unemployment is also higher in these other countries – although the figures he so often lists are not properly comparable with our own. But no comparison with other countries is worth anything that ignores the fact that those countries have reached the bottom of the recession, while the downturn in output and employment has only just started in this country.

Recorded history is full of examples of the failure of attempts to control inflation by legislating against individual pay and income increases. Instances go all the way to ancient China, the Roman Empire, the Black Death, the Elizabethan Statute of Apprentices and Europe after both world wars. No inflation has been brought under control, even in totalitarian countries, without a firm control of the flow of money demand. This still leaves a great deal to argue about: how this control should be exercised, what the balance should be between fiscal and monetary measures, how far the Budget should be allowed to go into a deficit in a recession and so on. It also leaves open what supplementary measures should be taken to diminish the impact of demand restraint on employment and bring forward the impact on wages and prices. The latter is the only role that incomes policy can play even in theory. One cannot help asking what there is in the economic record of this country since 1961 to make its rulers suppose that they have a special insight into inflation, which enables them to downgrade the monetary and fiscal weapons relied upon by others in favour of a patent medicine of their own.

I have often emphasised that the two main requirements for a rapid reduction in the rate of inflation would be a ceiling on monetary demand and a shock to expectations. The £6 norm is certainly a shock to expectations, even though it does not go far enough for a quick kill. There is no stated ceiling to monetary demand – that is the sum total of spending by the public and private sectors. This is because the package is thought of by its framers – and has so far been publicly discussed – in almost exclusively incomes policy terms.

The greater is the apparent short-term success of direct pay control, the less is the chance of the cash flow approach being taken seriously. There are hypothetical circumstances in which I would support a temporary incomes freeze or ceiling as an adjunct to a monetary clampdown. But in the current situation I would hope MPs will vote against the £6 ceiling, (a) because as a matter of hard UK political fact pay norms and cash control are alternatives rather than complements; (b) because the norms are to be implemented in a harmful way with harmful accompanying measures; and (c) because most incomes policy advocates wish to use the present measures as a gateway to permanent wage and price controls as a mode of life.

To be very specific: the cash ceiling on public sector wages is now regarded as a pay norm set out in fashionable language, with the intention of giving everyone £6. Indeed, anything else would be a breach of the Government's stated intentions. It is only if Parliament rejects pay control that there will be a chance for a genuine cash limit under which a department or public service can grant more than the norm if it can save manpower.

There is no patriotic duty for MPs to vote for pay controls that will do more harm than good. There is no reason why they should support an intensification of price control designed to make all firms pay the same wage increases irrespective of efficiency or market forces. We have had continuous dividend and price control since 1972, which has provided an overwhelming incentive for business management to play safe, avoid risks and keep out of the limelight. But the controls have not prevented inflation escalating to 25 per cent. If we are now to have a further enforced narrowing of pay differentials, there are likely to be all sorts of results not envisaged at present, ranging from emigration and a retreat from commercial activity to the pricing out of jobs of the least skilled and most disadvantaged people. The tragedy is that it is all so unnecessary, as the increased supply of white-collar and educated workers is itself eroding differentials against manual workers through market forces in a more sensitive and selective manner than is possible with a national formula.

If pay and price controls are introduced, the advocates of incomes policy will not stop there, as they are nearly all on record in favour of a permanent machinery to determine pay relativities. A little theoretical reflection, of the kind that some people find un-British, would show that there is no logical justification for any particular pattern of income and wealth inequality – or equality, for that matter. A 'fair relativities' approach would not merely create shortage in one place and unemployment in another; it would also aggravate the social tensions it is meant to cure. Moderate MPs from all parties will be making a great mistake if they go into the the lobbies in favour of pay and price controls simply because the Labour Left is opposed to them. Non-extremist politicians can surely find a more sensible approach than looking at what the Tribune Group is doing and voting the opposite way.

The £6 pay limit of 1975 was reasonably well observed, as is often the case during the initial uniform phase of pay controls. There was more erosion of the Phase 2 limit for 1976–7, which was supposed to be $4\frac{1}{2}$ p.c., and when the actual earnings rose by about 10 p.c. But despite the tailoring of most Government policies – and those of the CBI as well – to obtain TUC consent for Phase 3, the Chancellor failed to obtain a pay pact for 1977–8. Indeed the compression of differentials and distortion of the labour market over the two-year period, was bound to lead to a catching-up phase of higher wage increases.

The Government's official target was a 10 p.c. limit to the average increase in national earnings. But key official advisers regarded 15 per cent as a far from pessimistic estimate of what was likely to happen. Because the Government's monetarism was so 'unbelieving,' the Chancellor failed to use his monetary guidelines to influence expectations about prices and about what employers might be able to afford.

The rate of increase in retail prices fell from 24 p.c. in 1975 to $16\frac{1}{2}$ p.c. in 1976 and looked like averaging 14 or 15 p.c. in 1977. This was little if any better than might have been expected from monetary policy alone; indeed maladroit handling of sterling in both 1976 and 1977 unnecessarily delayed the reduction in inflation rates. The more sophisticated pay policy advocates claimed that, without wage controls, monetary restraint would have led to soaring unemployment – a claim that is hardly corroborated by the rise from 1 million to 1.4 million in the number of jobless in the two pay control years following July 1975.

12   Prospects for the 1980s

The period from the 1970 general election until the IMF loans and sterling balance agreements of the winter of 1976–77 was widely regarded by people of many different persuasions as a series of economic disasters. The New Year of 1977 opened with hopes that a period of better fortune had arrived and that the nation would benefit – because of better luck, or because policy-makers had learned from previous errors, or from a combination of both reasons.

But how much had fundamentally changed? Professor David Laidler has identified the crucial error of the early 1970s in the following way. 'In 1972 fiscal policy, accommodated by monetary expansion and a flexible exchange rate, was combined with wage and price controls in an attempt simultaneously to reduce unemployment, increase real growth and reduce the inflation rate.' He was writing in early 1976 and was scarcely more optimistic about the future. 'The current condition of the British economy is the direct consequence of this policy,' he remarked, 'but because this diagnosis is not widely accepted in Britain, there is now a grave danger that the error of 1972–73 might be repeated.'

Prime Minister Callaghan and his leading economic ministers would have rejected these forebodings with vigour. It was their proud boast that, in contrast to the Heath–Barber regime, they did not administer large fiscal or monetary stimulants in the face of the 1975–6 recession and a rise in adjusted unemployment to 1.4 million.

Who was likely to be right? Rather than engage in a guessing game, it is better to pick up what clues we can from actual events.

Mr Callaghan made a much quoted speech to the Labour Party Conference about the impossibility of spending ourselves into full employment. But this was an utterance the wording of which lacked the personal Callaghan flavour, and which did not turn out to be a reliable guide to ministerial attitudes. Government opposition to demand expansion was directed mainly against an excessive stimulus to *domestic* demand. The Prime Minister and Chancellor were constantly hoping for a stimulus from export demand and were exhorting countries with strong currencies, such as the United States, Germany and Japan, to boost spending. Ministers were still relying mainly on incomes policy to prevent an inflationary explosion at home.

The official order of priorities became clear when Chancellor Healey took a deliberate risk with the borrowing requirement in his 1976 Budget by offering tax concessions of nearly £1 billion conditional on a Stage II pay agreement with the TUC. The risk was smaller than that undertaken by the Heath regime, but it was still indicative of official thinking. Scarcely had the ink been dry on the agreement with the TUC in June 1976 before the emergency package of July was announced, which took back in public expenditure cuts and in a surcharge on employers' contributions aimed at 1977–8 nearly £2 billion – or twice as much as he had conceded in return for the pay agreement. In December 1976 Mr Healey took back still more. But it was the thinking behind the bargain that was more telling than the runs on the pound which prevented the Chancellor from observing the spirit of it.

The conversion of the Treasury to monetary targets in the course of 1976 was very much a matter of *force majeure*. The various batches of public spending cuts and monetary curbs announced at intervals in 1976 were embarked upon reluctantly in response to a series of sterling crises, which undermined earlier strategy and shattered morale at both the political and official levels. The first run on the pound occurred as a result of a notorious mishap on 4 March, when the authorities sold sterling to prevent it rising too far above $2.00. A day later the MLR fell by a quarter of a point as the result of the downward movement of market interest rates. The foreign exchange markets rightly interpreted this sequence as a sign that the British wanted to engineer a decline in the pound – which both the economic side of the Treasury and the Chancellor personally indeed wanted to do. But the decline went further than intended; and the authorities took fright when it continued after the April Budget – in which Mr Healey made a bargaining bid for lower pay norms than he expected, and received a predictably adverse public reaction from union leaders.

In June 1976 a $5.3 billion central bank standby was granted to the United Kingdom. It was deliberately limited to six months, because the countries concerned, and particularly the United States, were adamant that Britain put its own house in order, and that if it did not do so it should be forced to go to the IMF and accept IMF conditions. The July package was due to the continued weakness of sterling and the large rate of drawing on the standby. Upward revisions of the forecasts for output and employment were published as a pretext for the curbs. But the new forecasts were not widely believed and were soon belied by events.

It is probable that the July package would have been sufficient without further measures if it had been announced at the time of the April Budget and been accompanied by a firm monetary budget. Even when it was announced, it would quite likely have been enough if the Treasury had not muffed the monetary side of its measures. The July statement was originally supposed to contain a commitment to a 12 per cent limit on monetary growth in 1976–7; but this was vetoed at a late stage at a high official level, and the 12 per cent figure became something between an aspiration and a forecast. The potentially favourable effects on confidence and on inflationary expectations were thus thrown away.

The expression 'unbelieving monetarists' was coined to describe the attitude of high-level officials and advisers who came to advocate monetary targets mainly to satisfy overseas opinion and restore financial confidence, both of which were thought to be dominated by irrational beliefs. The point of talking about unbelieving monetarists was not any morbid fascination with the innermost thought processes of the men sitting around the Chancellor's table, but the effect of this unbelief on policy. It is, for instance, extremely difficult to believe that the period of over 30 per cent growth at an annual rate in the money supply between June and September 1976 would have been allowed to occur if the 12 per cent objective had had priority from the start, even at the expense of higher interest rates. Indeed, the effect of delaying the announcement of a firm monetary objective was to worsen expectations about inflation and sterling and thereby make necessary emergency increases in MLR and further fiscal restraints which could otherwise have been avoided. The monetary explosion of the summer and early autumn of 1976 did more than anything else to confirm the suspicions that the three previous years of stability had been an accident due to the ease of financing the Budget deficit.

The monetary explosion and further plunge in the sterling exchange rate were highly interrelated, each stimulating the other. To allay the anxieties of sterling holders, the IMF, and creditor governments, the 12 per cent monetary objective had to be made into an official target with great suddenness in October, and MLR jerked up from $11\frac{1}{2}$ to 15 per cent with a ferocity that would have been avoidable if the authorities had acted in time. As in 1968–9, the main reason for limiting monetary

demand was fears about sterling and the balance of payments. There
was little real sign that the inherent dangers of demand management
geared to target unemployment rates had been realised.

The crisis atmosphere continued even after the monetary tightening,
and rumour followed rumour. The adverse confidence spiral was also
related to the behaviour of the official sterling balances of the oil
producers. These were run down from £2.9 billion in September 1975 to
£1.5 billion a year later. The rapid fall in sterling made the balance
holders uneasy; and news and rumours about their withdrawals undermined confidence in sterling, which in turn increased the nervousness of

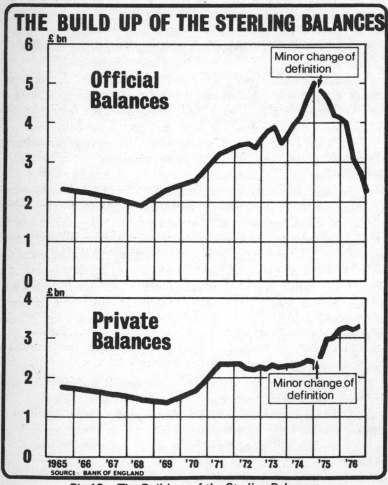

Fig 13.   The Build-up of the Sterling Balances

balance holders. Sterling holders were looking for two pieces of reassurance: a domestic package which would be approved by the IMF as a condition for a $3.9 billion standby, and an international agreement to cushion the pound against further withdrawals of the sterling balances. It soon became clear that the two were closely connected, as the governments and central banks of the creditor countries made it clear that an agreement with the IMF was a precondition for a sterling safety net.

It would be absurd to pretend that there was any scientific precision – or even much reasoned argument – about the figures that circulated in the financial markets and in overseas capitals about the required cutbacks in the British public sector borrowing requirement (PSBR). The view that got into circulation was that a cut of £3 billion was required in the PSBR, with the *arrière pensée* that £2 billion might be accepted as a compromise. There was no better way of stopping a lunchtime conversation dead in its tracks than by asking people why this particular cut was right, or how they knew what was the correct figure for the PSBR. The underlying thought was that, as the United Kingdom was in trouble at the existing PSBR, a lower one should be tried. So far as the £3 billion figure for cuts could be traced back, it was to some calculations that had been made in the US Treasury and Federal Reserve in the summer of 1976.

The Government was not helped by the official presentation of the PSBR. The £11 billion level at which it was supposed to be running in 1976–7 greatly exaggerated the true size of the Budget deficit. Public sector investment was running at an even higher figure; and, although questions could be asked about the value of that investment, it was not zero. More important was the fact that, in a period of rapid inflation, the real burden of interest payments was at least £5 billion less than the official figure, which would have been very clear if the Government had financed itself on an indexed basis. The Treasury was also handicapped because it did not publish a measure of the Budget deficit that abstracted from the business cycle. Such a measure would have shown that the shock November forecast, revealing a deterioration of the PSBR for 1977–8 to £11 billion from the £9 billion previously expected, was due mostly to the worsened outlook for employment and activity. This would have been much more satisfactory than the 'leak inquiry' that actually took place into how the figures reached the *Financial Times*.

But I do not want to exaggerate the effect that any presentational changes might have made at that late stage. The size of the PSBR that can be financed without resort to the printing press or an upheaval in interest rates is not given in heaven, but is heavily influenced by confidence factors, such as beliefs about future inflation and exchange rate movements, or political fears. The spectacle of a Labour Party Conference unable to prevent its left wing from defeating the Government in a proposal to nationalise the banks, and the obstinate adherence of the two main political parties to a first-past-the-post system, did as much harm to sterling as any technical mistake.

Meanwhile, mainstream Treasury economists were working on alternative packages of public spending cuts and tax increases which ran counter to their intellectual convictions. On their own analysis, demand required a stimulus rather than a check. The upsurge in both the world and domestic economies had proved disappointing and the forecasts for 1977 had been revised downwards, indicating a further rise in unemployment even without a package. In conventional terms there was a dilemma of a most extreme kind between external and internal needs, and a particularly intractable one because the textbook solvent of exchange depreciation had already been used on a massive scale.

The first attempt to deal with the dilemma was one on the lines of 'I'll fall down dead if you don't help me.' This was the phase when the Americans and Germans were told that further so-called 'deflation' would bring down the British social fabric and NATO with it. Neither the Americans nor the Germans were prepared to accept the argument. What clinched matters was that soundings among the Carter entourage after the November presidential election produced a strikingly similar message to that which had emanated from the Ford Administration.

Public discussion of the issues was clouded by a politically inspired smear campaign against 'monetarists' of almost McCarthyite dimensions. Enlightenment was not helped by newspaper attacks on the Treasury – of all organisations – as being a hotbed of monetarism. All monetarists were supposed of course to be hard-line and intent on 'savage deflation'. Writing as I did as a soft-line monetarist, there was no chance that I could contribute to that particular debate.

The true case for a tightening of the Budget in no way depended on a desire to depress real demand any further. The point was that a given monetary target could be achieved at alternative levels of interest rates, according to the size of the Budget deficit. In the short run the mix between high interest rates and spending curbs would make little difference to employment. But looking further ahead, the argument for lower interest rates and easier borrowing conditions was that this would encourage investment and raise the sustainable employment level in the years ahead.

In the end the Government compromised with the IMF on an £8.7 billion borrowing requirement for 1977–8 together with monetary limits and a phased reduction for future years. But it was the knowledge that British policy was to be monitored by the IMF, and that a sterling balance agreement was on the way, that precipitated the turnround in the sterling market. The reduction in the PSBR has been achieved partly by trimming the forecasts, partly by cosmetic items such as the sale of BP shares held by the Government, and partly by trimming some capital projects and other marginal adjustments in public spending.

Within a few weeks of the Callaghan–Healey package of 15 December, overseas holders who had gone short of sterling proceeded to purchase pounds; financial institutions that had held off the market rushed into gilt edged; and quite early in the 1977 New Year the authorities became worried about the speed of the fall in interest rates and the danger of the pound climbing too high in the foreign exchange market. After years of understandable scepticism, holders of sterling began to take seriously the potential effect of North Sea oil, expected to make its first really large contribution to import savings in 1977.

Manna from the North Sea?

North Sea oil was in fact an excellent topical illustration of the dangers both of the balance of payments approach to policy and of the political overload on the Government. There were some who saw it as manna from heaven, and others as yet another temptation to an orgy of spending on borrowed money. There were Treasury estimates of net benefit to the British economy of £12–£15 billion per annum by 1985 (in sterling estimated to be worth then about half its 1977 value). The actual benefit could turn out much higher than officials expected; on the other hand the oil cartel could collapse, leaving the United Kingdom with a lot of expensive oil the extraction cost of which would be high above the world market price.

It helps to see the matter in perspective if we value the benefit from the oil as a proportion of the national product rather than as an addition to the current balance of payments on some arbitrary assumption about prices and exchange rates. The £12–£15 billion official figure for benefit in 1985 assumes that the OECD internal prices rise at an average of 8 per cent per annum and that the UK prices follow suit. Analysis in GNP terms avoids the need to guess the course either of international inflation or of sterling. But it cannot eliminate the need for an assumption about the real price of oil relative to other commodities, and whether it will remain at its 1975 ratio.

Table 1. External Payments: Impact of North Sea Oil and Gas: Treasury Estimates (£m. at current prices *

Oil	1972	1975	1976	1977	1978	1979	1980	1985
1 Oil exports/imports saved (incl. surance and freight)	0	40	1,090	2,250	3,400	5,150	6,600	14,300
2 Imports of goods and services for North Sea programme	−75	−870	−1,130	−900	−850	−850	−800	−1,300
3 Imports/exports displaced by North Sea programme	20	230	270	300	300	350	450	1,200
4 Interest, profits and dividends accruing to overseas	0	−30	−200	−750	−750	−1,250	−1,750	−2,600
5 Interest on extra reserves (as measured by the cumulative total of 1-4 and 8)	0	20	60	150	350	550	900	4,300
6 Net effect on current account	−55	−610	90	1,050	2,450	3,950	5,400	15,900
7 (6) as a percentage of Gross National Product	−0.1	−0.7	0.1	0.8	1.8	2.5	3.1	5.2
8 Net effect on capital account	15	910	1,060	950	850	650	400	100
9 Net effect on overall balance of payments/reserves ((6))+((8))	−40	300	1,150	2,000	3,300	4,600	5,800	16,000
10 (9) as a percentage of Gross National Product	−0.1	0.3	1.1	1.6	2.4	2.9	3.3	5.2
Gas								
1 Net effect on current account	170	1,610	2,250	2,600	3,100	3,500	4,100	8,100
2 As a percentage of Gross National Product	0.3	1.7	2.1	2.2	2.2	2.2	2.3	2.7
3 Net effect on overall balance of payments/reserves	200	1,800	2,350	2,700	3,200	3,500	4,000	8,000
4 (3) as a percentage of Gross National Product	0.4	2.0	2.2	2.3	2.3	2.2	2.2	2.6

* Oil price is assumed to rise at the same rate as the world price of manufactured exports. The UK price level is estimated to rise at the OECD average, which is taken to be 8 per cent.

Source: Treasury, Economic Progress Report (July 1976)

On the assumption that it will so remain, the net gain from oil gradually rises, according to official estimates, from zero in 1975 to under 3 per cent of the GNP in 1980 and then to 5 per cent in 1985. This is equivalent to little over $\frac{3}{4}$ per cent per annum additional growth in each of the years 1977–80 and about $\frac{2}{5}$ per cent in the quinquennium to 1985. These are substantial additions to an underlying growth rate of 2–3 per cent, but they are not revolutionary. Whereas in the decade after the 1967 devaluation, sterling sank somewhat faster than justified by purchasing power parity, it might henceforth perform somewhat better. But its movements will still be closely related to differences in international inflation rates past and expected.

Are we to believe these North Sea estimates? Or is something likely to go wrong? It may be that we have had so many disappointments that we are inured to the possibilities of success. But contrary to the conventional view, *this is not something on which a political decision needs to be taken.*

If international holders of funds really believe that the United Kingdom will gain a large stream of foreign exchange earnings from oil, then sterling should be a good investment; and we would get all the overseas finance to take us through the late 1970s without riots in the streets. For overseas investors would put their own money where their mouths were; and their action would finance any current deficit without an excessive drop in the exchange rate until the oil arrives. The recurrent question during all the discussion of North Sea oil was: why, if the prospect was so good, was it so difficult to attract sufficient overseas investment on commercial terms to bridge the current payments deficit in the years from 1973 to 1976 inclusive? And why was it necessary for the Treasury to borrow in the international capital markets (before 1977 via the nationalised industries and local authorities which served as a front) under an exchange guarantee and also to borrow up to the hilt from the IMF?

There might, even without oil, have been good reason for a torrent of inward overseas investment. For during most of the 1970s Britain had been one of the few low-wage countries in the industrial world, reckoning either in dollars or units of constant purchasing power. Why did such an inflow not occur in, say, 1976; and if it appears to be occurring by the time this book is in the reader's hands, how durable is it likely to be? Will any new-found strength of sterling relative to its purchasing power disappear once domestic output begins to grow and excess unemployment starts to dwindle?

Past collapses of confidence have had a great deal to do with erratic and unpredictable official intervention in the foreign exchange market. These suggest that managed floating is better in theory but free floating is better in practice. Official intervention, combined with an erratic money supply policy, has helped to make sterling a highly speculative currency in which to hold assets. On past experience an improvement in sterling and the repayment of international credits would be the signal for another domestic spending spree dignified by talk of growth, industrial strategy and incomes policy.

Another unnecessary deterrent to overseas investment in the United Kingdom could turn out to be the interpretation placed on the decision to end sterling's rate as a reserve currency. By the time of the Basle agreements for this purpose in January 1977, the most volatile of official sterling balances had already been withdrawn – another example of locking the stable door when the beasts have bolted. Unfortunately, however, the Government indicated that it would take

Fig 14. UK's International Competitiveness

extensive steps to discourage both private and official holders of funds who wished to put some of their cash balances into London voluntarily. The theology about ceasing to be a reserve currency joined forces with a determination to prevent an excessive appreciation of sterling, almost as fanatical as the earlier determination to prevent a depreciation in 1976.

The distinction sometimes made by some between 'speculative' short-term funds and long-term investment is largely spurious. There is no hard and fast line between short- and long-term funds. Balances may first be put on short-term deposits, then in long-term securities and – as confidence is gained – into financing new investment. But even if no such transmission takes place, any overseas lending to this country makes available real resources to sustain an increase in British domestic investment, and by its effect on interest rates creates an incentive for that investment to take place.

What our rulers were really saying at the beginning of 1977 was that, if people in other countries wanted to lend us some of their savings, we were going, puritanically, to turn them away, and that we were interested only in an overseas balance achieved by physical exports. The point is a very practical one. The OPEC countries were still running, in 1977, a current surplus of around $40 billion, which means that they had a net savings surplus of that amount. We had moved from the 1974 extreme of pleading for as much of this surplus as possible, to rigging markets the other way round to say that we wanted no part of it. This was the route to a quite unnecessary depression of British living standards below what they otherwise would have to be.

The Main Questions

The key question was whether governments would switch to expansionary financial policies once the improvement in sterling and the reserves had gone far enough, and they were no longer under the influence of the IMF. One is irresistibly reminded of 1969, when Roy Jenkins's credit squeeze brought a sharp payments improvement, but did not prevent a wage explosion. If the monetary limits had been kept on into the 1970s, inflation would in due course have subsided; and after several winters of discontent we should have been better off with less unemployment than subsequently occurred. But the Heath Government opened the monetary floodgates; and the temptation for another government to do so in the late 1970s will also be great. North Sea oil, although helpful in other ways, will lessen the balance of payments constraint on monetary excess.

One worrying sign apparent in 1976 was that in the realm of ideas, if not actual policy, the official Treasury view was actually less advanced than that of its political masters. An illuminating instance was the reaction to House of Commons Expenditure Committee report early that year. The Committee had recommended that, subject 'to the first priority of demand management, controlling the rate of monetary expansion should be the prime aim of economic and monetary policy'. The recommendation was, of course, internally contradictory. The Treasury in its reply early in 1976 prised apart the contradictions by making it clear that traditional demand management was indeed the first priority and monetary control took a back seat by comparison.

Indeed, the Treasury threw down the gauntlet in its last sentence by saying 'controlling the money supply is not an end in itself'. This was a characteristic misunderstanding; for the real point of the Treasury's critics – still not taken on board – is that monetary flows, i.e. money times velocity, are one of the few things that overall economic policy can determine. Output and employment – which are what the Treasury means by demand management – cannot be so determined. This continued adherence some thirty years later to what was the progressive thinking of 1945 was depressing.

Of course, other views were being aired. The overseas side of the Treasury was in favour of strict monetary control largely on the grounds of foreign confidence. The Bank of England was in favour of monetary targets in principle, although for traditionalist reasons it tended to oppose technical changes such as index-linked securities or the auction of gilt-edged issues, which would have made it easier to control the money supply in periods of difficulty. Very similar statements, in favour of controlling the money supply in principle, were in fact being made by Lord O'Brien when Governor of the Bank of England in 1970–1 to those that his successor, Gordon Richardson, was making in 1976–7.

One difference between the two periods was that experience of how easily things could go wrong had accumulated. A second difference was that there were now a few young Turks among the middle and junior levels of Treasury officials who had become sceptical of demand management and were serious about monetary control. But a third difference, acting in the opposite direction, was the prospect of oil revenues which could lessen the external pressures towards sensible policies.

The domestic credit expansion (DCE) limit adopted in the United Kingdom at the behest of the IMF in December 1976 was a potential disaster. DCE is roughly equivalent to the growth of the money supply plus the balance of payments deficit (on current and private long-term capital accounts). This is a sensible formula for creditor organisations such as the IMF, interested in repayment, but it can be very harmful for domestic stability. It means that, if the balance of payments is worse than expected when the limit is set, the money supply is held back. But if it turns out better, the money supply can increase faster. The DCE limits fixed for 1977–8 involved, on government calculations, a money supply growth of about 9–13 per cent, which implied stabilising the inflation rate at just below double percentage figures. But as the balance of payments forecasts were cautiously modest, especially on private capital account, there was a very good chance that the DCE formula would permit a very much faster growth of the money supply. Gordon Richardson spoke very sensibly, at the biennial dinner of Scottish Bankers on 17 January 1977, about switching back to a money supply target when the balance of payments started to gain large benefits from North Sea oil. But that was before the event. The external improvement increased the temptation to indulge in a monetary policy that accommodated whatever level of costs and increases emerged from wage settlements.

If only British policy-makers could hold tight to the monetary growth rates of 1976–7 and not try to manipulate the exchange rate, the improvement in the balance of payments would eventually be followed by an improvement in domestic inflation; and as a third step in the sequence, domestic activity and employment would improve automatically without the Government having 'to do something' by way of increased Budget deficits and renewed monetary expansion. The Heath Government was not prepared to wait; nor were other Western governments in the early 1970s. Will the governments of the late 1970s have learned their lesson? The tedious, but probably correct, answer is: to some extent only. Chancellor Healey several times indicated that he would return to traditional policies of demand stimulus once the UK inflation rate was down to world levels. But perhaps an even greater danger was that British errors might be repeated internationally on a more modest scale but with wider repercussions. The election of President Carter was greeted with audible cheers by demand managers, fine-tuners and forecasters with large-scale models the world over.

It was difficult to escape a sense of frustration at the failure of so many governments to learn from experience and their continued faith that the disappointing behaviour of growth and employment could be remedied by injecting extra demand into the Western economy. There was a growing clamour for countries with strong currencies to stimulate their home economies, even though the international inflation rate was already 9 per cent in 1977.

There is certainly no room for dogmatism about the forces that have raised unemployment rates the world over and made industrial capacity indices misleading. But the fact from which we cannot escape is that world inflation was already very high and tending to get higher when conventional calculations showed a large amount of unused capacity. This suggests (a) that a conventional demand stimulus either would not work or would work only for a short period at the expense of trouble later, and (b) that Finance Ministers and even Heads of Government could no longer determine output and employment by the stroke of a pen. Their meetings would be more successful, but less exciting, if they abandoned their illusions.

The view taken by critics of the Keynesian wisdom is that governments individually or together have been trying for most of the time since the Second World War to spend their way into unrealistic employment and output targets by means of demand management. This points to a diagnosis of ever-increasing inflation peaks from one epoch to the next. It also points to at least the possibility of ever-increasing unemployment peaks. This would be because each temporary check to inflation requires a successively sharper application of the brakes, because of the difficulty of business in adapting to unpredictable changes in the inflation rate and because of the proliferation of controls as governments try to suppress inflationary symptoms.

This has indeed been the experience in each of the cycles since 1961–2. But mechanistic projections of past trends rarely work in the social sciences; and those of us who are critical of the direction of affairs should be particularly careful of them. Policy-makers have learned something; external conditions are different, and there are fewer illusions. In the United Kingdom the frustration of real wage hopes is likely to be less with even a modest bonus from North Sea oil and with public expenditure under control than it was in the middle 1970s when the oil factor worked the other way through the fivefold increase in import costs.

The real menace, to the extent that it is monetary, is not that inflation will advance like a juggernaut, steadily from one cycle to the next; it is rather that it will advance over an average of several business cycles – in other words, it will advance over a cycle of cycles – which is still a pretty sobering thought.

In the British case, the root of our special difficulties has been political rather than monetary. Prospective investors, overseas and external, have had to ask themselves about the non-market risks of development in Britain. Would the return on a successful investment be held down by price or dividend control? How secure was profit repatriation? Could outright sequestration of overseas assets with or without argument be excluded? Would tax laws permit companies to pay the international market rate for good managers? Would pay policies create shortages of some workers side by side with surpluses of others? Would unions be given a dominant say in corporate policy under the slogan of industrial democracy?

There were of course the traditional worries about industrial relations and shopfloor attitudes; but my guess is that overseas concerns, whose managers are largely outside the English class system, would be prepared to cope if it were not for the wider political worries. They have rightly been concerned with the risks of some future government wholly hostile to the market system, private enterprise or both. Understandably, they look more than one general election ahead; they are concerned at the weakening of faith in the political system and worry about the possibilities of an unrepresentative minority coming into office through some swing of the electoral pendulum.

These topics will be the themes of the final part of this book, where the object will be not to make historical prophecies, but to look at the tensions that give these fears currency, and the reforms that might help to reduce them.

References

Laidler, D., 'Inflation in Britain: A monetarist's perspective', *American Economic Review* (September 1976).

Treasury, *Progress Report* (July 1976).

Appendix: The Pound in your Pocket

Practical men have long suspected that a devaluation of the pound is reflected by a corresponding fall in the value of the 'pound in your pocket' and have remained obstinately resistant to official attempts to separate its internal from its external value. They can now comfort themselves with the knowledge that their suspicions have been confirmed by the work of distinguished international monetary scholars proceeding on rigorously mathematical lines. They have not yet converted all their fellow economists, but the tide is moving their way.

Someone who had stuck to David Hume's essays of the 1750s could have read about the subject in lucid prose and spared himself the intellectual U-turns of the intervening two centuries.

This new–old or revisionist doctrine is sometimes known as the 'law of one price'. The starting point is the common observation that there is an international price level for traded goods, i.e. exports, imports and import-substitutes. This price level is often expressed in dollars, purely as a matter of convenience. The sterling equivalent of the international price level goes up in full proportion to any depreciation of sterling; for British exporters can charge more in sterling, yet maintain their dollar price. British manufacturers competing on the home market with imports can also raise their prices. Goods and services that do not enter into international trade may react more slowly, but will ultimately rise in price as producers switch to the more profitable traded goods.

Price controls may hold up the process of adjustment to the new sterling equivalent of the international price level, but not indefinitely. A characteristic instance of the effects of controls is provided by the manufacturer of a well-known product, which has been held down by price control to a level of UK charges well below what he can obtain on the Continent, and who has been making plans for shipping the product to Belgium and re-importing it to the United Kingdom.

The conventional postwar view that has guided exchange rate policy is very different. It assumes that import prices rise in almost full proportion to a devaluation, but that sterling export prices do not change much, leading to a fall in dollar terms. Devaluation, on this view, improves the trade balance through a cheapening of dollar export prices to the overseas customer and through increases in sterling import prices to the British domestic buyer. But the cost of this improvement is a deterioration in the terms of trade, i.e. the ratio of export to import prices, whether expressed in dollars or sterling. By contrast, the upholders of the 'law of one price' see the main effects of devaluation (if any) as coming from the increased profitability of exports and import substitutes, with little lasting change in the terms of trade.

On the conventional postwar view, the impact effect of exchange depreciation on the price level depends entirely on the proportion that imported goods and services bear to total domestic spending. If this is reckoned at a quarter, it leads straight to the Treasury rule of thumb, reiterated many times during the series of runs on sterling in 1976, that each 4 per cent depreciation of the pound leads to a 1 per cent rise in

British prices. What happens after that depends on the extent to which a wage–price spiral develops, which is regarded mainly as a matter of incomes policy. The view of the revisionist school, on the other hand, is that a 4 per cent fall in sterling leads to a 4 per cent rise in British prices through normal market processes. If depreciation creates abnormally large profits, the competition of firms for workers would bid up wages to offset the devaluation, without any question of unions or wage–price spirals. Thus it is impossible to engineer a permanent payments surplus through devaluation.

The main value of devaluation is that, if real wages have got stuck at too high a level and profit margins are abnormally low, it then allows balance to be restored by a rise in prices rather than through the painful process of a fall in money wages (or too abrupt a check to their rate of increase). This was the situation in the United Kingdom on the eve of the rapid sterling depreciation of 1976. For real wages had never fully adjusted to the fall in the international value of an hour of British labour following the rapid rise in the price of oil and other commodities, relative to manufacturing, in 1972–4.

Clearly, both the Treasury view and the 'law of one price' are extreme ends of a spectrum of possibilities. The longer the time horizon, the more that exporters invoice in foreign currencies and the smaller a country's share of international trade in its main products, the more likely is the law of one price to be the better approximation. Some suggestive evidence in its favour is provided by the fact that, in the year up to November 1976, when the effective sterling exchange rate depreciated by 23 per cent, the terms of trade deteriorated by only 2 per cent (and this at a time when the dollar price level of imports into industrial countries rose by 5 per cent). We are thus likely to go less wrong if we assume that the *whole* of a 4 per cent devaluation is ultimately reflected in domestic prices than by using the official one-for-four rule of thumb.

The importance of this argument for policy can hardly be overstated. The repeated protestations of the authorities that sterling was undervalued when it fell to $1.58 in November 1976 were based on the view that, on the basis of the movement of dollar export prices, or comparative international wage costs, a truly competitive rate was a little higher. Similarly the concern to prevent sterling rising 'too far' when it climbed above $1.70 in January 1977 was the worry that if it went much further British goods would lose their competitive edge. But if international costs ultimately adjust to the exchange rate, rather than vice versa, both sets of protestations fall to the ground.

It is nevertheless extremely misleading to say, as so many financial commentators do, that devaluation 'causes' inflation. In fact, both devaluation and inflation are caused by excessive money creation at home. Obstinate fights to preserve the parity once this monetary expansion has occurred, such as (Sir) Harold Wilson's in 1964–7, are a costly waste.

When the pound is floating, the external depreciation and the corresponding rise in internal prices can go further than is warranted by the monetary creation that has taken place. This can happen if the markets fear further monetary expansion in the future, or if there is a portfolio shift from domestic to foreign currency assets on account of political fears. All these elements were present between June and October 1976, when there was a two-way relation between the abnormally rapid fall in sterling and the temporary monetary explosion. Because of political and currency fears, overdraft limits were utilised both as an insurance against a future credit squeeze and to stock up with imports. This in turn caused the money supply to expand faster and worsened the initial fears. Sterling began to improve soon after a monetary clamp-down was imposed, and rose still further at the end of 1976 in anticipation of an IMF and sterling balance standby agreement, which would be conditional on the observance of monetary guidelines.

The commitment to monetary guidelines meant that, the faster the British price level rose, the more the real money supply would be squeezed and the more severe would be the depression of output and employment. The chart shows how the real money supply has been an almost uncannily accurate indicator of the short-term course of domestic activity. As the British authorities did not have the freedom to let the money supply rise in line with the price level, their best hope for domestic economic recovery in 1977 was to restrain the rise in domestic prices which could best be achieved if market forces brought about an appreciation of sterling.

The conventional view, that depreciation is expansionary and appreciation a stimulus, is – as the experience of so many countries testifies – the reverse of the truth. It was plausible only because of a neglect of the effect of depreciation on real money balances – a neglect excusable when the authorities felt free to follow a purely passive needs-of-trade monetary policy, but highly misleading when numerical limits to monetary expansion were in force.

Unfortunately, 'the authorities' – in this case the Treasury more than the Bank – were almost as anxious to avoid an 'excessive' appreciation of sterling in early 1977 as they were to avoid a depreciation in 1976. This was because they wanted to manage the exchange rate to secure a competitive advantage for British goods. This flew in the face of the evidence that such an advantage cannot be achieved for long, and that it is soon eroded by the rise in domestic costs to fit the exchange rate.

In resisting sterling appreciation, the British authorities were throwing away their best chance of making a dramatic onslaught on inflation — both directly and through the effect on expectations. They were also, as just explained, intensifying unnecessarily the domestic unemployment problem.

The root of the trouble was the reluctance of officials engaged in economic management to admit in practice that it was impossible in a free market system to have separate targets for the money supply, interest rates and exchange rates. A target for any one of these predetermines what will happen to the others. Of course, official advisers could see the force of the proposition in theory; but a policy of leaving the exchange rate or interest rates to market forces — and simply buying dollars in the foreign exchange market at a preannounced rate to accumulate $1 to $2 billion per annum for official debt repayment — would have gone against the grain.

Postscript on Exchange Control

The Chancellor of the Exchequer was hinting in January 1977 about controls on the inward movement of funds and a two-tier interest rate structure. We were thus in danger of repeating the absurdities of 1971, when there were exchange controls on both the outward and the inward movements of funds from and to this country. The best way of putting a brake on any undesired appreciation of sterling would have been not inward exchange controls, but a gradual relaxation of outward exchange controls with the aim of eventual dismantlement. The phasing out of exchange controls would have restored sterling, not necessarily as a reserve currency, but at least as an international currency, which would have been able to compete on its merits on the lines of the Hayek proposal discussed in Chapter 17 below. Such a course would have made it difficult to get away with policies such as price and dividend control, which depress the return to capital unnecessarily; and redistribution policy would have to take the form of wider capital ownership or tax measures rather than destruction of capital values. All this helped to explain the tenacity with which governments, and their advisers, hung onto exchange control, a wartime emergency measure that persisted for well over a generation into the peace.

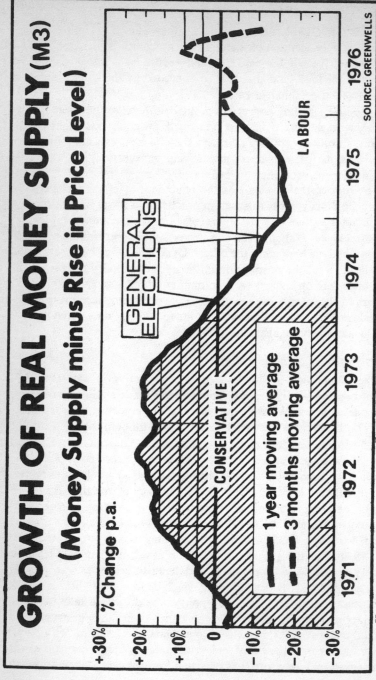

Fig 15.   Growth of Real Money Supply

References

Frenkel, J.A. and Johnson, H.G. (eds), *The Monetary Approach to the Balance of Payments* (Allen & Unwin, 1976).

Hume, David, 'Of the Balance of Trade', in *Essays: Moral, Political and Literary* (Oxford University Press, 1963 edition).

Calendar of Events

A The Background

1945	19 May	End of War in Europe
	11 August	Labour election victory: Attlee prime minister
1949	18 September	Devaluation of pound from $4.03 to $2.80
1951	25 October	General election: Conservatives displace Labour and remain in office for thirteen years
1955	1 June	Messina Committee on European Customs Union set up – UK does not participate
1956	26 July	Nasser seizes Suez Canal
1957	13 January	Macmillan succeeds Eden as prime minister
	19 September	Chancellor Thorneycroft raises Bank Rate to 'crisis' 7 per cent
1958	6 January	Thorneycroft resigns over government spending; replaced by Heathcoat Amory
1959	20 August	Radcliffe Report downgrades monetary policy
1961	5 March	First 5 per cent revaluation of Deutschmark
	25 July	Selwyn Lloyd crisis measures, including Pay Pause
	8 August	Foundation of NEDC
	10 August	UK application to join EEC
	16 November	Electricity Council breaks Pay Pause

1962	9 May	NEDC embarks on 4 per cent growth target
	13 July	Lloyd dismissed as Chancellor; replaced by Maudling
1963	14 January	First De Gaulle veto on British EEC membership
	19 October	Home succeeds Macmillan as prime minister
1964	15 October	Labour wins election: Wilson prime minister.
	26 October	15 per cent import surcharge; other crisis measures to cope with '£800 million deficit' (£300 million on current account). 'Statement of Intent' on prices and incomes
1965	16 September	National Plan published
1966	20 July	Crisis measures, including pay and price freeze, spending cuts and tax increases
1967	11 April	'Neutral Budget' – but large rise in government spending
	5 June	Arab–Israel War
	18 November	Devaluation of pound by 14.3 per cent from $2.80 to $2.40
	29 November	Jenkins replaces Callaghan as chancellor
	30 November	Callaghan Letter of Intent to IMF published

B From 1968 Onwards

1968	16 January	Jenkins public spending curbs
	18 March	Gold pool ended: two-tier gold market
	19 March	Budget – £0.9 billion of tax increases in full year
	8 July	$2 billion standby credits to offset sterling balance fluctuations; exchange rate guarantee for holders
	1 November	Hire purchase curbs
	22 November	End of unsuccessful Bonn conference on currencies; UK import deposits and tightened credit squeeze

1969	17 January	*In Place of Strife* White Paper
	15 April	Budget: £0.3 billion of net tax increases; but larger turnround in Budget accounts
	2 June	Labour Government drops proposed Industrial Relations Bill
	12 June	Announcement of under-recording of exports and improvement in visible and invisible balance
	23 June	Jenkins Letter of Intent to IMF for $1 billion standby; £0.4 million DCE ceiling for 1969–70
	29 September	Temporary floating of mark
	5 October	Abolition of Dept of Economic Affairs
	24 October	Mark revaluation
	6 November	End of dividend controls announced
	4 December	Public Expenditure White Paper limits real average annual increase up to 1973–4 to 3 per cent p.a.
1970	1 January	Abolition of foreign travel restrictions
	14 April	Budget: moderate tax cuts to boost real demand by ½ per cent, but little change in fiscal balance. 5 per cent monetary expansion target for 1970–1
	18 June	Conservative election victory: Heath prime minister, Macleod chancellor
	26 July	Barber chancellor after death of Macleod
	6–12 August	Ministers exhort nationalised industries and private employers to resist wage inflation
	20 September	IMF meeting in Copenhagen: floating rates anathematised
	27 October	Public expenditure cuts: 2½p off standard rate of income tax. Industrial Reorganisation Corporation abolished
	6 November	Scamp Report concedes 15 per cent to council workers, saying proposals are 'inflationary'
	3 December	Industrial Relations Bill published
1971	20 January	Post Office workers strike
	4 February	Rolls-Royce collapse: receiver appointed

10 February	Wilberforce Inquiry into electrical supply recommends topping-up of official offer
15 February	Currency decimalised
23 February	Rolls-Royce rescue begins
8 March	Post Office strike called off
30 March	Budget: tax concessions reduce revenue £0.7 billion in full year
10 May	Floating of mark to stem dollar inflow
14 June	Cabinet refuses further aid to Upper Clyde
15 July	CBI voluntary price increase limit of 5 per cent
19 July	Reflationary 'package' including £0.4 billion of purchase tax cuts
15 August	Suspension of dollar convertibility into gold; US import surcharge, and prices, wages and dividends freeze
23 August	Temporary floating of major currencies including pound
10 September	*Competition and Credit Control* published; banks to compete on rates; automatic support of gilts by government broker to stop
25 November	Public Expenditure White Paper announces major increases in spending
19 December	Smithsonian Agreement: new fixed parities. Dollar devalued against major currencies

1972	9 January	Miners' start strike
	18 January	Britain completes entry negotiations with EEC
	18 February	Wilberforce Inquiry; end of miners' strike
	4 March	Rescue of Upper Clyde begins
	21 March	Budget and tax reductions of £1.8 billion in a full year, mainly from income tax cuts
	23 June	Pound floated as 'temporary measure'
	28 July	National dock strike against Industrial Relations Court commitment of five dockers to prison
	26 September	Heath 'anti-inflation' proposals for voluntary agreement: £2 limit to pay increases and price limit of 5 per cent

	3 November	Breakdown of tripartite attempt to reach voluntary pay agreement
	6 November	Counter-inflation Bill; ninety-day statutory stand-still on most increases in pay, prices, rents and dividends
1973	17 January	Stage II of 'Counter-inflation': pay increases limited to £1 a week plus 4 per cent with rigid price controls until autumn. Pay Board and Price Commission to be established
	13 February	Second devaluation of dollar (by 10 per cent)
	4 March	Generalised floating against dollar
	6 March	Budget: no overall change; Value-Added Tax set at 10 per cent
	4 April	Government limits building society rates
	21 May	Public spending cuts (£½ billion in 1974–5)
	2 July	Gordon Richardson takes over from O'Brien as governor of the Bank of England
	9 July	After sharp fall in pound, Chancellor Barber claims sterling 'undervalued by objective criteria'
	18 July	Government announces cost-of-living threshold proposals for pay
	20–27 July	Crisis rise in Bank of England's MLR from $7\frac{1}{2}$ per cent first to 9, then to $11\frac{1}{2}$ per cent
	11 September	Limit to bank interest rates on deposits of under £10,000 to help building societies
	6 October	Outbreak of Arab–Israeli War
	8 October	Government Phase III proposals: maximum increases of 7 per cent with flexibility margin and £350 per annum maximum
	10 October	Rise of two-thirds in posted price of Arabic light crude oil announced by Gulf States
	18 October	Cut of a tenth in oil supplies order by Saudis
	5 November	Cut of a quarter in Arab oil supplies
	8 November	Miners decide on overtime ban
	13 November	Crisis rise of MLR from $11\frac{1}{4}$ to 13 per cent
	13 December	Three-day working week announced
	17 December	Crisis measures to cut public spending by £1.2 billion in 1974–5, property development tax, surcharge on surtax and imposition of

		limit on interest bearing deposits ('corset')
	23 December	Gulf states' decision to increase posted price of oil again, which quintuples over year
1974	9 January	TUC suggests 'special case' treatment of miners: rejected by Barber
	9 February	Miners' strike begins
	4 March	Wilson becomes prime minister after Conservative election defeat; Healey chancellor
	6 March	Miners' settlement
	26 March	Budget: aims to increase revenue by £1.4 billion; rises in income and corporation taxes
	30 April	Bill to repeal Industrial Relations Act
	26 July	Reflationary package: cut in VAT, food subsidies, etc.
	21 November	Budget: PSBR for 1974–5 estimated at £6.3 billion, compared with £2.7 billion March estimate
	19 December	Business rent controls to end
	31 December	Government rescues Burmah Oil
1975	28 January	Indexed-linked savings schemes for very small savers
	31 January	National Enterprise Board proposed
	15 April	Budget: tax increases to yield £1.5 billion in full year; nationalised industry subsidies to be phased out; public spending to be cut by £0.9 billion in 1976—7
	23 April	British Leyland shares suspended. Negotiations for rescue
	5 June	EEC Referendum
	11 July	Pay limit of £6 a week and extension of Price Code
	5 August	Temporary employment subsidy introduced to defer redundancies
	24 September	First £175 million job creation scheme
	5 November	'Industrial strategy' launched
	7 November	Application to IMF for loan of $2 billion – $1.2 billion under oil facility and $0.8 billion from first tranche

	17 December	Easing of HP controls and minor 'employment creation' measures
1976	12 February	Further minor package of £215 million to encourage investment and to reduce growth of unemployment
	19 February	Public Expenditure White Paper aim to keep volume of spending roughly flat between 1976–7 and 1979–80; cut of £1 billion in 1977–8
	5 March	Sterling falls below $2 for first time after Bank of England sale of sterling and MLR cut
	5 April	Callaghan becomes Prime Minister
	6 April	Budget: conditional income tax cuts linked to second stage of pay policy. Revenue loss of £1 billion in full year
	5 May	Government and TUC agree on £2.5 to £4 pay limit ('4½ per cent') for year to August 1977
	7 June	Sterling crisis: central banks standby credit of $5.3 billion for six months only
	22 July	Further cuts of £1 billion in public spending for 1977–8 announced; rise of nearly £1 billion in employers' national insurance contributions from April 1977
	10 September	Crisis rise to 13 per cent in MLR
	29 September	Healey announces application for remaining $3.9 billion from IMF
	15 December	Third major package of public spending cuts in less than a year. £1 billion off expenditure in 1977-8 and £1.5 billion in 1978-9 to keep public sector borrowing requirement around £8.7 billion in both years. Sale of part of government holding of BP shares. DCE limits up to 1978-9
1977	10 January	Sterling balance agreement in Basle: $3 billion standby facility and conversion offer into foreign currency denominated securities for balance holders

23 March	Government saved on no-confidence motion by new pact with Liberals
29 March	Budget. Reduced estimates for P.S.B.R. in 1976–7 and 1978–9. Adjustment of allowances. Conditional reduction of basic rate from 35 to 33. Increased indirect taxes. Net cost £1.5 billion in full year, £1 billion in 1977–8
5 May	Petrol tax increse withdrawn because of Liberal opposition
14 June	Government defeated on Finance Bill Committee on increase in, and index taxation of, personal allowances
8 July	T.G.W.U. Conference votes against wage restraint
15 July	Statement by Chancellor concedes failure to agree on fresh pay controls with TUC. Emphasis on 12 month gap and desirability of 10 p.c. earnings ceiling
28 July	Royal Assent to Finance Act. Basic rate 34 p.c. But higher personal allowances and qualified indexation of tax starting points

PART II

Interventionism in Theory and Practice

13　The Deceptive Attractions of the Corporate State

What should be produced and by whom? How should incomes from employment and profits be determined? How should the labour force be distributed between different occupations and who should make the decisions? On the one side are those who believe that these should be made by citizens freely choosing to buy or sell in the market place, subject to impersonal general rules laid down by Parliament. Resources should be allocated through trade and competition, as in industries where firms strive for the consumer's vote. On the other side are those who believe that decisions should be made by the principal interest groups concerned, whether by agreement or with the aid of the State as referee. As will be shown below, this view forms the background to the Heath–Walker Industry Act of 1972, the Wilson–Benn Act of the same name of 1975, to the 'industrial strategy' adopted by the Labour Government the same year and to many versions of incomes policy.

Members of this school tend to favour: nationwide job evaluation; 'sensible' price controls; a symbiotic relationship between 'industry', the unions and Whitehall; 'export drives', and purposive intervention to save energy, foreign exchange or whatever happens to be the fear of the moment. They tend to call their opponents 'old-fashioned classical economists', 'nineteenth century liberals' or other epithets which are more flattering than they intend. They believe that the state is a business, 'Great Britain Ltd' which has to be managed rather than ruled; hence the label 'corporatist'. The roots of the notion go back, however, to the guild system of feudal times.

The central tenet of corporatism is that a society is an organisation with collective goals to be pursued by its managers. This tenet is linked to a view of how the various interest groups should fit in with the common purposes of society. The following quotations throw light on the essential conceptions:

119

Organised groups of producers must be recognised as essential and on the other hand, they must be placed firmly beneath the control of the state, which must lay down their precise functions and ensure that their role of watchdog and guardian should be held within certain fixed limits, in the form of independence without excessive licence. But above all it is necessary to change them from aggressive bodies defending particular interests into a means of collaboration to achieve common aims. The unions and the employers' organisations must join together within each industry to form one single mixed association .... We should abandon the rigid dogma which is given the lie every day by the facts that wages and systems of labour are determined by the law of supply and demand, and instead adopt the concept of a fair wage.

Many people would think these passages more useful than most political utterances heard today; and if only common sense would prevail over doctrine, bodies such as the National Enterprise Board (founded by the Wilson Government in 1975 and about which the Conservatives were uncertain) could be the instrument of a gradual co-operative reorganisation of industrial society, with the State acting as the umpire of last resort. The ideal would be neither the inequality of the market nor equality between individuals, but 'disciplined control of inequality and hierarchy within the state'.

The passages above do not come from a leaked interdepartmental report, a PEP pamphlet or some NEDC back-room thinking, but were in fact written in 1920. I hope it will not temper anyone's approval if I add that the author was Alfredo Rocco, who later became one of Mussolini's most influential and able ministers. Rocco was no mere technocrat, divorced from mainstream Fascist thinking: he also preached an 'activist outward looking imperialist nationalism' (his own expression). He contrasted the 'ephemeral value of the individual' with the 'indefinite life of society'. He added that 'war takes precedence since it requires the individual to make the supreme sacrifice'. Rocco was not only a successful minister, but a highly perceptive analyst who would stand head and shoulders above most members of either front bench in the House of Commons today.

Still, we must not go in for guilt by association. Almost every conceivable permutation of beliefs on different subjects has at one time or another been grouped together by different political movements. Might it not be possible, as another Italian writer, Mario Einaudi, put it, to implement the social and economic ideas just cited 'without ideology, war and concentration camps ...' in a 'depoliticised' society that would 'turn its back on the rhetoric of the 19th Century, but not on deeply felt national sentiments and seek its way under the guidance of stable and efficient leadership'?

For the record, Mussolini had by 1939 established on paper the system Rocco advocated, culminating in the formation of a Chamber of Corporations. But, according to Einaudi, vinegar producers and butter manufacturers alike saw in the system a chance to use 'the immense Roman bureaucracy', as public bodies have always been used, 'by anxious capitalists in trouble, that is, as a prop to keep them going until better times'. Thus the ideal was tempered by a little Latin realism.

The corporatist aim could be translated into contemporary British terms in the following way. The TUC should in the long term be responsible for forming and enforcing a collective view on relativities among its own members, and the CBI should be given similar responsibility for price control, with the object of dividing up the available share of profits in the most advantageous way. There would still, according to this view, be a need for a central division of resources between profits, wages and other uses. But the two sides, with the assistance of government experts, could go, it would be said, a long way towards agreement in a non-ideological atmosphere, leaving either to ministers or to some independent body the job of making the final adjustments. This approach was summarised by Mr Heath's famous 1973 offer to employers and unions to 'share fully with the Government the benefits and the obligations involved in running the national economy'. Once agreement along these lines has gone a certain way, it might be necessary to reinforce by legislation the authority of the CBI and TUC over their own members to prevent a few black sheep from wrecking the arrangements. There would be built into the whole structure an agreed hierarchy of pay and other differentials running from top executives to the shopfloor, which would draw heavily on social survey data of public evaluation of different professions.

The way would then be open – it is supposed – for a co-operative effort by government and industry, in which strategic decisions would be made about which industries should be backed in world markets; and these would be given all the state aid, back-door and front-door, that ministers could discreetly provide without provoking excessive overseas retaliation. Such 'planning agreements', deprived of their present class war implications, would largely replace the indiscriminate weapons of exchange rate movements or overall financial control. The whole edifice could be rounded off by a second chamber chosen to represent various interests, professional and occupational groups (including, perhaps, 'consumers') which could either evolve out of the NEDC or replace the House of Lords. This last is the proposal by which wholehearted corporatists so often give themselves away.

It is not necessarily a condemnation of corporatist ideas to say that their leading twentieth-century exponent was Mussolini. Some industrialists might regard them as the acceptable face of fascism. Nevertheless, the reader will not be surprised to learn that I do not think such corporatist plans are either desirable or even workable without going much further towards a totalitarian state than even Mussolini was prepared or able to do.

Some advocates of corporatism see it as a second best. They profess to favour the use of market forces, reinforced by monetary, fiscal and social security policy, to harmonise individual and social interests. Where such a general approach is, or appears to be, inadequate, then the instinctive reaction of many politicians and businessmen is that industry and the unions should 'control themselves', although in consultation with government. This is regarded as a superior alternative to state regulation.

Yet it is in fact the worst alternative of all. If specific controls are unavoidable in an emergency they should be brought in not by backdoor pressures, but by an elected House of Commons. Otherwise, one is in the dangerous state of regarding the mere wish of a minister as having binding force and, instead of giving the State a monopoly of coercion, of setting up systems of private law.

The favourite reply of Whitehall officials to this line of argument is that no law, prescribing for example a freeze or a ceiling, could work without the approval of public opinion and in the absence of more than token opposition from the more moderate trade union leaders. This is true but irrelevant. The law against theft would be a dead letter without the support of public opinion: and the police can only enforce it because they are called in as a last resort in a tiny minority of cases. But no one suggests that theft should not be a matter of law or that we should rely on voluntary organisations to create a climate of opinion not conducive to stealing.

Is it, on reflection, really the job of the trade unions to restrain wages or of employers' associations to keep down prices? This is the job of trade unions in the Soviet bloc; but elsewhere their job is to look after the interests of their members. This does not mean that one must stand idly by in the face of their monopoly powers, which harm both employment and civic freedoms, any more than one should connive at employers' price rings or restrictive practices. But is the correct way to deal with excessive power, or the abuse of power, to make the parties concerned a part of the government machine? They cannot represent and police their own members without being unsuccessful at one or both of these tasks; and it would be difficult to invent a better way of transmitting power to militants at shopfloor level.

Advocates of the corporate state – or of concordats between the government, trade unions and industry – also make the fundamental mistake of assuming that, if there is a fair balance between business and labour interests, and betwen different regions and industries, all will be well. Indeed, they regard the clash of interest groups as itself part of the working of the beneficent invisible hand.

The reason why such a balance would be grossly wasteful and inefficient has been exposed by Mancur Olson in the following words:

> Even if a pressure group system worked with perfect *fairness* for every group, it would still tend to work *inefficiently*. If every industry is favoured, to a fair or equal degree, by favourable government policies obtained through lobbying, the economy as a whole will tend to function less efficiently, and every group will be worse off than if none, or only some of the special interest demands had been granted. Coherent, rational policies cannot be expected from a series of *ad hoc* concessions to diverse interest groups.

Where do the inefficiencies come from? Not from simple monopoly pricing, as this would tend to cancel out if practised universally to the same degree. The inefficiencies result from what one might call a fair exchange of restrictive practices: a tariff for one industry, in exchange for quotas for another and a government subsidy for a third; an agreement to restrict recruiting to one occupation, in exchange for higher entry qualification in a second and subsidies to maintain the labour force in a third; tax subsidies to house owners to balance council house subsidies; and price controls to please the organised consumer interest, with Ministerial task forces to investigate the resulting shortages.

The 'corporate State' rests on the fallacy that the national interest is the sum of the interests of trade unionists, farmers, employers, shopkeepers and so on. Even if it were true that everyone was a producer, and there were no such people as housewives and pensioners, it would still be a fallacy. For it ignores the interest that everyone has as a consumer, which is diffused among thousands of products and activities aside from his own particular industry. A producer-orientated society is likely to make its own members worse off, because of their apparent mutual interest in shoring up each other's special interests and restrictive practices. The result on the international scale leads to tariffs, quotas, trade wars, competitive devaluation and similar aggressive phenomena which cause political as well as economic harm.

Let us assume that all producers are also consumers, and that the network of lame-duck subsidies, prestige projects, state intervention to 'save' specific jobs and so on receive not merely majority, but unanimous, approval. In what sense can the libertarian economist object? Does this not mean merely that people value their quiet life as producers more than the extension of their choice as consumers or the benefits of faster growth? An economic commentator has no business to impose a long-run view on those who prefer to take a shorter one.

But do they really prefer to take a shorter view? It could well be that many people, if they had the necessary information and opportunity, would be prepared to phase out their particular interest group privileges as part of a bargain in which a sufficient number of others did the same thing, and all gained something. Unfortunately, such a bargain is quite unfeasible because of the extremely high costs of information, decision and organisation involved. One has only to try to imagine the miners, the farmers, the beneficiaries of Rent Control, Concorde workers *et al* attempting to bargain away their privileges and secure copper-bottom guarantees that all the other interest groups would keep their word. These difficulties are aggravated by the fact that the professional leaders of producer groups have a personal interest in securing a compromise based on an exchange of privileges – rather than in bargains to abandon them, which would reduce their own role and perhaps even eliminate their jobs.

There is a further point. The basic ideal of the corporate state is that of professional and occupational self-regulation. This is made explicit in Rocco's blueprint. But there are already powerful elements of this in the Anglo-American tradition. Lawyers practise self-regulation through the Law Society and the Bar Council; doctors have the General Medical Council. Teachers are more than halfway to such recognition for their own bodies. The essence of the Donovan Report in the early 1960s and of government policy in the 1970s has been that the unions should regulate and reform themselves. 'Industrial self-government' was a frequent suggestion put forward by Conservative businessmen in the forty years up to the Second World War as an alternative both to state socialism and the supposed 'chaos' of free competition. We may hear more such calls – with perhaps some sweeteners in the form of union participation. Its equivalent today is the form of sectoral planning now in vogue which could result in market-sharing and cartels with backup support from import controls.

The opposite point of view is nearer the truth. We have too much rather than too little professional self-regulation. If power can be abused, it will be abused. Unless compelled to serve the general interest in the competitive pressure of the market, or by the laws and enforcement bodies of an elected Parliament, professional groups will, in the nicest possible way, feather their own nests. Even when there is some market competition, as in private medicine, the patient is hampered by the convention that one practitioner does not criticise another. Dog does not bite dog. If there is an unpleasant incident in a local authority housing department, police force, school or old people's home and we read 'an inquiry is to be held', we should be very suspicious until we find out who is carrying out the inquiry. No doubt if in sixteenth-century Nuremberg there had been an inquiry into the practices of the Guild of the Meistersinger, it would have been an internal one, with Beckmesser as secretary; and a heavy-handed report would have endorsed the decision to ban the prize song as a flagrant breach of the regulations.

As for the 'fair wage' and the 'fair profit' no man possesses the ability to determine the merits of another. Indeed, it is one of the advantages of a market economy enjoying basic bourgeois liberties that a man's livelihood does not depend on other people's valuation of his merit. It is sufficient that he should be able to perform some work or sell a service for which there is a demand. In fact, a society based on a full-blown system of national job evaluation could prove even less acceptable than the present.

The basic reason, however, why the corporate state would be unlikely to work lies in the weakness of its self-regulating machinery for setting incomes. There is no need to discuss in this chapter whether and in what way union behaviour is relevant either to our inflation or unemployment problems. *If* it is in any way relevant, then any form of voluntary policy, or statutory policy relying largely on the consent of particular unions, cannot help very much as it is likely to break down eventually. This is because the benefits from restraint in the use of group market power consist of things such as price stability, fuller employment or faster economic growth, which are thinly diffused among the whole population, while the costs are incurred by the group that exercises restraint. It is therefore in the interest of each union group that other unions should show restraint while it exploits its own monopoly power to the full.

For it is clear to any particular union leader that most of the gains from price stability and fuller employment spill over to members of other unions and the general public, while the costs of settling for less than he could obtain are highly concentrated among his own members. The chance that an example of restraint by himself will be followed by others is so small that his best bet is to pursue his members' own interests. If the leadership of a union is prepared to look beyond the (fairly short-term) self-interest of its own members, it is likely eventually to be thrown out of office. One does not have to look for 'reds under the bed': the 'militant' moderates will do the job, and rationally so, from the members' point of view.

Thus there is no possibility of putting teeth into a long-term version of the Social Contract. Relativities Boards and national job evaluation schemes are false trails. But they are not harmless. For the illusion that we have a direct instrument for controlling incomes and prices for more than an emergency period is likely to lead to inflationary – and perhaps hyper-inflationary – monetary and fiscal policies under some 'needs of trade' doctrine or other rationalisation which we always receive on these occasions.

No doubt a benevolent dictator could find many ways of improving on the available market place. But in a society like Britain, discretionary industrial intervention is more likely to prove a recipe not for the regeneration, but for the degeneration, of Britain. Funds are provided to preserve existing employment and existing enterprises against change, with special emphasis on constituencies of interest to the government of the day. The preservation of existing employment can be defended as a stop-gap measure to help older workers; but when it is taken to the extent of recruiting new and young workers, who would be more profitably and securely employed in enterprises that can pay their way, the process is difficult to forgive. The least successful capitalists are to be kept in business and made respectable with taxpayers' money and state directors. Perhaps we should talk about 'The Road to Economic Slumdown' – although we are likely to get the serfdom as well, if the slumdom goes far enough.

There is however no such thing as historical inevitability. In the larger task of defeating the corporate state, the more thoroughgoing advocates of competitive private enterprise have a common interest with libertarian radicals who wish to 'do their own thing' and lead their own lives. If only these two groups could overcome their mutual pre-judices – in one case about non-bourgeois life-styles and in the other about the profit motive – the remainder of the twentieth century could see an unexpected turning of the tide towards individual freedom and limited government. There is no one less realistic or more likely to be wrong than the short-term 'political realist' who refuses to argue with the trend of events. By refusing to accept the apparently inevitable, we can yet change it.

In the following chapters alternatives to the corporate state based on competition and individual choice are outlined, not merely in the abstract but in relation to specific problems. But perhaps the most decisive considerations for the political realist are to be found in the examples of interventionist policies, as they have actually worked in practice.

References

Centre for Studies in Social Policy, *The Corporate State* (1977).

Congdon, Tim, 'Smith as a Critic of Corporatism' in *The Relevance of Adam Smith* (Institute of Economic Affairs, 1977).

Einaudi, Mario, 'Fascism', *The International Encyclopaedia of Social Sciences* (Chicago, 1965).

Hayek, F.A., *The Road to Serfdom* (Routledge, 1944).

Hayek, F.A., *The Constitution of Liberty* (Routledge, 1960).

Lyttleton, Adrian, *Italian Fascism* (Jonathan Cape, 1973).

Olson, Mancur, Jr., *The Logic of Collective Action* (Harvard University Press, Cambridge, Mass., cased 1965 and paper 1971).

14 Choice and Competition – the Untried Roads

What is the Social Market Economy?

What is the social market economy? It is a German expression that sounds ungainly in English, but is difficult to avoid using. One can talk about competition policies or competitive private enterprise; but the social market economy is both more and less than these things. Owing to an accident of history and personalities, the social market economy has been promoted in Britain by one section of the Conservative Party and vigorously opposed by other sections. This has had the unfortunate effect of misleading some people about the political aspects of the notion, or of the range of viewpoints it covers.

The 'social market economy' is not in fact a 'right-wing' or Conservative approach at all. The words are a literal translation of a term that was coined by Dr Ludwig Erhard, the economics minister at the time of the so-called postwar German economic miracle. The concept was however embraced by his Social Democrat successors (despite dissent from the old and the new Left) and was for many decades virtually a bipartisan doctrine. Even so, it would be wrong to tie it too closely to the details of specifically German policies or to the institutions and way of life of that country. Indeed, American and British economists have contributed at least as much as German ones to the underlying ideas, although often without using the label.

The starting point of social market doctrine is that there are only three known ways in which people can be brought to co-operate for their mutual benefit – through spontaneous good behaviour, through mutual interest in the market, or through commands backed in the last resort by force. Spontaneous good behaviour is rarely sufficient outside small groups such as families. This is not only because of insufficient mutual love; even if we were all prepared to do our best for our fellow citizens, it would not be immediately obvious what they require, or who would be best at providing it. A command system faces

128

the same information problem. A market economy, working on a basis of profit and loss, provides both the signals and the incentives. It is thus the nearest that fallible human beings can provide to a system of non-coercive co-operation.

Why 'social'? This is to indicate that markets, like other institutions, require a framework of laws and government services if they are to work satisfactorily. There will always be people who will not be able to earn in the market a sufficient income to provide what the rest of us regard as a tolerable minimum. There are services, such as defence, which only the State can provide; and others, such as education and health, where the State has a role, but should certainly not be a monopoly supplier. The price mechanism will in some cases need to be corrected, or property rights redefined, so that the market gives the right signals – for example, by charging for road space to discourage congestion. Again, the framework of laws must provide for such things as the preservation of areas of natural beauty or historic city centres.

Stated in this form the 'social market economy' would command the support of Harold Lever as well as that of Keith Joseph; and it would not be all that distant from the outlook of Roy Jenkins (but the same could not be said of all his followers from his parliamentary Labour Party days). I am of course referring to general outlook. Practising politicians are pulled by the supposed exigencies of events to support, for instance, incomes policies, which do not sit happily with their other beliefs and actions. The political aspects have been further obscured by the fact that Labour in the mid-1970s was passing through a highly interventionist anti-libertarian phase. The Conservatives on the other hand were reacting against their own involvement with state intervention of a particular disastrous variety in 1970–4.

Exponents of the social market economy disagree with each other on a great many points. They may be radicals or conservatives, sceptics or enthusiasts. The common starting point of their philosophy, which allows them to differ, is a belief that, although individuals may not be good judges of their own interest, the state or a committee of wise men is not likely to be better. In other words, people should be able to 'do their own thing'. If people want a 'bourgeois' pattern of life, concerned with their own career and that of their children, it is up to them. But these are individual preferences. Under a social market economy people are free to opt out of the puritan ethic and embrace a bohemian, hippy, aristocratic, communal or any other life-style they choose (a choice denied them in Russia, China and Cuba alike). These facts are sometimes obscured by the fact that many Conservative political leaders who talk about free choice and competition inconsistently condemn the results of such choice in the personal and social sphere. This underlines the point that the social market economy is not the property of any one political party or side of the political spectrum, and if it is promoted mainly by the Right it is likely to become disfigured.

There are, however, important legitimate differences of opinion among social market economists. Some of the most important concern income and wealth redistribution. Sweden is (or was until very recently) very much a 'social market economy' in terms of possessing an overwhelmingly private enterprise economy and of refusing to protect obsolescent or loss-making sectors from the winds of change. On the other hand, there is a great deal of deliberately redistributive taxation. West Germany is a 'social market economy' with excellent social services, but much less interested in removing income disparities. Among British social market economists there are some, such as Professor James Meade, who believe in equality as an ideal. But they are very concerned not to pursue this to an extent or by methods that destroy incentives to efficiency or freedom of personal choice.

Some social market economists are against equality as such, but do favour redistribution towards the least well-off. Another position, which I personally favour, would be concerned to spread the benefits of property more widely than would occur either through trusting to *laissez-faire* or through concentrating property in the State. My own interpretation also involves the distribution (as soon as we are over the immediate economic hump) of a modest minimum 'social dividend' for all. People would then have the choice of opting out temporarily or permanently from commercial society, with no attempt either to hunt them down as scroungers or to pretend that they are genuinely 'unemployed'.

The unifying theme among the many variants of social market economics can perhaps be seen best by looking at the ideas to which they are opposed. The two main ones are comprehensive economic planning and a 'corporate state' run through tripartite agreement between the Government, CBI and TUC. Each of these require central agreements or decisions on the areas in which to invest, the goods that are likely to sell abroad, the firms that should be backed and the degree of worker participation. In a market system, such choices and risks are widely spread; taxpayers' money is less involved; and different individuals and organisations can back their own judgements without political conflict or the use of state coercion.

It is reasonable to hope that a freer economy would be a more prosperous one. There is no knowing what would happen if neither high profits nor large losses among risk-takers carried a moral stigma, and if personal financial success were not denounced and taxed as much as possible. But no particular results for the growth rate can be guaranteed. Economic performance, as judged by statistical indicators, or even the visible proliferation of material objects, does not depend on policy alone. East Germany may have lagged behind West Germany, but judged by the standards of most other countries it is still an economic success story. In the British case, the comparative slow growth rate goes back at least a century.

The case for using markets has at bottom little to do with measurable growth rates. It is the case for allowing individuals more say in their own lives. A market economy, with at least a substantial private sector, is not a sufficient condition for political and personal liberty – as we see in so many military dictatorships. But it is at least a necessary condition for such freedom, as can be seen from the absence of any examples of centrally planned economies which allow free speech or provide for the peaceful change of regime.

Consumerism

Supporters of a competitive economy will instinctively champion the consumer; but organised consumerism is an uncertain ally best kept at a distance. Just as there are producer pressure groups, there can be consumer interest groups with equally deleterious effects. The case for competition is ultimately that of the general citizen rather than that of a group with a concentrated interest in the supply or purchase of a particular service.

The pressure for cheap mortgages, for instance, is a demand by one group of taxpayers for a subsidy from the rest of the community. This is over and above the tax privileges they already receive. The main privilege is not, as is so often assumed, the tax exemption (up to a limit) of interest payments. It is the abolition of Schedule A – the former tax on the notional rental value of a house. That this is a privilege can be seen by considering the deterioration in the tax position of a householder if he sells his house and puts an equivalent capital sum into marketable securities. House and security prices tend of course to move in such a way as to offset the disadvantages of such an exchange at the margin. But the artificial incentive to own houses rather than other forms of property remains.

Generally speaking, pressure for below-market prices for any product is the expression of some consumer interest group, with no *prima facie* claim to more attention than comparable producer pressures. One insidious kind of 'consumerism' consists of lobbying producers or legislators to insist on standards or specifications that individual consumers do not desire – either because they do not think the change worth the money, or because they positively dislike them. This has reached its apogee in the American cars, which emit a piercing scream and refuse to start if the safety belt is left unfastened. The dividing line between insisting on information for transmission to customers and forcing some people's values and tastes down the throats of others is a very tricky one, which consumer bodies are always in danger of crossing.

Then again, the supposed interest of consumers in lower prices is deceptive, if they are imposed at the expense of quality, availability or future supplies. There is all the difference in the world between promoting competition by uncovering collusion, and attempting to roll back the share of profits or make a stand against inflation. Cutting competitive margins and resisting inflation are beyond the power and the competence of consumer bodies; and if they have any influence in these directions it will be to endanger future investment and employment and – paradoxically – to promote a pattern of resource allocation different from that desired by consumers themselves, as shown in their market place behaviour.

The Industrial Strategy Myth

Preachers are fond of saying that the trouble with Christianity is that it has never been tried. The same may be said about competition. In a large part of the economy is has never been applied, and the idea of applying it seems almost equally heretical to both our main political parties.

The Labour Party's fondness for the public sector and the public corporation is, of course, well known. The Conservatives retaliate by trying to gain or regain territory for private enterprise. But this is not the same as promoting competition. Markets and prices are important as signals and incentives for producers as well as a means of allocation among consumers. The case for profit is often put in entirely the wrong terms, such as a source of funds to finance investment, or to provide savings for industry.

If this were the main case, a completely collectivist system could pass the test. If freeing resources for investment is the main requirement, all that is necessary is that a gap be created between total production and private and public consumption. Taxation and a budget surplus will do just as well for this purpose as company profits. Whether the state then invests itself or lends conditionally through a National Enterprise Board becomes secondary. The potentialities of collective saving have never been better demonstrated than in Stalin's Russia, where the investment (or savings) ratio far exceeded anything achieved in capitalist countries.

The real value of the profit yardstick is as a *criterion* to guide investment in the direction of customer requirements, home and export, as well as a source of information about the efficiency of alternative techniques and methods. In a world of change and uncertainty, some firms will make abnormally high profits and others low profits (or losses).

Both the signals and the incentives are atrophied in the present-day climate of opinion, where high profits are stigmatised as 'obscene' and losses as 'failing the nation', and as an excuse for nationalisation. Moreover, no better method of discouraging risk-taking than price controls has been devised. Why go for an untried process or product, and all the heartaches involved, if success in the form of high profits is suppressed by the Price Commission *while failure continues to carry a penalty*? All the incentives are to play safe and avoid trouble.

Supporters of a competitive private enterprise market economy have drawn comfort from surveys showing that a majority of workers are against more nationalisation or any large extension of government controls. But economists who emphasise the 'competitive' and 'market' aspects of such an economy should not be over-sanguine. Some 69 per cent of the sample questioned in one such survey thought it 'should be the object of the government to help British companies'. To remove any ambiguity, 54 per cent thought that this should take the form of 'financial help' or 'lending money to firms when they need it' and most of the others wanted cash assistance in one guise or another.

It is doubtful if most people in the poll realised that *they*, as taxpayers, would be providing the resources for this help. Politicians and economists who are sceptical of open-ended rescue operations for 'lame-duck' industries are customarily reviled as right-wing and even (such is the debasement of language) as anti-liberal. The essential point, rarely grasped, is that citizens are being coerced by the tax system to support the car, electronics, aircraft and many other industries at a scale they are not prepared to support from their own pockets as consumers.

Whatever else can be claimed for the National Enterprise Board (NEB) , the 'regeneration of industry' is no more likely to result from it than from previous industrial intervention by governments of all parties. If there is a shortage of entrepreneurial skill, or knowledge, or expertise related to particular industries, why should the creation of a new central body bring them into existence? If past experience of such ventures is any guide, the main role is likely to be the injection of taxpayers' cash into ailing concerns, plus the undertaking of a few regional showpiece projects that have not succeeded in attracting profit-seeking private funds.

There is, moreover, not the slightest reason to suppose that help for 'lame ducks' or for enterprises of doubtful profitability is a transfer to the poorest members of society. Many people who pay the subsidies in taxes are almost certainly worse off than those who receive the aid. The one coherent justification for such assistance – and the most generous interpretation of the poll findings – is the desire to cushion people from the effects of change. But in that event the subsidies should be temporary and degressive and not be misrepresented – as the National Enterprise Board has been – as a programme for reform and innovation. And it should always be considered whether cash compensation will not give better value to taxpayer and 'lame duck' employee alike.

Above all, there is the myth that insolvency is the ultimate disaster – which the Labour Party prefers to tackle by state ownership and the Conservatives by propping up with public funds. No physical assets are destroyed when a concern goes bankrupt, not even the goodwill attaching to component units. The assets are available to new purchasers who see a way of putting them to profitable use. Instead of long-term rescue operations and grants and cheap loans for favoured companies, it would be better to have (a) a reform of the bankruptcy laws to take some of the sting out of insolvency, without preventing the winding-up of the firms concerned; and (b) an agency to take an active part in breaking up insolvent concerns into smaller components, with perhaps some public funds to prevent a chain reaction among suppliers and creditors, and to avoid sudden mass dismissals of labour while new owners are being sought. This function could be performed by a reformed NEB. It is absurd to suppose that there is no constructive compromise between indefinite public subvention and instant closures. The NEB could also be entrusted with the short-term cushioning functions mentioned in the next chapter, once it was shorn of its more grandiose ambitions.

Meanwhile, as Geoffrey Owen has suggested, the NEB should concentrate on its task of managing its very extensive portfolio of investments inherited from the earlier government interventions. These cover aircraft engines, computers, machine tools, motorcycles, cars (including British Leyland), trucks, construction equipment and electronics. In Mr Owen's words, 'This is surely enough to satisfy those in the Labour Party who favour competitive public enterprise as a spur to the private sector .... If the NEB can demonstrate that it is making a better job of these investments than the previous managements and owners, then and only then will it be appropriate to think about extending its empire into new fields.'

My own suggestions would be that the criterion of success should be the *ability* of the NEB to sell off these investments at a profit to the taxpayer. Whether they *should* then be sold is a political matter, but potential saleability is a purely commercial test. To take an analogy from a different area: the size of the returns from new roads, if tolls were imposed, would be an aid to road investment decisions, even though there may be good (economic as well as political) reasons for not imposing the tolls. (Up to the point where congestion occurs, a new motorway has the characteristic of a 'public good', in that its use by one person does not restrict the amount available to another; and charging then results in wasteful under-use.) The same argument applies to museum charges on non-crowded days – but only on such days: on crowded days use by one more person restricts the space and enjoyment available to others in a museum, so that it is not a public good and pricing is advisable.

The Nationalisation Controversy

The game of awarding marks for the relative performance of public and private industry is a futile one. I can still remember the scorn that Aneurin Bevan used to pour on those Labour moderates who tried to make out a case by case argument for nationalisation based on the specifics of particular industries. The traditional socialist believed in public ownership because he wished for a wholesale transfer of power and ownership from private capital to representatives of the people. The basic contention was debatable; but it was self-deception for Labour politicians to pretend that their bias in favour of public ownership was due to an esoteric argument produced by Professor X about the efficiency of the iron filings industry. To argue in this way makes for bad economics and confused political argument alike.

Similarly, those whose bias is in favour of private industry do not need to claim that publicly owned undertakings are incapable of producing efficiently certain goods or services, such as gas, electricity, rail services or even steel. The problems of these industries are much the same all over the world irrespective of the form of ownership. The real argument for private enterprise is that a society in which the State owned most of the means of production would be unfree in all but name; that there are positive advantages in the existence of private wealth and independent centres of decision; and that the answer to over-concentration of private wealth is greater dispersion rather than total abolition. The economic arguments for private ownership are of a subtle kind; the main superiority of private enterprise lies in discovering new wants, new products and activities, and of bringing to the fore new people in new schemes in a way that does not (and should not) come naturally to publicly accountable hierarchical corporations.

The economic and social impact of the British public sector depends on its character rather than on minor variations in its size. There were two clear reasons for the great improvement in the performance of the public sector between the 1950s and the 1960s. First, the nationalised undertakings lost much of their monopoly power as competition was intensified. Secondly, the state-owned industries were provided in their second decade with much more precise financial objectives. They were given target rates of return; and a bipartisan doctrine was adopted under which they were required to be run on commercial lines with specific state subsidies for those loss-making services that they were expected to provide for wider national reasons.

The breakdown of this 'commercial' doctrine as a result of government attempts to use the nationalised industries as an anti-inflationary spearhead, and the consequent deterioration of their performance in the 1970s, is one of the themes of an excellent Fabian pamphlet by Christopher Foster, who was director of economic planning in the Ministry of Transport in 1966–9. Ironically enough, the Heath Government interfered much more than either the previous Labour Government or the Macmillan Administration in the operation of the nationalised industries, and for the first time treated them as 'commanding heights of the economy' to be manipulated for the sake of national objectives. This interference took many forms. While private industry used the year up to mid-1971 to rebuild its badly squeezed profit margins, the nationalised industries were not allowed to do this, and in July 1971 were 'persuaded' to conform to the CBI price restraint pledge, which they were much less able to afford. On top of all this they were 'asked' to invest more than they thought profitable as part of the Government's reflationary drive. Few would quarrel with Foster's verdict that the resulting severe losses of these industries had a harmful effect on financial control and responsibility.

Foster discusses these and many other less obvious topics in his study. Nationalised industries suffer from a great deal of interference and arm-twisting from government departments; but paradoxically ministers and their advisers have little power over strategic policy. It is possible to tell the chairman of a nationalised industry that he must postpone a price increase or stand up to a wage claim in the national interest, or even to persuade him to bring forward investment projects of dubious profitability. But Foster found few if any instances of major investment proposals being turned down or a Board's long-term commercial strategy being rejected. As a good social democrat, he comes to the conclusion that these things should not be, and puts forward proposals for clarifying objectives and for returning to the emphasis on profitability. The basic trouble with this approach is that the very act of nationalisation transforms every commercial decision in the industry concerned into a potential political issue; and as politics is not going to change its nature, there are always going to be backsliding; and shortsighted expedients; and no government of any political complexion is going to abide very long by the principles of enlightened economists.

Without in any way intending to do so, Christopher Foster has written a more profound tract against nationalisation than anything ever published by the Institute of Economic Affairs. For what shines out of every line of his work is the way in which nationalisation transforms the most humdrum commercial decisions into major political issues. The most dramatic cases arise of course from resistance to wage claims. With the Government in the end writing the cheques, a completely neutral policy is extremely difficult. Either it leans on the public sector to buy off strikes – and is accused by private industry of caving in – or it uses the public sector as a battering ram against wage claims, and every dispute in the public sector becomes a major national crisis. Even if the Government could find the ideal middle course, it would have no way of demonstrating that it had done so.

The fact that political activity is bound to increase in some areas, such as the control of the physical environment, is all the more reason for governments concentrating on those areas where political intervention is indispensable and for abstaining from activities that do not have to be inside the political arena. There is, in fact, a crude pragmatic case for some genuine denationalisation where this is possible. It would show that the boundaries of the state sector can retreat as well as advance; and this might lessen some of the political hostility to the establishment of *new* public enterprises either where these are the best way of offering competition to a private monopoly or where a technical case can be made for this form of ownership.

But it is much more important to promote competition than to make marginal changes in ownership. If I were minister for industry, trade or transport, I would ask for a review of all the nationalisation and other statutes preventing private concerns from competing with the public corporations. One example would be the restrictions on the private generation of electricity. Another would be the monopoly position of the public urban transport undertakings.

A Note on Public Spending

Some advocates of a market economy tend to summarise their viewpoint by calling for less public spending. I prefer to focus on the basic policy errors themselves, which are sometimes, but not always or to a reliable extent, reflected in government expenditure. Table 2 may help to explain my hesitation in joining the hue and cry. It shows the movement of public spending according to four different definitions. Given enough space, time and patience, there could have been 44 lines, or 444.

The wide gap between the percentages on the various definitions shows that the differences between them are no mere quibbles. The lowest of the percentages consists of the spending of all public authorities on goods and services at market prices. This reached $26\frac{1}{2}$ per cent in 1975–6. The next lowest uses the Government's new definition, which includes all cash transfers. It is expressed as a proportion of GDP at market prices and corresponds most closely to the basis used by OECD for international comparison. This reached 46 per cent in 1975–6. The old definition, jettisoned by the Treasury in 1976, included all the investment of the nationalised concerns, while the new one includes only investment financed from government funds. The old one also included all public sector debt interest gross, whereas the new one excludes interest financed from public sector prices, rents or charges. A switch back to the old definition takes the 1975–6 proportion up to $51\frac{1}{2}$ per cent. A seemingly technical change – that of expressing the total as a proportion of the national product at factor cost instead of market prices – takes the proportion up to $58\frac{1}{2}$ per cent – the source of the famous 'nearly 60 per cent' estimate.

But this is by no means the highest estimate that is possible. The

Table 2. Public Spending as a Percentage of GDP

	1965–6	1975–6	1978–9 (official forecast, Jan. 1977)
	%	%	%
On goods and services at market prices	21 *	26½	23-4
Goods and services at factor cost	24 *	30	27
Total public spending at market prices	35½	46	42-3
Total public spending at factor cost	40½	51½	48
Total public spending at factor cost, pre-1977 definition	45½	58½ *	n.a.

* Estimated

Source: The Government's Expenditure Plans, Cmnd 6721 (HMSO, January 1977) and Treasury estimates.

transformation of child tax allowances into positive cash benefits will add another $1\frac{1}{2}$–2 per cent to the public spending proportion. The inclusion of other allowances and reliefs, including insurance and mortgage relief and the non-taxation of income from owner-occupied residences, would add a further 5 per cent or more. The inclusion as tax expenditures of 'free depreciation' and other industrial reliefs would take the total higher still. Indeed, the distinction between concessionary tax relief and positive government spending is largely one of administrative and accounting convenience, and by operating differently it would have been easy to bring the public spending ratio well above 70 per cent. (Theoretically it could go above 100 per cent.)

On all definitions, public spending is a very different animal from the size of the public sector. An economy with 100 per cent state enterprise could as a matter of logic have extremely low public spending, if people were left to buy out of their own incomes the products of these state enterprises, and if taxes and the 'social wage' were both low. Conversely, a largely private enterprise economy, such as Sweden, could have heavy public spending. And in the United Kingdom there would be many ways of cutting public spending, such as raising charges, cutting benefits or slashing capital spending, which would have no effect on the number of people working for central or local government.

It was true – and disquieting – that public spending increased so much on all definitions in the decade up to 1975. Too rapid an increase in the public spending proportion is a source of social strain and also of wage-push. Nevertheless, the ease with which the Treasury switched from one definition to an equally plausible lower one shows how difficult it is to find any single absolute percentage as an index of excessive government control. More than definition is at stake. It is easy to think of policies that reduce public spending statistics without lessening government intervention. The 1970–4 Conservative Government switched to protecting farmers by import levies in the hope of saving subsidy payments, as well as for EEC reasons. A switch to protecting Leyland by import quotas instead of government cash would work in the same way.

But there is a more pragmatic point. There has been a reaction against the squeeze on take-home earnings produced by government outlays and handouts. On the programme presented to the IMF, real public spending (excluding debt interest) in 1978 will actually be a shade lower than in 1976. Even allowing for some slippage, the government spending ratio is more likely to fall than to rise. While calls for less public spending might have been a rough-and-ready short-cut slogan for social market economists a few years ago, they are so no longer. The bigger danger to both freedom and efficiency rests in the controls and restrictions on all manner of things – from closed shops and employment contracts to prices and pay beds – that are rapidly proliferating. It is in these areas (and in measures justified only by pure envy, such as penal taxes that produce negative revenue) that the real adverse comparisons with other countries lie, rather than in public expenditure pure and simple. Some, but not all, of the instances in the following chapter involve wasteful public expenditure. It was a concern with the market mechanism and the rule of law that led me to investigate them rather than as an *a priori* concern to hold down public spending as such; and it is in returning to these fundamentals rather than through wild axe-wielding that our best hope for future improvement lies.

References

Brittan, S., *Capitalism and the Permissive Society* (Macmillan, 1973).

Foster, C.D., *Public Enterprise* (Fabian Society, 1972).

Meade, James, *The Intelligent Radical's Guide to Economic Policy* (Allen & Unwin, 1975).

ORC (Opinion Research Centre) Poll, *The Times* (13 and 14 January 1975).

Owen, G., 'Priorities for the National Enterprise Board', *Financial Times* (17 February 1975).

15 Invest in Failure – a Bipartisan Style

The Road to Industrial Serfdom (29 July 1971)

The Constitution of Liberty, published in 1960, was a profound inquiry by Professor F. A. Hayek into the principles by which liberty could be preserved in a modern industrial state. It did not receive the attention it deserved, partly because some of the practical conclusions were uncongenial to the temper of the time, and partly because the fashion for 'pragmatism' and impatience with all arguments based on principle was then at its height. Yet after a decade it remains one of the most contemporary books that I know; and looking through the 1960s press cuttings, it is the critics who sneered at Hayek's warnings (for example on the dangers to full employment of union monopoly power), not he, who should feel discomfited by events.

Professor Hayek's most important conclusion relates to the overriding importance of the 'rule of law'. By this he means that the individual citizen (and this includes the company director) should be free to pursue his own interest and purposes as he sees fit, provided that he conforms with known laws. This in no way involves a commitment to *laissez-faire*, or a belief in the perfection of market forces. But it does mean that the rules should be laid down in advance and that the law should not depend on the discretionary judgement of ministers or officials. It also means that the Government should have a monopoly of coercion and that there should be no system of private law.

Hayek's doctrines should certainly not be swallowed hook, line and sinker. In particular, as I have argued at length elsewhere, his conception of the rule of law is a necessary, but not a sufficient, condition for establishing a free society. The voluntary price control initiative by the CBI is a good example of what can occur when the belief in the rule of law burns low. The CBI has proposed a voluntary undertaking by the two hundred largest firms to limit their price increase to 4 per cent or less in the coming twelve months and to report to the CBI

142

Director-General, Campbell Adamson, if for any reason they find themselves unable to comply. This undertaking was sold to members on the grounds that it encouraged the Government to take its reflationary measures in July; and the CBI sent out a circular to members with a *pro forma* pledge to sign.

[Subsequent inquiries confirmed my original belief that the CBI offer had a negligible effect on official demand management policy, which was governed entirely by the usual combination of Treasury forecasting and political fears.]

The whole undertaking is, of course, nominally a voluntary one. But it is pretty obvious that considerable moral pressure is being put on the remaining doubters to sign. The price ceiling has never been enacted by Parliament and does not have the force of law. It is being implemented by a series of informal pressures and by bodies without any legislative authority. Yet those who do not conform will risk incurring government displeasure; and the CBI is being transformed into an organ of government policy – partly in the hope that the TUC may undergo the same transformation. If this does not turn out to be a system of private law, it will not be for want of trying on the CBI's and Government's part. Organisations like the CBI are subject neither to the discipline of the market place nor to political control; and 'industrial self government' is in the literal sense irresponsible. If a price ceiling is necessary in an emergency, it should be introduced by an elected Government by means of an Act of Parliament which states the forbidden courses of action clearly.

Even on the narrowest economic grounds, the case for the CBI move is dubious. It is based on the attractions of the short-term and the seemingly expedient. If prices are going up too quickly, the natural inclination of the interventionist mentality is to decree a slower rate of advance. It is the longer-term and indirect consequences of such interventions that are overlooked in the search for immediate results that often prove most important.

It is of the essence of the free market case that many of the consequences of intervention are unpredictable and often different from what its supporters expect. But some of the dangers of the present move can be seen even now. The most obvious is that, after many years of a low and falling rate of return on capital, 'voluntary' price restraint is likely to force it down even further. In that case investment is bound to suffer, as both the funds available and the incentives to invest will be reduced.

Those who do not find Professor Hayek's views to their political taste will find the dangers of low profitability spelt out by two New Left economists, Andrew Glyn and Bob Sutcliffe. They document in impressive detail the fall in the share of profits in net corporate turnover and in the pre-tax and post-tax rate of return on capital. The present state of affairs is, in the authors' view, incompatible with the ability of British capitalism 'to make profits and maintain a reasonable share of investment'.

The share of profits has fallen heavily as a share of the total domestic product; and the rate of return on capital has fallen even further. [According to Department of Industry estimates, it fell on a replacement cost basis and after providing for stock appreciation from 13.2 per cent in 1960 to 7.8 per cent in 1970 and 3.9 per cent in 1975, before recovering a little lost ground.] Doubtless there has been some rebuilding of profit margins in the first half of 1971 after the cyclical dip of the previous two years; hence the support of the CBI for voluntary price restraint. No doubt, too, the Confederation also hopes that the Government's reflationary measures will raise turnover enough to offset the effect on margins. This view ignores the fact that profits are very cyclical in their behaviour and that a temporary in-

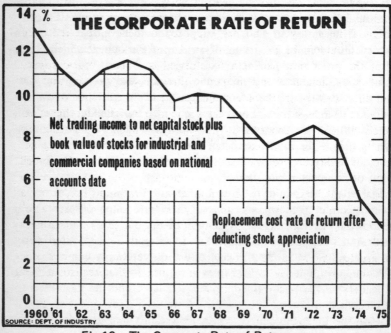

Fig 16.   The Corporate Rate of Return

crease in the recovery phase of the cycle is compatible with a longer-term trend towards insolvency.

[The CBI's reward was that the voluntarily restrained margins became part of the basis for the official price control imposed in 1972 which remained in force for several years afterwards. The corporate profit ratio and rate of return were both falling steeply in 1973, two years after the CBI initiative. Free depreciation and investment allowances provided some post-tax help but did not upset the falling trend shown by these figures.]

Whatever the case in the private sector, no one has pretended that the price ceiling can be offset by higher turnover in the nationalised industries. The Government's statement about financing more of their investment from the National Loans Fund shows that ministers are resigned to running heavy deficits. The effects of this policy on the government borrowing requirement and the money supply are not the most important. More worrying still is the effect on the morale of these industries. As Christopher Foster has pointed out, their managements now know that any good they might achieve by the careful scrutiny of investment projects, or more efficient running of their affairs, will be swallowed up by government-enforced losses. For the sake of a doubtful short-term tactical advantage, a dozen years' work to instil financial discipline into the nationalised industries has been thrown away — and by Conservatives, who are supposed to believe that these industries should make profits and 'stand on their own feet'.

But the point that needs to be stressed is that no moral stigma should be attached to any managing director who decides that his main duty is to the shareholders and that he is not equipped to act as an amateur judge of the nation's economic interest. The fact that is extremely difficult for economic writers — myself included — to take to heart is that more harm can often result from the well-meaning activities of highly civilised and sophisticated people such as Campbell Adamson than from the more blunt approach of unco-operative industrial rough diamonds who would regard Professor Hayek as a foreign Communist. Innumerable studies have shown that, when freedom has been lost, it was often because the victims had already lost their self-confidence and the desire to determine their own affairs. The greatest threat to the British free enterprise system has not been overt socialism, but the lack of faith in its principles demonstrated by the leaders of the business community.

Freedom and the rule of law have long been under pressure from those on the Left who cannot see that economic freedom is a crucial part of the wider liberty that they profess to value. But it is in equally great danger from those on the Right who are suspicious of general principles and who believe that 'if Government is in the hands of decent men it ought not to be too much restricted by rigid rules'.

The Private Use of Public Money (May–August 1972)

Towards the end of 1971 the Prime Minister appointed a committee of top officials to work out a crash programme for dealing with unemployment. The belief at the time was that unemployment would not yield easily to normal monetary and fiscal stimuli or even to general regional incentives, and that an emergency programme of special assistance was required.

The result was very much what would have been expected from a committee of this kind, and was embodied in the Industry Act. Up to £600 million [in 1972 pounds] is to be made available to selected private firms at the discretion of government departments, aided by yet another advisory board. No criteria are given and cases are to be examined 'on their merits'.

Since this policy was accepted, and the 'lame duck' doctrine ceremonially buried, the situation has changed. Unemployment has fallen faster than expected; inflation has emerged as the greater problem; and a carefree attitude to government spending and borrowing no longer seems so appropriate. Yet policy changes carry a momentum of their own; for good or ill, selective aid to private industry is emerging as the theme song of the Heath Government, and Labour's main critical contribution is to urge yet more of the same.

European industrial and regional policy is taking a similar turn; and the one major statesman who stood out for a socially responsible market economy, Professor Karl Schiller of West Germany, has been forced out of office by an increasingly familiar coalition of industrial interest groups, central bankers and Eurocrats.

It is worth setting out what precisely is wrong with the new type of Conservative industrial intervention, which is far from being the non-doctrinal common sense that its adherents suppose. There has to be a regional policy, in the sense of an attempt to load the dice in favour of the high-unemployment areas. Because of the existence of unused labour and a certain amount of unused social capital, the real costs of expansion in these areas are lower than the money costs. Conversely, the industrialist who expands in the South-East and Midlands imposes congestion and other costs on others for which he does not have to pay himself. Regional policy has to be a compromise between preserving the existing geographical distribution of the working population and leaving everything to natural forces.

The mistake is not that regional incentives are being given, but that they are of the wrong kind. The new and generous depreciation provisions give incentive to capital-intensive methods throughout the country. On top of this, there are to be investment grants, unrelated to employment. Labour MPs may mistakenly cheer this as an act of repentance. But the result is that those firms and projects that are heavy users of capital and modest users of labour are being given a special inducement to move to areas of labour surplus.

Moreover, the one measure that directly reduces labour costs in the regions, the Regional Employment Premium, is being phased out. The faults of the measure could have been remedied by making it into a proportional payroll subsidy applicable to all activities including services. This would have made it into the equivalent of regional devaluation plus a cash transfer, and also would have rendered it proof against erosion by inflation. Unfortunately, this suggestion was turned down; and even the discrimination in favour of manufacturing and against services inherited from Labour remains in the investment incentives. Thus the price mechanism, so far as it is being applied at all, is being applied perversely.

[The Labour Government, elected in 1974, began by reprieving the Regional Employment Premium; but by 1976 it too was in the process of phasing it out to make way for more selective intervention.]

There is no need, however, to pretend that general economic policies, or even regional ones, can be fully adequate to deal with workers whose livelihood is suddenly threatened by changes in world markets or by corporate mismanagement. There are two approaches that could help here. One is the German concept, developed in Erhard's day, of degressive subsidies phased out over a stated period of years to give workers time to adjust. The other is straightforward compensation. This would not be appropriate for equity capital, or for those occupations such as football or film-acting, of which risk is the essence. But there are many kinds of work to which it could apply; and, if it did, the Government would then be forced to ask whether it would pay to compensate redundant workers in this way rather than to sustain their existing occupations indefinitely. The Industry Act makes it all too easy to confuse 'full employment' with preserving the same employment.

Even this, however, is not the heart of the matter. The worst fault of the Industry Act is that special assistance is to be provided on no known principles, but simply according to the discretion of ministers and officials. This misinterprets the role of government intervention: it ought not to be to usurp the entrepreneurial function, but rather to adjust the structure of rewards and penalties so that it pays businessmen to act in a socially desirable way. There is no hidden supply of entrepreneurial talent available to Whitehall which private industry is unable to tap; and much of the vogue for selective intervention reflects the experience of countries such as France and Italy which have not had a fully developed capital market. With the system that is now developing it may become more important to keep in with Whitehall than to show good independent commercial judgement. Too much discretionary power is being given to ministers and officials to spend taxpayers' money according to the political pressures, fashions or hunches of the moment.

Not the least important aspect of the latest turn in government policy is the almost irresistible temptation it presents to the Labour Party to outbid it in a still more interventionist direction. Thus both parties become committed to a form of state-supported capitalism in which both shareholders and trade unionists have their immediate interests protected at the expense of consumers — which all of us are.

Why Look in the Crystal?

If we are to embark on this type of conservative socialism, the least we can do is examine the results of such policies. This has been done by the House of Commons Expenditure Committee. Its report does not attempt to go at all deeply into the validity of the various arguments for government intervention, nor does it consider the pros and cons of general incentives as against discretionary assistance; but what it does say is important enough.

The Committee found it impossible to pin official witnesses down on the reasons why assistance should be given to one firm or industry rather than another. Indeed, the criteria were constantly shifting, even while the Committee was sitting. It was originally told by the Shipbuilding Industry Board (subsequently abolished) that the only major justification for aid to shipbuilding was that other governments, especially the Japanese, subsidised their own shipbuilding industries. Without these artificial handicaps the British industry could, according to the chairman of the Board, Sir William Swallow, 'in general compete right away'.

The Committee was therefore surprised that by the beginning of 1972 British representatives at OECD were 'distinctly cautious' about

Table 3. The Changing Cost of Concorde

Date	Estimates of total develop- ment costs (£m)	Estimates of UK share (£m)	Actual UK expenditure to date (£m)
Nov. 1962	150-170	75-85	
July 1964	280	140	
June 1966	500 (incl. 50 for contingencies)	250 (plus 30 at R&D establishments)	
March 1969			170
May 1969	730 (no provision for contingencies)	340	
Oct. 1970	825	405	240
April 1971	885	440	280
March 1972	970	480	330
June 1973	1065	525	
Dec. 1973			406
March 1974	1070	535	
July 1975	1096	548	
March 1976	1154	564	
Oct. 1976			515

The above figures exclude production costs of the 16 aircraft manufactured from 1971, of which the net cost to the UK was £200 million. Therefore, up to the end of October 1976, the total net cost to public funds of the Concorde project was £715 million.

Source: Department of Industry

an international programme of phased reductions in subsidies. The Japanese import duty, which was the main example given of unfair overseas help, was eventually abolished and the Board could only say that other countries' practices were 'very devious and involved'. The all-party committee was unconvinced that the general run of British shipbuilding would be viable once unfair international practices had ceased. Sir Ronald Edwards was however a lone voice when he doubted whether it was logical to respond tit-for-tat if another country supported a particular industry.

A similar confusion was noted by the Committee on whether project receiving special assistance were expected to become profitable after a time. Upper Clyde was the clearest, but far from the only, example where commercial forecasts were too optimistic and the employment motive understated. As Lord Beeching observed, governments sometimes wanted to be deceived. 'They wished to see a project carried out for various non-commercial reasons, and would then want somebody to carry the responsibility for persuading them that it was going to be profitable.'

Interestingly enough, the long-run profitability argument was more often advanced for make-work projects in declining industries than for advanced technological projects. As the Committee tactfully notes, 'Whatever reasons may have been uppermost in the minds of Governments in supporting Concorde and the RB-211, the expectation of a solid return on the money can hardly have played much part.'

Indeed, the whole advanced technology argument emerges rather battered from even the mild investigation of a Committee wanting to be unanimous and to avoid doctrinal disputes. The Society of British Aero-Space Companies emphasised that it was normally about eight years before any surplus on a civil project was earned and it was therefore not possible to finance the cash calls from the market. One did not notice a similar inability to raise finance privately for a distant return for land purchase or office buildings, or gold shares [or North Sea oil]. The size as well as the distance of the return is clearly relevant.

Scepticism about the Treasury's power to check the supply of feeding stuffs for white elephants, lame ducks and similar fauna is expressed by the present report. A previous Commons committee was struck as early as 1963 by the contrast between the careful technical study devoted to the Concorde and the lack of detailed attention to its financial implications.

An annual White Paper on each major assistance project, in a form to be agreed with the appropriate parliamentary committee, is recommended. Departments and beneficiary companies too often invoke commercial confidentiality as an excuse for avoiding financial control and criticism. The Expenditure Committee believes, however, that firms in receipt of government assistance should 'accept some loss of confidentiality in the interests of full Parliamentary scrutiny'.

There is one general conclusion that strikes me forcibly after reading this report. Policies of active government industrial intervention came back into fashion in the early 1960s as a means of speeding up economic growth and raising living standards in the face of the imperfections of the market-place. In practice, they have proved just the opposite. Selective intervention has more often than not diverted manpower and investment to areas of low or negative return. Sometimes this has been done for prestige or international political reasons. Nothing can be said against this, provided it is really true that people would rather have the prestige than the cash in their pockets. The other main reason for selective intervention is to slow down deliberately the process of industrial change to reduce the burdens on people who would otherwise have to find new occupations, move their homes or live on the dole. It is perfectly reasonable for an affluent society to pay a price to protect the victims of change, but what stands out a mile is the lack of any attempt to quantify the costs and benefits of alternative ways of doing this.

Selective Intervention – British Style (December 1974 – August 1975)

Until recently, state rescue and support were concentrated overwhelmingly on three industries – shipbuilding, aerospace and machine tools. The three workers' co-operatives to which Mr Benn offered finance in 1974–5 were fairly modest in terms of cash although important for the principles raised. They were Meriden, the *Scottish Daily Express* and IPD. The Industrial Development Advisory Board were publicly overruled in all three cases. The unemployment situation in Glasgow and Merseyside was the Government's main justification in two of them. Mr Benn's use of public money caused anxiety among his own officials; and in at least one of these cases a permanent secretary is believed to have put a note of dissent on file. [P. Carey]

But all these cases fade into insignificance by comparison with the British Leyland rescue. The original company was itself sponsored by Mr Wilson and Mr Benn, and lubricated with Industrial Reorganisation Corporation money in 1968. During the period up to 1974, its trading profits (after interest) as a percentage of sales averaged 2.3 per cent. These profits were arrived at without setting aside funds for replacing a substantial part of BL's plant, and thus overstate the true results.

With such a record, there would have been a strong case for liquidation to put assets and manpower to more fruitful use. Nevertheless, it would be politically understandable if the Government wished to postpone these changes until the national unemployment trend was reversed, and so extended its bank guarantee for a year or two. But the present rescue operation goes breathtakingly further. The official intention now is that fixed capital spending should rise from £77 million in 1974 to £381 million in 1978 (assuming that inflation settles down at $12\frac{1}{2}$ per cent by 1976–7). In the period up to September 1978 the Government is expected to provide or guarantee £900 million in addition to finding up to £60 million to buy out existing shareholders.

For the longer period up to 1982, some £2.8 billion is to be provided in fixed and working capital. The Ryder Committee hopes that, some time after 1978, half the capital will be generated from within the new state-controlled British Leyland, but it wisely refrains from going into detail that far ahead. It would be a complete break with precedent if the actual sums did not turn out much higher, as they have for nearly all previous state-sponsored investment projects.

On the highly optimistic assumption that only half of the £2.8 billion programme would need to be financed externally, the best the Ryder Report can forecast from 1982 onwards is enough profit to pay interest at 12 per cent, with nothing over for dividends after retentions. The Ryder Report is also based on certain assumptions about world markets and the British share of them. I have not the faintest idea whether these forecasts are right. But I do know that the whole postwar period has been littered with industrial forecasts by official committees that have been wildly wrong – dollar shortages that have turned to surpluses, predictions of chronically 'high' and chronically 'low' commodity prices alike belied by events, phases of over-optimism and over-pessimism about the prospects of coal, oil and atomic energy.

The provision for annual reviews from 1976 onwards before further loan transfers are granted is a very limited safeguard. As we know from experience with Concorde, the inevitable argument will always be: 'Having sunk so much, it would be wasteful to stop the expenditure mid-way just because the return has been delayed.' This is known as the 'Treasury bounce'.

It is time someone pointed out that Sir Don Ryder and his team are not engaged in the same activity when they rush out an advisory report for the Government as when they are working in their own businesses: then their own careers and reputations are more directly involved, and they have to back their views with their shareholders' money. The astonishing fact is that no economic analysis of any kind is presented to justify the preservation and expansion of BL in defiance of the judgement of the market. The Committee simply reiterates that 'vehicle production' is the kind of industry that ought to remain an essential part of the United Kingdom's economic base.

There are really two considerations that seem to have weighed with the Ryder Committee and the Government. The first is that BL employs 170,000 people and provides orders for components and suppliers which Mr Wilson grandly aggregated into 'a million jobs'. The other is the magic word 'exports', which amounted in 1973–4 to £485 million, and fears that some of BL's home sales of £483 million would be replaced by imports.

Mr Wilson made it very clear time and again that critics of the rescue operation will have 'a million jobs' thrown in their faces; and they will deserve it if they allow themselves to be so intimidated. It really is not good enough for a prime minister who once taught economics to play up to the illiterate assumption that, if some particular jobs disappear, no others will take their place. Anyone with knowledge of the future looking ahead in 1959 would have been able to predict job losses far exceeding anything involved in BL. Between 1959 and 1973 the fall in the numbers employed in agriculture – or 'jobs destroyed', in populist jargon – was 325,000. Over 400,000 jobs disappeared in mining; nearly 230,000 in textiles and over 200,000 in the railways. But although these jobs were not 'preserved', total employment expanded by 1.2 million over the period.

The fallacy is that their is an entity called 'the UK' which decides which industries should expand or decline, and by how much. The motor industry was not created by a government decision. Nor were most others. The Government does not have to decide which product 'we' opt in or out of. There are any number of halfway houses, such as manufacturing trucks and specialised cars, or components, or final assembly, or leaving small car production to Ford; but if the motor industry declines, other industries will take its place, *provided that government policy allows a market return on capital.*

Harold Macmillan, although far wiser than his successors, displayed the essence of the politician's (or industrial stateman's) approach when, discussing 'demand management' with some economic journalists, he asked: 'Demand for what?' It is a mistake even to try to answer from the centre how consumers at home and abroad are going to spend or invest their income. They will decide for themselves. It is not governments that create jobs but customers, here and abroad. Similar arguments apply to exports and imports. If British and overseas customers spend less than the £1.3 billion they have recently been spending on BL cars, they will have spare resources to spend on something else – or to finance investment – and, provided that excess demand is avoided and the exchange rate is competitive enough, this will go on British goods. It is time to point out that nearly all industrial rescue operations involve the coercion of taxpayers and consumers, who are forced to devote a part of their income to supporting activities on which they are not prepared to spend their money voluntarily.

A particularly unfortunate aspect of the present emphasis on protecting jobs is that (apart from emergency periods of wage freezes and ceilings) unions are encouraged to put forward inflationary wage claims in the knowledge that the State will come to their rescue. This is, in the not-so-long run, bad for employment itself. For it means that any given level of money demand will be associated with higher wages and lower employment – although the loss of employment may occur in the non-rescued companies or take the form of lower recruitment even in the rescued ones.

Of course a world recession is a special situation. It is very difficult to distinguish between perfectly sound commercial operations, threatened with destruction by a temporary tempest, and unsound operations that have been artificially protected by the excess demand of the previous boom. There are some much-needed changes which, if not made in a recession, are not made at all. But even if the benefit of the doubt is given to threatened enterprises at such times, the argument is one for temporary assistance and not permanent state involvement. The latter brings politics into every commercial decision and makes every change in prices or in the pattern of employment a positive government action for which ministers are accountable.

Quite apart from periods of recession, there is a perfectly respectable case for some attempts to compensate the victims of industrial change. This is, however, a very different matter from preventing change or forcing on consumers, at home or abroad, products they do not want. Instead of reacting to each case on an emergency basis, there should be a permanent Adjustment Assistance Board with funds to help those adversely affected by market or technical developments. The NEB could form the basis for such a board. We could learn something from the continental habit of adapting old institutions to new purposes, instead of destroying them and recreating them under other names with little underlying changes in policy.

Unlike the present National Enterprise Board, the reformed body I am suggesting would have no illusions about speeding up industrial development. It would have the conscious job of imposing a brake for social reasons. It could give assistance in the form of grants or even specific job subsidies. The main condition would be that all assistance should be temporary and phased out according to a preordained timetable; and the Board would always have to calculate whether financial compensation might not be cheaper than supporting employment.

By contrast, British industrial policy is now based on two principles: bribing or cajoling private and state concerns to invest in new plant, and making sure that as many workers are required to man the new plant as the old. The best comment I heard on our situation was by Captain Shotover in the National Theatre's excellent production of *Heartbreak House*. 'The captain is in his bunk, drinking bottled ditchwater, and the crew is gambling in the forecastle. She will strike and sink and split.' But the crew has a shrewd suspicion that the ship is headed for the rocks and is much readier to respond to a new leader and a new course than the ship's officers realise.

The Not-So-Hidden Cost of Import Controls
(Spring 1975–Summer 1976)

The advocacy of import controls by a group within the Labour Party, with strong backing from some government economic advisers, reveals how certain things go together in the interventionist mind: protection of the existing job pattern and of inefficient capitalist concerns with taxpayers' money, the conservative dead hand of union control, insulation from foreign competition and departure from the EEC to promote collectivism in one country.

The great temptation of controls is that they appear costless on a superficial view: imports are replaced by domestic output; total production grows by a multiple of the imports replaced; there is no exchange rate pressure on the cost of living; and extra resources are whistled up to meet real wage claims in an anti-inflationary way. Nevertheless, I am worried that the opponents of import controls are resting their case on dubious arguments. Although these arguments may be easier for politicians and industrial leaders to follow than the true ones, they are also more vulnerable to sceptical probing.

Dubious Argument No. 1: Overseas Retaliation

Too much weight is being placed on overseas reactions by the opponents of import controls. The basic 'New Cambridge' reply to the retaliation argument is that, if in any case UK imports have to be limited to what Britain can earn and borrow overseas, it makes little difference to other countries if we limit imports by quotas or by restricting home demand. Some countries gain and others lose from this difference of method, but the total effect is the same.

One might argue about indirect and remote repercussions, but our trading partners might take the view that a country that accounts for a mere $8\frac{1}{2}$ per cent of manufacturing trade, and is beset with inflationary and payments problems, will not bring down the world trading structure if it restricts imports, and they might agree reluctantly to help get the United Kingdom's problems off their backs. If import controls are to be stopped, the argument must be made out on domestic grounds.

Dubious Argument No. 2: Leave it to World Trade

The case presented by officials against import controls has been highly dependent on their forecasts of a world trade recovery. The implication has been that, if only we could sit tight and refrain from stimulating home demand, exports would – for once – take up much of the slack at home. The trouble with this approach is that it is related to specific predictions of an unreliable kind; and it leaves the door open for politicians to argue for import controls if world trade falls below the forecast path.

The danger is particularly great because so many British leaders believe that world output and trade depend on political decisions to stimulate demand, This makes one wonder how world trade grew in the nineteenth century, when no finance minister ever knew what it meant to 'stimulate demand'. But while the belief persists, ministers are likely to have for the time an excuse for import controls on the argument that the stronger countries have not played their part in maintaining world growth.

If there is excessive slack at home then exchange rate depreciation, backed by an appropriate and controlled once-for-all monetary expansion, can help to remove it even without a boom in world trade. On the other hand, the amount of slack and the speed with which it can be taken up may be less than the crude unemployment figures suggest. In that case an external stimulus to demand, from a growth in exports, is likely to be just as inflationary as an internal stimulus arising from import controls and a switch to home-produced articles.

Dubious Argument No. 3: Import Controls are Inflationary

This argument should be used with great caution. It has been defensive value against the charge that the devaluation alternative is inflationary. In a pioneering study two economists, R. A. Batchelor and A. P. C. Minford, compare the effects of the import controls and the equivalent devaluation that would have been needed to eliminate 80 per cent of consumer good imports in 1975. To do this would have required either very severe import controls or a sharp devaluation. The authors assume that import licences would be auctioned to the highest bidder and would be transferable. This would minimise the damage from the controls and prevent the quota holders from reaping windfall profits. If, according to normal practice, licences were given on the basis of historical shares, the real costs would be higher; and either prices would rise in fringe markets, or queues and shortages would penalise the home buyer even more severely. The latter would be the equivalent to a hidden price increase expressed in the form of a deterioration of service.

The desired effect on the trade balance could, it is estimated, be accomplished by import controls equivalent to a 144 per cent tariff on consumer goods or a 28 per cent general devaluation. In both cases it is necessary to take account of the switch in demand to home-produced goods, which would rise in price. The effect of both measures would, according to the authors, be an increase in the price level of 7 or $7\frac{1}{2}$ per cent. Thus import controls raise prices just as much. It is, I hope, unnecessary to emphasise that it is not the exact figures that matter but the demonstration that import controls do not magically escape the disadvantages of devaluation. The calculations take account of the impact effect only. The eventual effect on the price level is likely, of course, to be greater. But this qualification applies equally to the devaluation and important control route.

Why then should one be cautious about saying import controls are inflationary? In both the devaluation and the import control case, the effects on the price level are once-for-all. There will not be a continuous inflation unless monetary demand is permanently boosted. This is more than a quibble about the academic use of the word 'inflation'. The price level over the next ten years is going to depend far more on whether the money supply remains the same, is doubled or quintupled (different possibilities which reflect differences in the rates of monetary expansion in various recent years) than it will on the severity of import controls or the height of tariffs. The inflation argument against import controls is thus vulnerable to the first person who points out that better monetary control than we had in the first half of the 1970s is likely to make more contribution to curbing inflation than any amount of free trade.

The Real Arguments Against Controls

An attempt can in fact be made to quantify part of the cost of import controls in terms of curtailing choice and the shift to less efficient home-produced substitutes. This has been done in the study by Batchelor and Minford. The authors begin with a schematic projection of the national accounts in 1980, of a now-familiar kind. It is assumed that any attempt to achieve 'full employment' would lead in that year to a £3 billion current payments deficit assuming 'constant competitiveness'. The two options (apart from doing nothing or borrowing) appear to be further devaluation and import controls.

The authors assume that controls are imposed on consumer goods and on 'light finished goods purchased by firms' such as tables, stationery or clothes. Import penetration of consumer type goods is estimated at 17 per cent of the domestic market (21 per cent for consumer goods narrowly defined). The imports in question make up 28

Table 4. Tariff Equivalent of Import Controls

Cumulative deficit to be eliminated (per cent of GDP)	Required tariff rate (per cent)
0.5	6
1.0	13
1.5	22
2.0	33
2.5	47
3.0	66
3.5	96
4.0	144
4.5	260

Source: Batchelor and Minford op.cit.

per cent of total imports of goods or 5 per cent of GDP equivalent to about £5 billion at 1976 values. [In 1976 £1 billion happened to equal about 1 per cent of GDP.]

The clue to quantifying the effect of import controls is to convert them into hypothetical tariffs of equivalent effect. Table 4 gives the authors' estimates, based on standard international trade elasticities, plus an assumption about the price response of domestic suppliers, of the extra tariffs required on these consumer-type goods to save different amounts of imports. To save imports equivalent to 3 per cent of GDP would require a tariff of 66 per cent. To save $4\frac{1}{2}$ per cent., which may have been nearer to what the Cambridge Economic Policy Group had in mind when it advocated import controls in 1976, would require tariffs of 260 per cent. As mentioned above, Batchelor and Minford themselves assume import controls equivalent to a 144 per cent tariff. Thus quotas on imports are far from being a painless alternative to relying on monetary control plus a flexible exchange rate. Batchelor and Minford produce calculations to show that the deadweight cost of the import control alternative is a good deal higher.

In fact, the damage resulting from more extensive import controls would be more severe than such essentially static calculations are able to show. While devaluation involves across-the-board stimuli to both exports and import substitutes roughly in proportion to international trading advantages, import controls would, as the authors stress, be a deliberate distortion affecting one side of the account only. However, once the economy has become adapted to them they could not be removed without creating severe local pockets of unemployment – an effect extremely difficult to quantify in advance. Calculations confined to the trade balance by their nature ignore the possibility of changing the balance on capital account, in particular the attractiveness of a low-wage country such as the United Kingdom for international private capital, if only a modicum of confidence could be restored.

Moreover, no kind of static analysis can take into account the long-term effects on efficiency of insulating British industry from international competition. The Cambridge Economic Policy Review in its frequent pleas for massive across-the-board import controls had up to 1977 given no programme or time-table for their removal; and the more honest advocates of such controls as a major economic weapon do not envisage them as being at all temporary or stop-gap. Static calculations cannot take into account the big improvements in competitiveness – at an exchange rate that did no more than reflect international differences in monetary growth and inflation – that would occur from the restoration of the profit motive to British industry and to individuals as well as companies.

The truth is that import controls are undesirable because they force British consumers to buy expensive, low-quality, long-delivery or otherwise unsatisfactory British goods. By doing so they perpetuate the inefficiency of the home producer in a vicious circle, which will be reinforced by NEB subsidies, planning agreements and all the rest.

There are two theoretical roads to import controls: the creeping and the galloping. The creeping road is the one British governments tend to take. Its principle is to extend protection wherever this can be done without causing too much fuss. Controls are accepted *de facto* internationally on items such as textiles and shoes, or on Iron Curtain imports; and here the Government has tightened up already. Another area is Japan, where our EEC partners share our prejudices; and there is always the search for evidence for so-called dumping, which is another pretext for discouraging imports.

Postscript on the Green Pound

Between January and April 1976 the wholesale price of raw materials purchased by the manufacturing industry rose by an annual rate of over 50 per cent. During the same period the price of products purchased by the food industries rose by an annual rate of just under 20 per cent. The big discrepancy is largely due to the behaviour of the 'green pound', which governs certain food prices under the Common Agricultural Policy (CAP). In contrast to the ordinary pound, the 'green pound' was not devalued after October 1975 for the remainder of the year [and the whole of 1976]. If the green pound had fallen immediately by the full amount of sterling depreciation, wholesale prices of those foodstuffs where EEC intervention effectively governs the price would have been 19 per cent higher, retail food prices perhaps 5 per cent higher and the retail index about 1 to 2 per cent higher than they were in April 1976.

The basic features of the green pound are in fact simple: it is the mechanics, exceptions, administration and anomalies that provide the nightmares. Let us suppose that we had a dual exchange rate, with one rate for the great bulk of sterling transactions and another specially high rate for agricultural products. The differential could be maintained by subsidising agricultural imports and putting a levy on farm exports. In a food-importing country such as the United Kingdom, the subsidies would exceed the levies. The only difference between the ground pound and a straightforward dual exchange rate is that the net cost of the subsidies is paid out of the EEC Budget rather than by the British Treasury. That is really all there is to it. Germany maintains an opposite kind of dual exchange rate with a lower rate of agriculture than for other transactions and is a net loser to the EEC.

Green currencies first arose when the French devalued and the Germans revalued in 1969. The French were not prepared to see the cost in francs of their food rise by the full amount of the depreciation; and the Germans were not prepared to see the prices in marks received by their farmers fall. Subsidies were therefore provided for French consumers and German producers. The United Kingdom has taken the same attitude as France in 1969. Unfortunately, the agricultural price levels that are lowered in the United Kingdom by the green pound and raised in Germany by the green mark are not world market prices: they are so-called 'common prices' fixed by Community ministers in Brussels and enforced by a network of intervention boards.

It would thus be very superficial to conclude from the figures in this article that the Common Agricultural Policy has, contrary to expectations, turned out to be a source of benefit for Britain. EEC prices are above world market levels. The savings on the food bill through the green pound are just a partial offset against being deprived of the right to buy food in the cheapest market – which is a genuine deprivation, even if only a minor contribution to the United Kingdom's economic problems.

References

Batchelor, R. and Minford, C., 'Import Controls and Devaluation' in *On How to Cope with Britain's Trade Position* (Trade Policy Research Centre, London, 1977).

Brittan, S., *Capitalism and the Permissive Society* (Macmillan, 1973).

Corden, W. M., and Fels, Gerhard (eds), *Public Assistance to Industry: Protection and Subsidies in Britain and Germany* (Macmillan, 1976).

Foster, C. D., *Public Enterprise* (Fabian Society, 1972).

J. Bruce-Gardyne, and Lawson, N., 'How Whitehall Grew Wings', in *The Power Game* (Macmillan, 1976).

Glynn, A., and Sutcliffe, R., *British Capitalism* (Penguin, 1973).

The Future of British Leyland ('Ryder Report') (HMSO, 1975).

16 Social Tokenism at Home and Abroad

How to Create a Shortage

There is a popular fallacy that economic writers have nothing to say on subjects such as housing, social security, defence, higher education, television, aviation policy and so on. They ought therefore to argue away among themselves about crawling pegs, fiscal drag, borrowing requirements, and other arcane topics. This misunderstanding is probably unavoidable. Economists and commentators themselves work in a market place; and in the public arena at least the demand is for pronouncements on highbrow monetary topics which many people find puzzling.

It is very tempting for the commentator, whether professor or journalist, to fall in with this stereotype. After all there are only twenty-four hours in every day and no one whose prime job it is to unravel the mysteries of the US Federal reserve or the Treasury's attempt to fine-tune the British economy can possibly hope to be at home with the facts of dozens of social or industrial problems. Unfortunately, the acknowledged experts in such fields are far too often mainly experts in the extraction of taxpayers' money for special interest purposes, or in the operation of a vast network of controls and regulations designed to increase their own powers and feelings of righteousness.

A book of collected articles by Professor Milton Friedman has attracted a great deal of attention because of his prescience (not complete, but greater than that of most policy-makers) on the money supply, inflation, incomes policy and related topics. But the most interesting lesson to be learned is not to my mind in this area, but in Friedman's repeated demonstration that so much of the legislation and expenditure designed to help the poor, the minority groups and the under-privileged has the opposite of the intended effects, and the net result is partly to help the better off (in an arbitrary and illogical manner) and partly a net destruction of income and wealth.

Examples of the effects of social tokenism are legion. The United

States has on paper a progressive tax system in which – thanks to special exemption and avoidance opportunities – the higher-income classes pay a smaller percentage in tax than the less well off. In a recent year only 626 US citizens reported a taxable income of over $1 million – which is clearly absurd. Friedman describes the latest US tax legislation as the 'Accountants and Lawyers Relief Act'. Other examples include farm price supports, which raise the cost of living of the poor and enrich the landowner while doing almost nothing to help the poorest farmers. Perhaps the most tragic example is the US minimum wage law, rightly described by Friedman as the 'most anti-Negro law on our Statute books'. A recent increase in this minimum wage produced, as Friedman predicted, unemployment percentages of over 30 per cent among male Negro teenagers.

The best way to help the poor is by cash benefits. Ideally these should take the form of a negative income tax, but a better-than-nothing approach to this can be made under present institutions by sufficiently high (and taxed) child benefits, supplementary benefits, rebates for school meels and so on. The problem of providing sufficient generosity to the poor without inadvertently creating tax disincentives to work – the poverty trap – is a delicate one, which is a reason for trying to replace as many as possible of the present mass of unco-ordinated benefits by one or two simple cash payments whose impact is known and which can be set off against the tax bill. There will however always have to be a safety-net for discretionary payments to hard-pressed families not covered by the rules. There will be a case for increasing benefits not merely when the general price level rises, but when items that loom disproportionately in the budgets of the least well off, such as basic foodstuffs or the cost of home heating, show especially heavy increases. Although no panacea, the payment of cash benefits is almost invariably better than attempts to control or subsidise key items in the 'cost of living'.

Indeed, one of the least remarked, but most insidious prices of rapid inflation is that it enormously increases public misunderstanding of, and hostility towards, the price mechanism as a source of incentives and a method of allocation of resources. It would be a fair guess that most people confronted with the word 'prices' think of the 'cost of living', which, so it seems to them, always goes up and adds to the problems of life. Changes in *relative* prices, which are necessary to guide production and consumption, thereby become confused with the upward movement of the *general average* of prices associated with currency debasement.

It is in this general climate that a clamour for subsidies, especially for 'essentials', develops. Unfortunately, subsidies are a way of treating the symptoms that makes the disease worse. If a product, say beef, is scarce, a high relative price signals to people the amount of other goods that has to be foregone to pay for a pound of beef whose price has risen, perhaps because of what is happening in world markets. A subsidy, by contrast, encourages profligate spending precisely when the need is for economy. It is moreover a peculiar redistribution of income that favours consumers with an above-average taste for beef, rich and poor alike, and (because of its tax cost) penalises consumers with average or below-average tastes or requirements.

The food subsidies introduced by the Labour Government in 1974 and then gradually phased out after a series of sterling crises illustrate the point. At their 1975 peak they were running at a rate of £1 billion. Let us assume they were financed from the increase in the basic and higher-income tax rates in the 1974 Budget. On this basis, far from the sum being concentrated among the poorest families, the middle-income groups secured the lion's share, when subsidies were 'netted out' against tax. The effect on income distribution was almost identical to that of raising the tax rates and distributing nearly £2 per head in cash to everyone, tinker, tailor, tycoon, sailor, you and me. But the result was inferior to such a transaction as the grant was not freely spendable but had to be used on the purchase of specific products.

Because subsidies are expensive, there is a temptation to resort to physical rationing, either formal or informal, to reduce the financial outlay. In a world of scarcity some form of rationing is always with us. Rationing by coupon has the disadvantage of ignoring the different (and changing) tastes and circumstances of different people and firms. We have seen that there are more efficient ways of redistributing resources *between* income groups; while, *within* a given income group, coupon rationing discriminates against people with certain preferences and in favour of those with others. Just as important, physical rationing is a form of coercion, preventing people from spending their incomes in ways they prefer. This can be most clearly seen if we imagine a world in which everything is 'rationed'. Then money left after buying the ration of food, clothing, and so on is useless, and everybody is compelled to adopt the same life-style irrespective of preferences, and is forbidden to spend his income in any except the one way approved by the powers that be, whoever they are.

One of the worst examples of the control, subsidy and allocation approach is the artificially created problem of 'housing'. Public housing expenditure in the United Kingdom on loans subsidies and grants of various kinds was running at £2 billion in 1977. Local authority rents covered on average 43 per cent of the total housing outgoings, and looking ahead to 1980–1, the Labour Government intended to do no more than raise this proportion to 50 per cent. The best and most sophisticated point that can be made on the Government's behalf was that local authority interest payments were much exaggerated in conventional accounts; and during an inflationary period much of what appears as interest is really refinancing (see chapter 12). But if we really wish to conduct the discussion rigorously, the level of subsidy should not be measured by central and local government outlays at all, but by the difference between council rents and the free market rents of the same properties. On this basis the 43 per cent figure is likely to be an underestimate rather than an overestimate – at least of impact effects, for if there really were a free market in rented houses, rents might, after the initial shakeout, settle at surprisingly low levels.

But this is very far from being the complete bill. On top of these programmes, purportedly designed to help those who cannot buy their own houses, there is another set of programmes designed to help those who can. Tax relief for owner-occupiers was running at around £1½ billion in 1977. The cost of the absence of any Schedule A tax on the annual income from home ownership has never been estimated. These are concessions that not only help the better off, but help them more than in proportion to their wealth.

The use of improvement grants, which has at times helped the better-off to make a huge capital gain at the taxpayer's expense – of which we hear so much from the Left – is characteristic of the unintended effect of so much 'do good' legislation. But the home purchaser, affluent or otherwise, is not the main beneficiary from the tax subsidies and special help. For the ultimate effect is to raise the cost of land. If the whole of the so-called housing programme – both that part which appears as foregone revenue and actual expenditure – did not exist, it would be possible to free millions of the lower-paid workers from tax, greatly increase social security benefits and in all probability improve our whole urban environment.

The worst advertisement for rationing by administrative allocation is rent control. If the price of any commodity is held below the market level, the result will be more demand and less supply – thus creating a self-perpetuating shortage. If the price of clothes or bananas had been arbitrarily fixed on supposedly social grounds, we would have had a banana or clothing shortage with black markets, privileges for those who happen to have contacts in the trade, queues and all the rest. Rented accommodation has been controlled to an increasing extent for nearly sixty years; and privately rented accommodation has fallen from about 90 per cent of the housing stock at the turn of the century to less than 50 per cent in 1950, just over 25 per cent in 1960 and only 15 per cent in 1976.

With rents so far below free market levels, private rented housing is not available on the market, while council houses are allocated by local authorities under a waiting list system. The result is a serious misallocation of house room and an arbitrary redistribution of incomes, with many low-rent council homes in the possession of tenants a good deal better off than people who do not have such good fortune. The incentive to build for rent or even to let out spare rooms is killed off, and many people who would pay the market rent are homeless.

In Stockholm some poor families have waited for five to eight years for council flats, while better off people have got in quickly through contacts or key money. 'In fact next to bombing, rent control seems in many cases to be the most efficient technique so far known for destroying cities, as the housing situation in New York City demonstrates.' This quotation is not from Friedman, not from Hayek, but from a paperback by a Swedish Social Democrat economist, Assar Lindbeck, *The Political Economy of the New Left*.

The practical consequences for the United Kingdom have been spelt out by David Eversly, the former chief strategic planner to the GLC: '... no unfurnished rented property is now available, and furnished rooms only at exorbitant rents ... newcomers to the housing market are under more of a disadvantage than they once were.' Homelessness is on the increase:

> Local authorities are putting more people into bed and breakfast accommodation, and organisations catering for the young single homeless report a great increase in business. What this means is that local authority housing departments have no means of dealing with a section of the population who, a generation ago, would have found transitional accommodation in the private market. ...

Private tenancies are increasingly a privilege for

> those who need [them] least (just examine the National Trust's rent roll) ... what are we going to do to enable people to move house when they need to change jobs? What are we going to offer, besides

a council house after a very long wait, to young couples getting married and perhaps wanting to start a family? If the answer is 'nothing', then no one should be surprised if large cities cannot man their essential services, if homelessness is on the increase, and if fertility is falling faster than even the optimistic had demanded.

How many fires, floods and plagues would have wrought the havoc created by gradual destruction of the house-letting market by rent restrictions since 1915?

It is important to see what has gone wrong. Housing subsidies, whether for tenants or owner-occupiers, can be justified if it is believed that people cannot be trusted to spend enough on homes for themselves and their families. (Help for poorer families is not itself a sufficient justification.) But having made this paternalist judgement, central and local governments (and voters who elected them) have not willed the means.

If the public authorities were prepared to build enough houses and flats to supply to the full the extra demand created by their rent policies, more of the nation's resources would go into housing than citizens desire. But this would be the limit of state coercion; and once sufficient accommodation were built, rented housing would be available, like any other goods or services, without queuing or administrative allocation. A *permanent* housing shortage, and the power of public officials over individual lives, arises because a political commitment to rent (i.e. house price) ceilings in no way carries with it a parallel commitment by central or local government to build sufficient houses to satisfy the demand created by these below-market ceilings. The politicians have fixed the price without filling the resulting gap between supply and demand. This is an example of one of the many imperfections of the political process.

The evils of half a century cannot be undone overnight. The immediate lifting of all rent controls would inflict great hardships; and by the time the price mechanism had done its work and enough new homes were provided by drive down rents, many of those most cruelly affected would long have been dead. The individualist-liberal, who rightly condemns the authoritarians of Right and Left for being willing to sacrifice millions for some dubious long-term principle, must be careful not to make the same mistake himself.

Unfortunately the Conservatives chose the wrong reform in their 'fair rents' legislation of 1971, repealed in 1974. They took over, as they boasted, from Richard Crossman the formula of a 'fair rent' equivalent to the rent ruling in a market where there were no shortages and no surpluses. This is a completely circular process as the state of the market itself depends on the level of rents; and in practice valuers had to replace the formula by a rule of thumb.

It would be better to approach reform in terms of individuals and households. The main weapon for reform should be the decontrol of vacant dwellings, whether in the public or the private sector. Security of tenure at low rents should be given to all older tenants, who above all deserve to be protected from the effects of economic or policy changes. In the intermediate group of younger established tenants, a policy of predictable step-by-step increases is indeed appropriate, so that expectations are not suddenly shattered. But the final aim should be to a free market rent rather than to one decreed by the man from the council.

Even if such a policy were successfully adopted, one must face the fact that accommodation in highly prized central metropolitan areas is always going to be much more expensive than similar homes elsewhere. This is one of the drawbacks to living in the centre of London or Stockholm, to be balanced against the advantages by a young couple deciding where to live; and it is difficult to discover a principle of justice requiring those with a taste for metropolitan living to be subsidised at the expense of those who prefer to spend their money in other ways.

In fact, a large part of the effect of rent controls and subsidised council homes in the metropolis is passed on to middle- and upper-class residents in the shape of cheaper personal services of all kinds, whether domestic help, car repairs, newspaper deliveries or retail services. If subsidised homes were not provided, wages would have to be a great deal higher to persuade sufficient working-class people to live in town to perform such functions. Alternatively, they would come in from outside and their charges would reflect transport costs and travelling time. Either way, professional and business classes would have to pay more for services that are at present subsidised under the guise of 'social policies'.

A number of people who have, like myself, bought residences in, say, Islington or Notting Hill feel that central or local government should now intervene to preserve working-class tenancies and thereby to preserve a pleasantly mixed social composition. They tend to forget however that one of the main reasons why landlords are so anxious to evict tenants by whatever means they can is that letting is a mug's game under rent control.

The unthinking interventionist solution, which Labour tried as far as finance would allow in the years from 1974, is to buy up such houses and let them cheaply. This gives officials and councillors enormous powers to grant an extremely privileged financial position to a minority of applicants. Indeed, the chosen few would be something between pets, tourist attractions and sources of cheap labour – or perfect examples of social tokenism in place of genuine social reform.

Unfortunately, the preferred free market solution of a gradual decontrol of urban rents, sparing the older and more vulnerable, runs into difficulties in the realm not of pure economics, but of the political market place. After so many decades of controls and of occupying the role of political scapegoat, would private capital ever have sufficient confidence that the controls would not be reimposed to invest again in rented homes? Either there would be such difficulties of political credibility, or there would be windfall gains to those landlords (now very few in number) who had bought rented property expecting controls to remain. For such reasons market economists of a radical disposition have been attracted by municipalisation or some form of public ownership of rented homes. But it would be municipalisation with a difference; for the public authorities should then move towards free market rents in the way described and would use the resulting cash flow on their housing account to channel to the poor the kind of aid they need most – which is hard cash.

The trouble with this approach, as with most of the plans of 'market socialists' (with whom I have far more in common than with dirigiste capitalists) is that they depend on the existence of benevolent and enlightened rulers, only waiting to learn what the public interest is in order to enact it. Unfortunately, there is not the slightest reason to suppose that any public housing authority will act in the way prescribed. Such experiments as Labour has made with municipalisation have in no case been associated with moves towards market rents. This is not to speak of lower-level blunders, such as the planting by councils of compulsory purchase orders on some buildings, and the purchase in the market of others, which they have not had the resources to convert for tenant occupation, and thousands of which have consequently been lying idle and decaying as a result.

But even if by some miracle GLC bureaucrats and Whitehall planners were seen clasping to their bosoms the works of market socialists, I would still hesitate to leave anything as important as rented housing to a monopoly, however apparently enlightened. Does this mean that nothing can be done? Not quite. Price mechanism solutions of a second best kind tend themselves to emerge in the real world, unless they are thwarted by the heavy hand of the law and social convention.

The Case for Grey Markets

The principle involved in making the best of official restrictions may be labelled that of secondary markets. It states that, *if rationing by coupons or quotas is 'politically inevitable', the coupons and quotas should be transferable between individuals and firms at mutually agreed prices.* So far from being condemned as 'black market', such transactions should be recognised as increasing both the efficiency of allocation and the range of human choice.

The main points can be illustrated by imagining another energy crisis which results in the coupon rationing of petrol. Without such a scheme, petrol would still have to be rationed – by price. If petrol coupons can be sold in the open market, there is a rather peculiar redistribution in favour of motorists whose desire to drive is below the average, who benefit from the high exchange value of the coupons. That is why the situation is second-best compared with rationing by price and changes in tax and transfers designed to offset the impact on the distribution of income.

Nevertheless, having a secondary market in the coupons is far better than making their sale illegal, even if the prohibition could be effectively enforced. A motorist who sells spare motor coupons and the purchaser who is prepared to sacrifice other things for extra motoring (irrespective of whether he needs to or does it for pleasure) both gain. Otherwise they would not deal. Prohibition of such deals as 'black market' makes both sides worse off, and the only gainers are those who value uniformity of behaviour above the satisfaction of flesh and blood individuals.

Next, consider a secondary market in the right to purchase cheap EEC butter, recently exercised by British pensioners. Let us take a very emotive example: the sale of such coupons by a pensioner to a duchess. No one benefits from forbidding such a secondary market. The pensioner prefers the other things she can buy with the money proceeds of the butter coupons she sells; otherwise she would not sell them. Forbidding such transactions makes the poor even poorer than they otherwise would be.

A secondary market in 'rationed' services would probably be of most value in rented housing. The defects of below-market council rents, irrespective of means, could be mitigated if council tenants were empowered to sell their rights to dwell in the property on short- or long-term leases. This reform would release to the market many houses too large or otherwise not really required by council tenants, but clung on to at present because of the high cost of moving. A secondary market of this kind would undoubtedly bring down house prices and reduce 'key money' in the private rented sector.

The Conservatives have merely proposed that council tenants should be empowered to *buy* their houses at below-market prices. This is not the same thing, (a) because short- or medium-term leases would not be an option and (b) because the councils and not the sitting tenants would get the proceeds of sales; and such tenants could not move without losing the whole capitalised value of their right to accommodation at below-market rents.

At present a council tenant can arrange a mutual exchange ('MX') with another tenant but only with the consent of both local authorities. Some local authorities run exchange bureaus, and advertisements are placed in local newspapers. But as financial transactions between parties are not permitted, the system works only if there is a rare double coincidence of wants: A must want B's dwelling (taking into account size, quality and location) and B must want A's. (This is rather like a textbook description of a barter economy before the invention of money.) Not surprisingly, this facility does not produce much mobility. About 20 per cent of the tenants of both the GLC and Newcastle are on the transfer list at any one time, but only 3 per cent are transferred and less than $\frac{1}{2}$ per cent through MX.

A so-called scandal came to light in 1975 in the London borough of Tower Hamlets. Attention was drawn to it by the *Evening Standard* of 13 February of that year with a headline 'Council Flats for Sale at up to £800'. Immigrant families 'desperate for accommodation' were 'jumping the queue by buying council rent books'. One family was reported to have paid £460 for a flat and another £800, in addition to the normal weekly rent which they continued to pay to the Council. The press report showed a photograph of the eviction of a family who had lived for two years in a flat acquired in this way. They were 'being interviewed by a social worker and were now in council care'.

Would the legalisation of such transactions hit the people at the bottom of existing council lists? The answer is: only if the outgoing tenant would have departed in any event. If, as is often the case, he will not move without financial consideration, both he and the new tenant are better off and no one is worse off. But if we are determined to satisfy the purist a tax could be imposed on releasings (instead of prohibiting them altogether) and the proceeds could be used to increase subsidised house-building. Remember we are in the realm of the second-best.

The main preliminary reform required if such a secondary market is to be contemplated is a clear definition of the terms of existing council tenancies. At the moment they have no definite length of life and their disposition on the departure of a tenant (whether to a member of the previous family or not) is within the discretion of the local council, which means, in day-to-day practice, officials.

References

Eversley, D., 'Landlords' Slow Goodbye', *New Society* (16 January 1975).

Friedman, M., *An Economist's Protest,* 2nd edn (Thomas Horton, New Jersey, 1975).

17   Competitive Money Past and Present

The spectre of accelerating inflation, and our inability to cope with it, arises from the State's age-old claim to a monopoly of the money-issuing role. Reflection on this fact has caused Professor Hayek, after a lifetime of adherence to fixed exchange rates and the gold standard, to come out in favour of the much more libertarian alternative of allowing people to make their own choice between currencies freely circulating in the market.

Hayek no longer believes that a return to the gold standard will work. Governments will not agree to regard it as an 'absolute obstacle' to the clamour for more and cheaper money. The politicians responsible for popular policies of demand stimulation might not be the same as the ones who would be blamed for the subsequent wave of inflation and the ensuing slump. The rule 'In the long run we are all out of office' would sweep away any attempt to establish a new gold parity and discredit all such attempts in the future.

On the other hand, people would be able to protect themselves against the worst excesses of currency depreciation if the state monopoly of the money-issuing role were abolished. They would then be left to discover for themselves the most stable monetary unit in which to make contracts and settle debts. The gold addicts would have their chance; the EEC enthusiasts would be able to launch their Europa; those who would rather work in German marks, or who believe that in the last analysis dollars are best, would all be able to exercise their preferences. Even the pound sterling might improve its performance under the best of all pressures – that of competition. The early stages, while the good money was driving out the bad, might be confusing, but no more so than the present muddle, in which the task of devising a mortgage or business loan that will not clobber the debtor in the early stages and defraud the creditor later seems beyond the wit of our institutions. In many border areas of Europe – such as the

Geneva district or the Tyrol – at least two continental currencies are already in frequent use; and many traders are accustomed to dealing in a third, the dollar, as of course are many British stores.

Indexed contracts, whether related to a hard currency or cost-of-living index, are quite legal in the United Kingdom provided that these 'moneys of account' are translated into sterling and the sums handed over are in pounds. The House of Lords decided in a test cast on 5 November 1975 that foreign creditors could have their claims

Table 5: British Inflation Rates *

	% per annum
Long-run rates	
1936 – 56	5.1
1956 – 76	6.4
1936 – 76	5.8
Shorter periods	
1936 – 46	5.1
1946 – 56	5.1
1956 – 66	3.0
1966 – 76	10.0
1971 – 76	14.5

Inflation rate (% per annum)	Time taken for Money to lose 50 per cent of value (years)	Time taken for money to lose 90 per cent of value (years)
6	just over 11	just over 37
10	just under 7	just under 22
14.5	just under 5	just under 15

*Measured by change in retail prices

Source: London and Cambridge Economic Service and *Economic Trends*

recognised in their own currencies. The main deterrents to most indexed or foreign currency linked contracts, and especially loan transactions, lie in the tax system and informal official pressure backed by threats to bring back control over capital issues.

Foreign currencies are, however, not legal tender inside the United Kingdom. To change this an amendment would be required in the Currency and Bank Notes Act (1954) and the Coinage Act (1971). These lay down that sterling bank notes are the only recognised legal tender (which cannot be refused) for major sums. A much more important, practical obstacle to such contracts is, of course, exchange control, which makes it a punishable offence for UK citizens to hold foreign exchange or gold without authorisation.

Obviously, the proposal for 'free money' needs to be thoroughly debated and its many implications studied. But its mere unfamiliarity does not make it crankish, although cranks are irresistibly attracted by any proposal to do with currency.

Hayek has made his suggestion in two forms. The first is the free circulation of existing national money – and perhaps gold – across the exchanges. This, of course, involves the abolition of exchange control, to which the EEC is already committed. The second and more far-reaching one would be to allow the private introduction of currencies. This takes us into uncharted territory. There is no widely accepted theory of the results of free competition among privately issued currencies. Fragmentary historical experience has been with certificates or tokens representing gold or other commodities; and it is highly probable that privately issued currencies would have to be gold- or commodity-based. Most people would probably be satisfied with the first version of the proposal – the ability to make contracts and settle debts in Deutschmarks or Swiss francs or gold.

One of the most important practical difficulties relates to taxation. Both corporate profits and the yield on personal assets would be different according to the currency in which they were measured. Governments with the weaker currencies would lose, both from the unpopularity of their money as a store of value and from the loss of their power to extract excess revenue by taxing paper incomes due entirely to currency depreciation. If for instance the sterling price level rises by 10 per cent, the true revenue on an investment yielding 10 per cent is approximately zero, and the owner is at present the victim of a capital levy, however small his investment.

Governments and central banks would resist even the more modest proposal tooth and nail. The ancient arguments for giving the monarch a currency monopoly now appear in more respectable disguise as 'balance of payments considerations' or fear of pressure on the official reserves or the sterling exchange rate.

It has nevertheless been the rule rather than the exception for different kinds of money to circulate side by side at fluctuating exchange rates inside state boundaries, as well as on the foreign exchange market. The nineteenth-century gold standard, in which all kinds of money were convertible by the authorities into gold at fixed rates of exchange, and which still colours our conceptions, was a very untypical state of affairs. The earliest coins had indeed no measure of value and were simply conventional ways of carrying pieces of metal of standard (or not-so-standard) weight and fineness. In many places both gold and silver coins were in circulation and fluctuated against each other in accordance with the bi-metallic ratio shown in the chart. Token coins of base metal go back almost to the dawn of currency; and, because they were both inconvertible into precious metals and issued in excessive numbers, they tended to depreciate against both gold and silver coins, forming yet another alternative money. Medieval Genoa flourished with fluctuating gold and silver standards. Instances of gold and silver currencies circulating side by side at fluctuating rates did not come to an end until well into the nineteenth century, when the glut of silver made coins of that metal into tokens that depended for their value on the willingness of the authorities to convert them into gold currency.

In the first two-thirds of the nineteenth century different paper currencies fluctuated against each other in the United States. From the

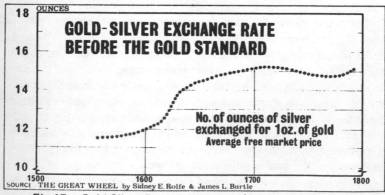

Fig 17. Gold-Silver Exchange Rate Before the Gold Standard

US Civil War until the resumption of gold payments in 1879, inconvertible 'greenbacks' circulated side by side with the gold dollar at a fluctuating discount. It is doubtful whether the establishment of the Federal Reserve in 1913 to regulate the supply of paper money and bank deposits brought greater monetary stability than prevailed under the so-called disorder that characterised the greater part of the previous century. The Federal Reserve certainly failed to prevent either the massive contraction of the money supply in the Depression of the early 1930s or the inflationary increase extending over a large number of years following the Second World War.

It is quite true that even in the ancient and medieval worlds many rulers were not content to see gold and silver circulating at fluctuating rates but attempted to fix an official rate between them known as the bi-metallic standard. The fluctuations of silver against gold in the free market were the subject of complaint, just like exchange rate fluctuations today; and the blame was, of course, put on speculators. But, just like today, 'chaos' and runs from one type of currency into another frequently resulted not from market fluctuations but from government attempts to freeze the gold-to-silver ratio. Even if the official ratio reflected market ratios at first, it could not stay correct very long, as changes took place in the relative scarcity of the two metals. Whichever metal was more favourably valued became the predominant currency and was presented at the mint for coinage, while the undervalued metal was exported (often illegally) or hoarded, and exchanges took place at black market rates. Because the same official ratio could sometimes overvalue gold and sometimes silver, changes in the predominant currency could occur with startling rapidity. The establishment of *de facto* gold standard in England so much earlier than anywhere else may well have been due to the accidential overvaluation of gold in relation to silver by the master of the Mints, one Sir Isaac Newton, in the recoinage of 1717.

Some historians praise the enlightenment of rulers for providing standardised denominations of coins through royal mints. In fact, the attempts of governments to establish a monopoly of the mints arose from their desire to charge a price – known as seignorage – for the basic costs of the operation higher than they could achieve if they had to compete with private mints. Any public benefit was a by-product and was more than offset whenever the monarch yielded to the temptation to debase – that is, to reduce the weight or fineness of coins provided in his mints. Citizens would put up with debased coins for the sake of working with a familiar currency; but if debasement went too far they would shift to other currencies, and the debased coin would depreciate in the market.

The ability of the ruler to benefit from large-scale debasement was greatest if he could force his subjects to use the debased coins and accept them at face value. Hence the age-old resort to legal tender laws and exchange control. The exceptional severity of British exchange control goes back a long way. In the words of the *Cambridge Economic History of Europe*, 'A very considerable variety of gold coins circulated together in late medieval Europe except England. The entry of foreign coins into England was prevented by the vigilant action of Royal Exchanges at Canterbury or London, of the mint at Calais and of the local authorities in seaports like Sandwich.' (Vol. III, p. 597). The freedom of the eighteenth and nineteenth centuries was an interlude in an age of control. Medieval observers noted the peculiar English habit of treating as identical silver pennies of widely different finenesses and weights, which on the Continent would have exchanged at very varying rates. This was due not only to England being an island, but to the less romantic fact that the degree of debasement tended to be less extreme than on the Continent and the incentive to make a careful comparison of weight and fineness less pronounced. But legal tender and exchange control laws were always difficult to enforce and tended to break down under stress even in England, as they did during the Great Debasement of Henry VIII.

The much proclaimed Gresham's Law, 'Bad money drives out good' (which is found already in Aristophanes *The Frogs*), is not a law at all, but a half-truth. It is more normal for good money to drive out bad. Gresham's Law holds good only when citizens are forced by legal decree to accept the debased money at a ratio higher than that prevailing in the international (or black) market. Then, of course, people will try to spend the bad money as quickly as possible, and hoard or export the full-bodied variety.

When the value of different sorts of money diverges too radically, it is impossible to talk about inflation rates without ambiguity. The notorious Roman debasements were of the silver *denarii*, which degenerated into copper coins with a silver wash and eventually into just copper coins. On the other hand the gold coins were debased very mildly if at all. The *solidus* was established by Diocletian and Constantine around AD 300, settling down at 24 carats (then a measure of weight) of pure gold. It continued to be minted unchanged in weight and purity for another seven centuries in the Byzantine Empire and became one of the great international currencies of the medieval world.

The worst aspect of the divergence between the two currencies was that Roman taxes were fixed in gold coinage, while payments to suppliers and soldiers were made in debased copper coins. In an emperor wished to curry favour with the army or celebrate his accession, he would make a special gold payment to the troops. It is as if British citizens in the inflation of the 1970s had to pay taxes in stated amounts of Swiss francs while government disbursements continued to be made in sterling.

A very old distinction is between the unit of account for measuring value and the actual currency used as a medium of exchange. These can be entirely divorced. Cattle were used by Homer to denominate wealth, but they did not necessarily change hands in normal commercial transactions. (The English word 'pecuniary' derives from *pecus*, the Latin for cattle.) Contracts in terms of heads of cattle were a primitive form of indexation and continued long after the development of the coinage. Pounds, shillings and pence (£, s, d) were the most widely used European units of account from the time of Charlemagne, even though in many times and places there were no coins corresponding to these units. It was simply a way of reckoning in which a pound = 20 shillings = 240 pence. In changing over to the decimal system, we have thrown away a large part of our monetary history.

Although it had the same name, a pound used as a unit of account did not mean the same in terms of one currency as it did of another. A pound was equivalent to 240 pennies in France, Genoa and Milan alike. But in 1500 it represented 22 grammes of silver in France, in Genoa 13 grammes and in Milan 9 grammes. In Venice there were two different pounds, one based on silver and the other on gold, circulating against each other. To make matters more complicated, there were even in some centres different silver pounds based on silver coins of different degrees of debasement.

Contracts in money of account did nevertheless provide certain safeguards. A merchant who wanted to safeguard himself against the debasement of the local silver unit could make a contract in one of the greatest international gold currencies such as the ducat or florin. Historians frequently bemoan the absence of common money of account into which all the main European currencies could be converted at known and stable rates. The confusion of fluctuating exchange rates, within as well as across frontiers, was indeed inferior to a fixed set of relationships between stable currencies. But they were a great deal better (even before the days of the pocket calculator) than forcing people to trade at false ratios or to use a currency that they feared would be debased. The present-day British subject is in one respect a good deal worse off than his counterpart in medieval Europe. Because of official pressure and tax discrimination he is not able to lend or borrow in indexed terms, and he is forced to take a gamble in all his domestic contracts on the rate of depreciation of a single paper currency.

The main difficulty at the moment – even of the modest proposal to phase out exchange control within the EEC – is the communications barrier between those who think in terms of the demand and supply of different types of currency and the official economists, living in a single home currency world, who would regard the suggestions discussed in this chapter as opening the way to a pointless balance of payments leak on capital account and a fearful complication of the public sector forecasts. The currency freedom movement needs people who can write and answer the sort of Treasury–Bank briefs that would knock out of the ring any front-bench politician who tried to advance the idea; but Whitehall equally needs someone who can explain without the ritual sneer the point of the competitive money school in acceptable national income terminology.

Exchange control has, however, never prevented confidence crises in the past. The United States, West Germany and many other Western countries do not have it. Draconian exchange control, often carrying the death penalty as a sanction against any breach, is, on the other hand, the trademark of communist states and Third World dictatorships, where it still does not prevent flourishing currency black markets.

A frequent reaction in the City of London to the competitive currency proposal was 'the authorities will never wear this', a sad reflection on the subservient attitudes towards the state of so many in the business community. Nevertheless, as experience in every runaway inflation shows, once currency reaches intolerable levels, natural forces start pushing towards the use of alternative forms of money, whatever the law states. Even in Britain in the middle 1970s, one heard many stories of small business and professional people insisting on being paid in kind, especially in rural areas; and a case of wine has always been a welcome 'gift'. One should in fairness add that these devices were used more to avoid taxes than to escape inflation. Competitive currencies would become 'politically possible' once the only alternative was seen to be a reversion to barter or to the use of cigarettes and bottles of cognac. The German authorities in the 1920s were no longer in a position to resist the use of foreign currencies when they themselves began to issue dollar-denominated loans and insisted on tax payments being linked to the dollar to safeguard their real value in the interval between assessment and collection.

Nothing will prevent a move towards unofficial money or barter if inflation continues to be rapid and unpredictable. Is it not better for such developments to be visible and above board rather than to take place furtively to the disadvantage of the weak and the law-abider?

References

Cambridge Economic History of Europe, Vol. III (Cambridge University Press, 1963).

Cipolla, C.M., *Money, Prices and Civilisation in the Mediterranean World* (Princeton, 1956).

Cipolla, C.M., 'Currency Depreciation in Medieval Europe', *Economic History Review*, XV, 3 (1963).

Corden, W.M., *Monetary Union* (Trade Policy Research Centre, London, 1976).

Flemming, J., review of Hayek's *Denationalisation of Money Financial Times*. Feb. 4 1977.

Friedman, M., 'Money' in *Encyclopaedia Britannica* (Chicago, 1970).

Gould, J.D., *The Great Debasement* (Oxford University Press, 1970).

Hayek, F., *Choice in Currency* (Institute of Economic Affairs, 1975).

Hayek, F., *Denationalisation of Money* (Institute of Economic Affairs, 1976).

Hicks, Sir John, *A Theory of Economic History* (Oxford University Press, 1969).

Jones, A.H.M., *The Roman Economy* (Oxford University Press, 1974).

Porteous, John, *Coins in History* (Macmillan, 1967).

Rothbard, Murray, *What Governments Have Done to your Money*, 2nd edn (Rampart College, California, 1974).

Yeager, Leyland B., *International Monetary Relations* (Harper and Row, New York, 1966).

PART III

Markets for Human Beings

18   Unemployment and Economic Policy

It was indignation at the absurdity of unsatisfied wants side by side with idle hands willing to satisfy these wants, which I thought existed before the Second World War and could occur again, that first led me to the study of economic policy. How could this come about? The purpose of this short essay is to use the freedom of the non-academic to classify what now seem to me the main types of unemployment problem and to make a few clear and simple distinctions.

A fierce controversy raged among economists in the interwar period on whether excessive unemployment was due to wages being too high or 'demand' being too low. The argument has flared up again, almost as fiercely, as a result of the crisis of Keynesian economics. The reader may suspect that these are two ways of saying the same thing, but there is more to it than that. It is convenient to divide unemployment, to the extent that it is a problem, into five categories:

1 *micro-unemployment*, due to wrong wage relativities;
2 *real-wage unemployment*, due to an excessive average leve of real wages;
3 *macro-unemployment*, due to money wages being out of line with monetary demand;
4 *disincentive unemployment*, due to a structure of taxes, social security benefits and other variables which amounts to a subsidy, to periods of leisure or to extensive 'search' between jobs;
5 *capital starvation unemployment*, due to shortage of capital of enterprise.

Needless to say, these are shorthand terms. Several of the categories are likely to be present at any one time. Only the first three categories – and perhaps only the first two – have any claim to be theoretically pure; the others are variants or combinations. But it is helpful to separate out all five for purposes of diagnosis and policy.

185

Micro-Unemployment

If the price of any product or service is above the market-clearing level there will be a surplus; if it is below it there will be a shortage. Like it or not, this applies to labour as well as other services. To remove all emotive questions about capitalism, let us think in terms of self-employed carpenters. It then makes no difference if the carpenter forms himself into a company and pays himself a wage, or charges directly for services performed. There is thus a wage for carpenters – or more strictly a range of wages, which will vary according to the skill, geographical location and other qualities of the individual craftsman – which will balance the supply and demand for carpenters' services. The prevailing wage may be too high because the demand for carpentry at existing prices has fallen – say because of a change of fashion towards brick or stone – or because carpenters may have formed an association and agreed to raise charges.

But to look at a single market in isolation is deeply misleading. A customer or employer looks at the price of carpenters' services and compares them with that of other kinds of workers, whether stone-masons, bricklayers, general labourers or even workers in unrelated trades such as processed food or motorcars. For it is the pattern of *relative* prices – which depends on the pattern of *relative* wages – that influences decisions both on what products to buy and what processes to use in making them. To say that carpenters' wages are too high to balance the labour market is the same as to say that other wages are too low. If the whole pattern of relativities and differentials is out of line with market-clearing levels, there will be extensive unemployment and also extensive labour shortages.

Although micro-unemployment is the simplest and most basic type of unemployment, it is in some ways the most intractable. The diagnosis and measurement of 'micro', as of other types of unemployment, is not a simple matter of counting people without jobs. Relative wages are never going to adjust so quickly to structural change that labour markets are cleared instantly without surpluses or shortages. Nor is it sensible that they should, any more than it would be sensible for restaurants to adjust their meal charges hour by hour so that there were no unfilled tables and no customers without bookings turned away.

The reasons why an element of price stickiness is desirable are related to uncertainty and information costs, about which there is a large and growing theoretical literature. A worker who has lost his job does not know immediately what is the best offer available. It will pay him to spend time searching through the labour market rather than take the first job that turns up; and it will pay the community, up to a certain point, that he should do so. Search effort and experiments with different jobs are particularly important for young people at the start of a career, so that it is not surprising that teenage unemployment tends to be higher than for adults. It is also higher among older people, because they are less adaptable and may have to choose between a long and dispiriting search or pricing themselves into a badly paid job – and the latter may be difficult in itself because unions object to minimum rates being undercut, or because employers find it pays to operate with standard wages rather than to incur the financial and human costs of investigating the proficiency of each new job applicant individually.

Clearly, policies that push relativities further away from market-clearing levels lead to micro-unemployment. These may take the form of minimum wage laws, incomes policies that compress differentials or other forms of pressure. Putting more money demand into the system would only re-create the problems at higher average wage and price levels if the same policies and pressures were still at work.

Real-Wage Unemployment

The next type of unemployment arises not from individual wages being too high relative to other wages, but to the average level of real wages being excessive. They would be excessive in relation to profits (and it will help to keep political emotion at bay if we postulate either state ownership or ownership by investment trusts in whose shares every citizen has an equal stake). In this situation it is equally valid to say that money wages are too high or that prices are too low. To put it yet another way, the price of labour is too high in relation to the price of capital.

If real wages are 'too high' employers will shed labour wherever they can; and – more important – they will give their investment projects an excessively labour-saving bias, so that there will be insufficient employment opportunities in the future. It has been argued that during booms both employment and real wages rise, relative to trend. But this is at most a trade cycle phenomenon. The trend around which employment fluctuates from one cycle to the next is inversely related to the level of real wages, and even in the short term a sufficiently large rise in real wages above the equilibrium level will assuredly depress employment.

If a politician were foolhardy enough to explain these matters, he might be well advised to talk about productivity being too low rather than real wages being too high; but it is clearly the relationship between the two that matters. A more subtle source of confusion is that the equilibrium level of the real wage may change for reasons far removed from the domestic labour market. An adverse swing in the terms of trade, owing say to an oil price explosion, will reduce the buying power of an hour of work in the United Kingdom. Conversely, an inflow of overseas capital which raises the sterling exchange rate will increase the equilibrium real wage.

There is still the question of how average real wages come to be excessively high. Why do not employers raise profit margins until equilibrium is restored? One answer may be price controls. Another may be a temporary inertia. If there have been large increases in money wages, it may take time for employers to realise that their competitors are being affected in the same way and that they can safely restore margins (monetary policy permitting). Or it may be due to delays in adopting inflation accounting. As already hinted, the disturbance is at least as likely to be due to some external force that reduces the real wage, or its rate of increase, below what workers have been accustomed to, rather than to any spontaneous outbreak of militancy on their part. Examples include not only a deterioration in the equilibrium terms of trade, but also an increase in the tax-take (indirect as well as direct) from the typical wage packet. Such phenomena are labelled, hardly surprisingly, 'real wage frustrations'. But it should be noted that it is an *increasing* and not a long-established high tax-take that has this effect.

Without government intervention in profits and prices, the forces making for an excessive level of average real wages are likely to be transitional. Expectations that prove excessive will gradually be adapted to realities in the economic market place, and thus the basis for frustration will gradually disappear, even though the process may take many years and cause much bitterness.

Macro-Unemployment

To come to grips with the third category of unemployment, the macro-variety, which is – often wrongly – at the centre of the national debate, it is helpful to make for a moment the artificial assumption that both relativities and profit margins are at a normal level without distortions. It is still possible that money wages and – on this assumption – money prices (often called *nominal* wages and prices) may be too high. Too high in relation to what? Either to the domestic money supply,* or to wages and prices in other countries (under a pegged exchange rate).

Again there is the problem of how money wages become too high in the first place. Pure cases are hard to find; but they are likely to arise from a disturbance on the monetary rather than on the wages side. An example would be a contraction of the money supply in the wake of a financial crisis, as in the United States in the early 1930s. Another example was the attempt of the Bank of England in the 1920s to lever up the exchange rate to re-establish in 1925 the pre-First World War sterling parity of $4.87 to the pound.

As a matter of practical policy, it may well be better in such instances to adjust the money supply or the exchange rate to the wage level rather than face the long, drawn-out agony of trying to depress the latter. Is it not better to adjust our watches for summer time than to ask everybody to get up an hour earlier? That is the essence of situations when it is reasonable to talk of demand deficiency, and it is what Keynes had in mind in the 1920s when he opposed the return to gold at an overvalued parity and advocated instead a monetary policy aimed at steady or very gradually rising prices at home. (There was the additional problem adumbrated in the *General Theory* of whether the interest rate could get stuck at an excessively high level, whatever was done to the money supply or to nominal wages. This is unlikely to be a major problem in an inflationary era when it is all too easy to have negative real interest rates.)

The difficulty of the Keynesian remedy is that in an inflationary period it is not just the *level* of nominal wages that is resistant to downward pressure, but their rate of increase; and it is more difficult to argue that the authorities should finance any established rate of nominal wage increase that happens to prevail and never try to reduce the inflation rate. If the rate of monetary expansion is increased in response to any chance acceleration of nominal wages but is never reduced, the rate of inflation will move ever upwards and reach Latin American rates by gradual stages. Nor is it likely that such a policy would help employment. It is well known that a reduction in the rate of monetary expansion, and of inflation, has depressing effects on employment. But so may an *increase* in the pace of inflation, because of institutional difficulties in adjusting business practices and the likelihood of more interference in wage and price setting by

---

* The lack of an agreed terminology suitable for public discussion can drive one to distraction. If one writes 'money supply', it infuriates those economists who think that variations in velocity are often the more important causes of disturbance. To avoid this particular issue, when it is not the problem on hand, it is helpful to think of money times velocity, MV, which is rendered in words as 'monetary demand'.

governments, to name only a few possibilities. The depressive effects of moving both to a higher and to a lower level of inflation are essentially transitional; but the transition may last many years; and at high rates of inflation it is almost impossible to generalise about which set of effects will be the greater.

Disincentive Unemployment

The fourth type of unemployment, which I have christened the disincentive variety, arises from the supply side. From the employee's point of view what matters is the real wage relative to the cost of not working. If the sacrifice involved in not having a job – or in not having a full-time job – is reduced, so will be the effective supply of labour. The difference between net pay (after taxes and expenses) at work and out of it represents both the net gain from work and the cost of leisure. This is an elementary point about rational behaviour and does not by itself imply anything about how high benefits ought to be or how strictly they should be administered.

Clearly, the more generous are the benefits available while not at work, and the less severe the pressure by the social security agencies on the worker to switch his trade or residence or sacrifice his accustomed standard of living to secure a job, the greater will be the number of registered unemployed during any particular phase of the trade cycle. There is no hard and fast line between voluntary and involuntary unemployment. Even with an American census-type system for calculating unemployment, the wording of the questions can be varied to obtain an enormously wide range of percentages. My own view (probably a minority one) is that it is right to err on the side of generosity in providing benefits to cushion the effects of job separation (whether initiated by employer or employee), but the price of so doing is the toleration of higher unemployment statistics than the ones to which we were formerly accustomed. There are nevertheless irrationalities in the way in which subsidies are given to those not doing paid jobs, which have nothing to do with true generosity and are certainly susceptible of reform. (Examples include the non-taxation of benefit and the tying of some of the means-tested specific benefits to pre-tax income. Another well-known aggravating feature is the very low tax threshold at which the full marginal rate of about 40 per cent in income tax and National Insurance contributions begins.)

Capital Starvation

The fifth kind of unemployment, labelled 'capital starvation', used to be regarded as characteristic of developing countries. It was also characteristic of Western societies in the early nineteenth century when the classical economists were writing, and is thus sometimes called classical unemployment. It occurs when there is a lack of other complementary resources to employ the labour force. The missing elements need not be physical capital; they could be business enterprise, or an insufficient supply of workers with scarce skills. Capital starvation may also occur because of structural shifts in the pattern of demand and supply, which make part of the existing capital stock obsolete.

There is a real wage at which anybody can find employment, however short or inappropriate the amount of capital or other resources; but this wage could be negative if people actually get in each other's way. More realistically, the wage floor is set by the social security minimum. The implication of the well publicised work of Bacon and Eltis is that investment has been so discouraged in Britain that there are simply not enough factories, offices and other capital items; so that it would be impossible for people to price themselves into jobs, even if real wages dropped substantially and so did the social security floor. If we are in this depressing situation, the sustainable level of unemployment will remain high until there is a far-reaching change in the environment for new investment.

In most actual unemployment problems several of the five categories are combined. The upsurge in British unemployment from 1974 onwards was partly due to the sharp deceleration in monetary growth from 20–25 per cent in 1972–3 to scarcely 10 per cent in subsequent years. This can be described either as demand deficiency or as the transitional cost of reducing the inflation rate according to taste. But unemployment levels were also much aggravated by the persistence of a level of *real* wages, which became excessive after the 1973–4 oil price explosion, and by the distortions of *relative* wages arising *inter alia* from the near flat-rate pay norms of 1975 and 1976. There was also in the course of the 1970s a steady reduction – sometimes to negative levels – of the incentive to work for at least some categories of social security claimants.

The monetary aspect is in principle the easiest to tackle, however difficult it may be in practice. Money wage increases are slow to adjust to a change in the pace of monetary growth because of the persistence of inflationary expectations which may have become built into long-term contracts. If prices have been rising by 20 per cent per annum, this rate will tend to be projected into the future. If only people's expectations about inflation could be transformed by a charismatic de

Gaulle or Schacht-like figure, price stability might be re-established without a lengthy transitional depression. Suitably designed indexation of wages, and of fixed-interest securities and other long-term arrangements, would help to take care of the contract problem and might even be a partial substitute for the hard-to-find charismatic leaders. By contrast, excessive *real*-wage expectations, or relativities that are out of line, are more intractable; for they require not merely a change in expectations, but sacrifices of real wages, either by the average wage-earner or by those who have gained from the distortion of relativities. Faced with successful pressure for unrealistic real wages or relativities, no monetary policy, not even if combined with the most brilliant political generalship and financial ingenuity, could prevent a high level of unemployment.

Some Bogus Remedies

There is simply not the space here for a specific and detailed discussion of the unemployment problems that have emerged either in the industrial world in general or in the United Kingdom in particular; and interested readers are referred to the works listed below. But the five categories listed above may be helpful as a quick aid in sorting out genuine from bogus remedies.

The thinking behind them is this: excessive unemployment is a sign of malfunctioning of markets – whether the labour, goods or capital market, or the provision of money for these markets – and the remedies must lie in the removal of obstacles to the successful operation. This stands in sharpest contrast to the 'lump of labour fallacy' – the view, held by many non-economists (and a few economists when they are nodding), that there is a fixed quantity of work to be done and therefore a fixed quantity of jobs, assuming no technical progress. On this view technical progress, or population growth, simply reduces jobs. Few people would own up to holding this view if really pressed. It could not explain the vast expansion of jobs in the last two hundred years, in which the British population has grown tenfold and we have had several industrial revolutions characterised by labour-saving innovations. Yet many policy proposals depend on something very close to the lump of labour fallacy.

An instance is the proposal for compulsory early retirement or the cutting of hours to share the available work. This will not remedy micro-unemployment owing to faulty relative wages and prices, and would be quite likely to make it worse by aggravating the shortages of capacity and skills that exist even at the bottom of recessions. If excessive real wages are the problem it will have no effect except by cutting overtime and thus lowering real wages per hour – a result that could be achieved less wastefully by adjusting the relation of overtime to normal wage rates. A reduction of total hours is inflationary – or 'reflationary' – in that it reduces productive potential relative to the money supply. But if this kind of boost is sensible it would surely be less wasteful to increase the money supply rather than reduce potential output. The disincentives to taking paid work rather than living on social security would also increase as real earnings per week would be reduced further towards the social security minimum. A reduction of man- or woman-hours would help only in the case of the fifth category: capital starvation. Even then it would be wasteful, as the degree of capacity shortage varies from trade to trade; and different sorts of capacity and skill are not perfect substitutes for each other. More fundamentally, a compulsory reduction of hours is highly irrational. So long as there is a surplus of labour relative to capacity, there is a potential profit to be made from creating new capacity to employ the people involved, if only we can do something about the deterrents to labour-utilising new investment. But if the effective labour force is cut back to fit the amount of capacity, then we can give up any hope of such capacity expansion.

References

Bacon, R. and Eltis, W., *Britain's Economic Problem* (Macmillan, 1976).

Brittan, S., *Second Thoughts on Full Employment Policy* (Barry Rose, Chichester and London, 1975).

Friedman, M., *Nobel Prize Lecture* (Institute of Economic Affairs, 1977).

19   The Impact of the Strike Threat

The clue to the economy-wide union problem is that it has at bottom very little to do with inflation. The power of the unions is that of producer groups who can shift the distribution of the national income in their favour and give the less powerful and the non-unionised the choice between the dole and lower real rewards.

The weapon that distinguishes unions from most other producer groups is the strike threat. Other monopolies confine themselves to setting a price higher than the competitive level, or putting a lower quantity on offer to maintain the price. A strike by contrast is a withdrawal of the whole of the unionised labour force – and in practice a ban on blackleg substitutes – until an agreement has been signed by the employers (who may be the State) to pay more per unit. This extra power, denied to most monopolists, is characteristic of what might be called *coercive producer groups*. Unions have not been completely unique in exercising this role: OPEC in 1973 and some of the US trusts at the end of the nineteenth century behaved in a pretty similar way.

The effect of a successful strike threat is to force the employer to pay a higher wage and therefore hire a smaller labour force than would otherwise be the case. The end result is similar to that of action by corporate monopoly, which can charge a price above the competitive level, but only at the expense of lower sales. The employment effect is not always obvious, partly because adjustment may be accomplished gradually by reducing recruitment. One politically unwelcome implication of the analysis of union monopoly power is that the gains made by trade unionists are normally not at the expense of employers, but at the expense of other workers, who are either non-unionised or are in weaker unions.

One aspect of the problem is the potential instability of the balance between different unions, and between the unions and the rest of the population. Economists have had the greatest difficulty in saying what it is a union negotiator might be trying to maximise corresponding to profits in the case of a firm. The normal situation is probably one of a reserve of unused short-run monopoly power available to raise wages at the expense of employment, or to prevent them from falling in the face of market pressures. Changes in outside circumstances or union objectives can call this reserve power into play.

American studies such as those of Albert Rees have suggested that strong unions raise wages by up to 25 per cent above the competitive level, with a typical figure being about 10 per cent. Professor Pencavel of Stanford concludes from some British investigations that the typical hourly earnings' differential between unionised and non-unionised workers is 8 to 12 per cent; Layard has estimated 25 per cent for manual groups. Small groups such as certain printers may gain higher differentials by various devices that restrict competition. One reason for these relatively narrow differentials is that, once the gain of the traditionally unionised reaches a critical threshold point, hitherto un-organised or weakly organised groups have an incentive to organise collectively to maintain their position. The main sufferers from union wage setting are probably individuals, or sets of individuals, rather than occupational groups.

There is no harm in the expression 'cost-push' for an increased use of monopoly power by either some or all unions, provided that it is realised (a) that, in the absence of accommodating monetary action, the inflation must eventually come to an end and (b) that, if monetary accommodation is *so* accommodating as to attempt to restore the pre-disturbance level of employment, it is likely to fail in its objective but in the process bring about a runaway inflation. Professor Milton Friedman has had no hesitation in his *Monetary History* in talking about wage-push in the United States for the period 1933–7 when union membership increased two and a half times and when there was government encouragement to raise nominal wages; partly as a result, the monetary expansion after the Great Depression was dissipated in higher wages for the existing work force, and unemployment remained obstinately high despite the New Deal.

More frequently, however, circumstances in which union power acts to increase unemployment are those that would make for abnormal unemployment even in the absence of unions. Unions have had con-spicuous effects on unemployment when they have resisted a reduction in real wages, or in their rate of growth, made necessary by a change in external circumstances – or when they have resisted anti-inflationary monetary policies, even policies merely designed to prevent an existing high rate of inflation from increasing.

In retrospect, the ability to appease union pressure by 'a little bit of reflation', or to drown relativity changes or the lack of them in a general rise in price levels, might seem the hallmarks if not of a golden, at least of a silver age. The balance of labour market power will become more precarious, and the difficulties of economic policy greater in times of adversity, as the last vestiges of money illusion disappear, and with it the power of extra inflation as a solvent for tensions.

The Political Threat

Nevertheless, the monopolistic distortions brought about by the unions can be lived with, just like industrial subsidies, agricultural protection and other restraints on competition. The real menace of the strike threat is political. Governments live in the knowledge that particular groups may hold up essential services unless their demands are met. The fear that people may starve, or freeze, or be faced with a mass breakdown in sanitation and health in the face of a showdown with one or more key unions has become the dominant force behind too many political decisions.

The present formula of government by trade union veto is not a durable one. A situation in which it is widely believed that a government cannot stay in office without union consent is inherently precarious. It is as certain as anything can be that the unlimited right to strike in all sectors at a moment's notice, exceptional legal privilege and the reluctance of governments to enforce even the existing law in industrial disputes will not be a permanent feature of our industrial life. These privileges will remain only if they are unused. They could fall into disuse if the TUC became a 'Soviet-style' instrument of industrial discipline; but this would be difficult as well as undesirable.

Some of the measures required have been conveniently summarised in a speech by Peter Walker in May 1976 as 'the abolition of social security payments to strikers' families, changing the law on picketing and training specialists to replace strikers in the maintenance of essential services'. Mr Walker's list is intended ironically; and the first suggestion is described tendentiously as penalising strikers' wives and children, without any mention of the possibility of converting payments to strikers' families into repayable loans, recoverable through PAYE. But whatever the author's intentions, the list is the minimum required to bring the unions very partially under the rule of law and to bring British practice nearer to that of most other non-Communist countries. One might add to it enforceable contracts with a definite termination date, a limitation of political and 'sympathy' strikes and effective measures to prevent the blacking of imports or other alternative supplies. Legal provision for postal ballots in union elections and strike ballots are often urged on industrial relations grounds. But they would also have the advantage of increasing the influence of the mass of workers who are probably more worried than the union activists about being priced out of a job.

The above list is by no means identical to the Industrial Relations Act of the Heath Government, which was concerned more with improving union procedures than with the monopoly and strike threat elements. I am not suggesting that another comprehensive measure can be attempted soon; and a step-by-step approach would, in any case, be preferable. Of course, one will have to wait for a suitable political climate to take even the most tentative of steps; but it is possible to become so absorbed in measuring the political temperature that one is caught without any plans when a suitable opportunity unexpectedly arrives.

An Interim Strategy

Why does union power present more of a problem in some countries than in others and in Britain most of all? We must not forget how much this power has been magnified by the exaggerated and trembling attitude to it of the British establishment. If the unions are told that they are all-powerful, that governments hang on every decision of their executive committees and that there is no way of resisting their slightest whim, they will begin to behave as if they have such power, and ultimately they will have it. This in a nutshell is the history of policy since the late 1960s.

It might have been best if Harold Wilson had managed to enact his *In Place of Strife* union legislation in 1969. The second-best state of affairs would have been for him never to have suggested it. Worst of all was his first putting forward legislation and then withdrawing it under TUC pressure. The role of the unions as overmighty subjects was again enhanced when the Conservatives went through a similar experience, first introducing the Industrial Relations Act and then undertaking in 1974 that they would not attempt to reintroduce it.

But even more important is the way that governments have staked their reputation on winning certain wage disputes, which thereby became matters of political face. These disputes were, moreover, entered with no satisfactory contingency plans for seeing them through, but relying only on the weapon of public opinion – which (a) is not as important in such matters as politicians think, and (b) likes to be on the winning side. The key episode was not the miners' strike of 1974, which brought down the Heath Government, but that of early 1972, when that Government had as yet no incomes policy, but relied on a so-called 'N minus one' strategy to bring down each successive major settlement. The Government's defeat, which took place in a recession, and which owed a great deal to activities such as the 'flying pickets', set the path for everything that followed. We have now moved to the other extreme, in which the authorities have almost let it be known that they are bound to lose any confrontation with a key union.

The advantage of concentrating on monetary and fiscal policy to prevent inflation from running away is at bottom political. It does not involve asking the unions not to use powers that they have; nor does it involve giving them extra power in the political arena. There is a distinction to be made between this form of monetarism, which is political, and a more technical form, which in its most extreme variant denies that the unions have had any role in the inflationary process at all – not even indirectly, through government reaction to the unemployment, actual or threatened, brought about by their behaviour.

No monetary guidelines are proof against a sufficiently large and widespread wage explosion, and they would not be even if they were written into the constitution. But let us remember too that, although wage demands can have political as well as economic roots, union leaders do not pick their claims out of a hat. Militant and ambitious union leaders will demand higher figures than moderate ones; but whether 5 per cent, 25 per cent or 125 per cent is a suitably high figure depends *inter alia* on economic forces and beliefs about financial policy. The relevant factors include price expectations, the state and movement of the labour market, the tax-take and (whether or not verbalised in that form) beliefs about monetary demand. One of the main reasons why the 1974–5 wage upsurge went on so long was that union leaders were given the impression that nothing they could do would price their members out of work. The very possibility of such an outcome was scoffed at by many economists close to the Government, and ministers kept on reaffirming their unconditional commitment to full employment, which they were in no position to meet, as events were to prove.

If monetary guidelines carried credibility – which they will never do when governments and their advisers are committed to an exclusively 'trade union' explanation of domestic inflation and reaffirm their devotion to 'full employment' three times a day – union wage militancy would be at least riskier than in the past. And the less frequently and blatantly union leaders challenge the guidelines, the more closely the guidelines will be observed, thus in turn making future challenges less likely. (This is very roughly the situation in Germany.) There is no iron law of economics guaranteeing success, but the risk of failure is even greater for the incomes policy alternative.

References

Brittan, S., 'The Political Economy of Union Monopoly', *The Three Banks Review* (September 1976).

Brittan, S., and Lilley, P., *The Delusion of Incomes Policy* (Maurice Temple Smith, 1977), pp. 63–8, 177–93.

Friedman, M., and Schwartz, Anna, *A Monetary History of the United States* (Princeton University Press, 1963).

Hutt, W. H., *The Strike-Threat System* (Arlington House, New York, 1974).

Layard, R., Metcalf, D., and Nickell, S., *The Effect of Collective Bargaining on Wages*. LSE Mimeo, 1977.

Pencavel, J.H., 'The Distributional and Efficiency Aspects of Trade Unionism in Britain', *British Journal of Industrial Relations* (1977).

Rees, Albert, *The Economics of Trade Unions* (Cambridge University Press, 1962).

Smith, D., 'Labour Market Institutions and Inflation', *British Journal of Industrial Relations* (March 1976).

20 Property Rights for Workers

Co-operatives for All? (22 January 1976)

Markets and socialism are not two words that are usually put together. Yet there has been a highly respectable body of economic
thought labelled 'market socialism'. The basic idea behind it is that
you can have the advantages of a market system, making use of the
profit motive and the price mechanism, without having capitalism, i.e.
private ownership of the means of production. To put it the other way
round, socialism in the sense of common ownership does not need
detailed controls, five-year plans, incomes policies or even an industrial strategy. Socialist firms can be guided by the profit motive in
deciding what to make and what to charge, with no more than the
minimum of regulation that, say, Professor Milton Friedman would
recommend for the United States. Indeed, with the emotive issue of
ownership of productive assets out of the way, profits would cease to
be a dirty word and it would be possible to make more use of markets
and prices than in most Western countries today.

Of course, there are snags in the argument. But it is precisely
because it is so much the opposite of the direction in which we are
travelling that it is so refreshing to examine. As Peter Jay says in his
Wincott Lecture:

> It is the logical, and potentially the political, antithesis to state
> capitalism, or corporatism, as now broadly favoured by the central
> establishment of contemporary political and economic thought,
> more or less indistinguishably under political regimes of either or
> any colour .... Anything which is the systematic opposite of the
> highest common denominator of conventional wisdom has a par-
> ticular presumption in its favour.

Market socialism comes in two main forms. The first is traditional
state ownership, but under which managers would be told to maximise

profits and pay competitive wages instead of to follow the national interest as conceived by the Government. The second, favoured by Mr Jay, consists of workers' co-operatives brought about by a change in company law that would give ownership of enterprises to people working in them.

Either form would require both main political parties – and other interest groups – to jettison most of their slogans. The Conservatives would lose 'private enterprise'. But, equally, Labour politicians would have to abandon their slogans about profiteering, speculation, 'rationing by the purse', property deals and so on. All these items in Labour's demonology would have to be dropped, as they would now become virtuous activities helping to further the national wealth and allocating it according to the will of the people. For as Mr Jay says, while the political process (or rather its idealised form) registers what most people want, the market registers what they want most.

The defects of the state ownership version of market socialism can be dealt with briefly, as it is certainly not recommended in the Wincott Lecture. The market system is not just a way of satisfying known wants by known techniques, as one might suppose from some textbooks. It is a discovery procedure in a world where tastes and techniques are changing and information is expensive. Under state socialism, some central body has to appoint managers and allocate funds. The variety of potential backers, available with different private holders of wealth, is missing if the competing socialist firms are all set up and financed by government authority.

Even more important, the incentives operating on the individual manager are very different in a state-owned concern. There is now a considerable US literature on the economics of non-capitalist concerns, whether charitable bodies or state enterprises. The upshot is that, because the managers cannot keep the extra earnings that their efforts might create in monetary form, they tend to concentrate on status symbols or non-monetary benefits for themselves, such as an impressive office, a pretty secretary and a pleasant working atmosphere, rather than on serving their ultimate clients. There are, of course, such tendencies in large private concerns; but a competitive market in management salaries (in countries where the tax system allows this) helps to keep them in check, as does the threat of a share takeover and the need to maintain a good rating in the capital market.

But the most important objection to state socialism is that political and personal freedom are not compatible with universal state ownership. The theoretical right to free speech is of little value if publishers, newspapers and theatres are all state-owned. If all wealth and patronage is in the hands of the government or its agents, a society will not be a free one, even if it does experiment with the price mechanism. East Berlin does not become a free market economy because it imposes admission charges for museums while West Berlin does not.

These disadvantages are not so acute in the workers' co-operative version of market socialism. The state does not have to appoint managers – they are hired by the workers on a basis that, one would hope, would differ radically from one jointly owned enterprise to another. The co-ops would keep all the fruits of entrepreneurial enterprise; and there would be more sources of power and patronage than under state socialism. Although Jay does not point this out, Tony Benn's experiments were not a fair test of co-operative market socialism. They were usually set up after illegal occupation of premises; they were subsidised by the taxpayer; and Mr Benn never showed the slightest interest in how an economy of co-ops would co-ordinate its activities for the benefit of the consumer.

A great difficulty in appraising co-operative market socialism is that only one country – Yugoslavia – has so far tried it. There, the Communist Party dictatorship preceded the co-operative system, which it introduced as an improvement over Stalinism – so one cannot say how the system would work in a politically freer environment.

Why, however, go to the trouble of making the change? There is nothing to stop workers' co-ops now; and in the present political climate considerable *cachet* would go to any private enterprise institution that financed a successful one. Their lack of success to date suggests that the difficulties of management control and other snags are too great; and that workers do not sufficiently value the extra rights to accept any resulting material disadvantages. As 90 per cent of consumption is financed from wages or social security benefits (and about half of all dividend income helps to finance pensions), quite a small loss in efficiency would soon swallow up any gain to the workers from expropriating capitalists.

At this stage it must be pointed out that Peter Jay's case for co-ops does not rest on utopian enthusiasm. He starts from the assumption that the present form of mixed economy is heading for disaster. The political and economic market places work according to incompatible criteria. Consumers spend their own money; but voters express intentions about what should be done with other people's money collected in tax; and there is no mechanism to stop unrealistic expectations about governmental activity. The worst of these is a demand for a level of full employment quite incompatible with the real wage that union monopolies insist on exacting for their members. The attempt to provide these employment levels by stimulating demand leads to accelerating inflation – not year by year, or even cycle by cycle, but over a run of cycles; and the result is likely to be anarchy followed by some form of strongman rule.

I would accept the broad lines of this thesis, but with some differences of emphasis. I am not, for instance, convinced that, left to themselves, the unions must inevitably insist on real wages that would be so high as to cause mass unemployment 'in anything short of a total buyers' market for labour'. Mr Jay suggests that we can discover whether there is a political solution through public tolerance and understanding of higher unemployment figures by following monetary policies in 1976 and 1977 'consistent with bringing the rate of inflation down to negligible levels' within two or three years. This is to confuse the 'natural' rate of unemployment, consistent with a stable rate of price change (and which the author has himself explained with exemplary lucidity on an earlier page), with the *transitional* rate of unemployment required to move down from the 1975 inflation rate of 25 per cent to something close to zero.

This, however, is a detail, although an important one. The essential hypothesis is that collective bargaining, backed by the strike threat, leads to an excessively high unemployment rate, whether or not accompanied by inflation. Mr Jay's basic hope is that, if the wage relationship can be abolished, it should be possible to restore a fully functioning market economy with the workers' co-operatives competing against each other.

The plan would seem to me to eliminate one, but not the most important, of the sources of conflict. At present wages are nominally set by employers. The only way a union can exert its plant monopoly power to secure higher returns is by forcing the employer to raise wages and prices. In a co-op the workers would set their own pay according to self-chosen criteria; and there would be no distinction between the wage bill and the remainder of value added.

There is, however, no reason to suppose that industry-wide monopolistic behaviour by organised workers would stop. It would, of course, take the form of raising prices rather than wages, but the distinction would be one of form. Indeed, workers' co-ops could more easily combine directly with each other to raise return by limiting output if they did not have to go through the inconveniences of threatened or actual strike behaviour first. Nor is there any reason to suppose that the tensions produced by an unstable balance of power between different groups of workers, and the resulting threat to employment and temptation to inflationary policies, would be any less than they are today. The most difficult wage issues and confrontations have even under the existing system been in the public sector, where the issue of profits has not even arisen, and where the argument is clearly one with the rest of the community over relative shares.

While there would probably be fewer strikes with workers' co-ops, because monopolistic aims would be achieved more directly, they are most unlikely to vanish altogether. So long as there is a state sector with custom to bestow; so long as there is a possibility of state subsidies, tariffs, import controls or official restraints on domestic competitors, workers in different industries will have demands for changes in public policy. I can see no more reason why they should abjure the threat to withdraw all output completely as a means of pressure on the authorities under the new regime than they would today.

It will not be enough simply to leave workers' co-ops alone if we are to maintain a competitive labour market. The whole syndicalist tradition has been based on the idea of producers', not consumers', sovereignty, and is naturally corporatist. The threat from union monopoly power arises not from the employer–employee relationship, but from the activities of coercive and rival producer groups; and a transfer of ownership will not make a decisive difference to whether or not we can live with these coercive rivalries.

The key question is whether it will be politically easier to apply anti-trust legislation to collusive action by workers' co-ops than to unions under the present system. An *Economist* poll published on 10 January 1976 showed 74 per cent agreement both with the statement that unions had too much power and that they were essential to protect workers' interests. It is not at all obvious why public support for self-help and direct action by producers would wither away with the disappearance of the large private enterprise.

Peter Jay does not himself raise the question of anti-trust legislation in a world of producer co-operatives. But his more general case is that, with the workers themselves running the means of production, their 'alienation' will end and they will cease to demand a level of remuneration so high as to undermine full employment. This assumes that hostile attitudes by workers to their place of employment are based on hostility towards the private shareholder rather than on the conditions of modern mass production, which can occur under a variety of ownership forms.

But there is a more fundamental difficulty. Alienation or not, it would still be logical for groups of producers to restrict output to improve their position relative to producers in other trades and relative to people looking for jobs. Jay's cataclysmic prognosis for democràtic mixed economies is based on the consequences of the collective pursuit of rational self-interest, and not on alienation. But the case for workers' co-ops depends on a completely different diagnosis in terms of alienation; and this crucial switch in the argument is not made explicit.

Even if alienation were somehow linked with resentment towards capitalist society, there would be many features of Mr Jay's world that would continue to encourage such feelings. It would not be an egalitarian one. People could still grow rich by starting small private firms (which would have to be bought out at a threshold size). A capital market would continue in which individuals could invest; and personal inheritance is not ruled out. There would thus still be plenty of scapegoat figures whose living standards could be compared with miners or nurses at crucial moments in the struggle for relative shares.

These elements are introduced into the proposals as a result of the author's commendable desire to introduce safeguards for personal liberty and efficiency. For Jay, of course, realises that these would be threatened in a system where all investment came from retained funds and all personal income from co-operative membership, and realises the totalitarian nature of a system in which no one had an opportunity to develop a business, however small, and where the form of ownership was laid down for all enterprises from ICI to the village baker. One of my worries is that those whose enthusiasm is for the common ownership rather than the free market aspects of the proposals will forget or ignore this all-important small print.

My own conclusion is that the idea of workers' co-operatives, whether on an experimental or a generalised basis, should be debated on its own merits rather than as a last chance for economic and political stability. But if one does reject the specific proposal to convert all major concerns into co-operatives by law, one should try to think of other institutional devices to move away from the system of industrial brinkmanship, which is what collective bargaining has become under the strike threat system.

Shares for Employees (21 June 1973)

The 'national capital-sharing scheme' just approved by the Labour Home Affairs Committee contains the germ of a good idea; and it would be a pity if it were lost to sight because it is buried in a rather bad plan. [In fact, no announcement had been made about it by early 1977, after three years of Labour Government.]

To be more precise, the capital-sharing plan is a compound of one good idea and one bad one. The good one is that the benefits of share ownership should be spread more widely; and that many of the defects of capitalism can best be mitigated by giving employees a chance to become capitalists themselves. The bad idea is to find a backdoor method of gaining centralised control of the main companies of this country — foothills as well as commanding heights.

The attractions of a wider spread of share ownership have often been stated. Instead of doing away with capital gains and 'unearned income' from equities, these would become available to the ordinary citizen. The advantage of having a nest egg to fall back upon, and the greater freedom arising from not being completely dependent on one's pay packet, would no longer be the privilege of a small minority. It was not the Labour Party that coined the slogan of a 'property-owning democracy', but the concept has a great deal to be said for it. The distribution of property is much more heavily concentrated than that of income (although the usual figures are highly misleading); and the goal of dispersing property more widely is inherently more attractive than that of wholesale takeover by the State.

There could also be specific advantages to the working of a market economy, if we ever reached a state of affairs where a typical wage-earner drew an appreciable slice of his income from equity ownership. To begin with, it would be very difficult for politicians and publicists to treat profits as a dirty word. The wage-earner would have a direct financial incentive to weigh up some of the costs of trade union wage-push; he might come to see some advantage in an interpretation of full employment that does not mean preserving all existing jobs; and he might even begin to see the point of allowing relative wages in different occupations to be influenced by supply and demand, instead of by a combination of bully-boy tactics and bogus moralising.

The idea of giving employees a stake spread out over the whole of industry and commerce is also a great advance over the traditional idea of profit-sharing or share incentive schemes. The big disadvantage of profit-sharing or share acquisition on a firm-by-firm basis is that all the employee's eggs are in one basket. For both his wage and the value of his capital assets depend on the prosperity of a single organisation. Yet another vested interest is thus created in favour of restrictions and subsidies designed to protect particular sectors from the effects of change. By contrast, the owner of a widely spread stake is more likely to identify his interests with the general prosperity than with a particular producer interest.

What then is wrong with the Labour plan? The fundamental fault is the suggestion that all the employee shares should be vested in a so-called National Workers' Fund whose Council would 'step in' to deal with companies whose behaviour it does not like. Presumably this intervention would take the form of either buying extra shares of that company in the market, or using its existing equity to oust or influence the management.

Any central body that aimed both to build up a majority stake in all public companies and to supervise their affairs would represent an intolerable concentration of power, unrivalled even on the other side of the Iron Curtain. Let no one be deceived by talk about worker representatives being in a majority on the Council of the Fund. There is no way in which twenty million workers can run the whole of British corporate industry. However they were appointed (and it is apparently to be by the TUC), council members would either become an arm of government or constitute a rival government of their own. In any case the two functions of looking after the value of the funds with which they had been entrusted and acting as an instrument of national economic policy would cause acute difficulties for the proposed body. This might well be wrecked by the attempt to carry out two incompatible functions. If the fund managers go into action to preserve unprofitable operations (plain English for attacking the 'asset strippers'), the value of their shares is threatened. The same would apply to any operations devised to push firms into any other activities – whether regional development, high technology ventures or the maintenance of a particular industry in Britain – where the planners' aims were in conflict with profit-and-loss calculations.

But rather than dismiss the plan altogether, it would be best to eliminate its centralising and interventionist aspects. This could readily be done, while preserving the principle of a wide spread of interest for each employee. It is worth remarking incidentally that, once the emphasis is placed on wider share ownership rather than on backdoor nationalisation, the 51 per cent target for employee shareholdings (which will in any case not be achieved until well into the twenty-first century) loses its magic significance.

The first essential change is to remove all temptation to use the Fund to further governmental economic fashions of the hour by eliminating the idea of a central agency altogether and setting up a variety of unit trust-type bodies. Quite apart from its possible misuse for political intervention, a central fund would be too large and unwieldy to manage its assets effectively without pushing the stock market against itself. This is a difficulty that some of the larger insurance companies already experience. The Labour Green Paper insists that the new 'Workers' Fund' will not 'play the market'. But if it does not switch between assets, except to bolster up unprofitable situations for 'social' and 'national' reasons, it will qualify for the booby prize as the worst managed investment or unit trust in the country and prove a poor bargain for its supposed beneficiaries.

Let us make the large assumption that some government would be prepared to take the Labour plan of 1973, but amended in the important ways suggested, as a starting point. What are the key features of the plan? In particular, how would workers acquire their equity stake? The basic instrument of the plan for spreading ownership would be an obligation on companies to issue each year new shares equal to 1 per cent of all outstanding equities for employees' capital.

Although companies would normally print paper rather than issue cash, the proposal amounts to a tax on existing shareholders. Each year they would receive a steadily smaller proportion of the available dividend income, and the rate of appreciation of all shares – new and old – would be reduced as a result of this watering of capital. This will have implications for profit margins and investment, whether one assumes that a company is run on behalf of its existing shareholders or adopts a managerial model. A shareholder-run company will attempt to preserve the previous rate of return on the original shares by raising margins and prices. If its competitors are behaving in a similar way, and international competitiveness is preserved by monetary or exchange rate policy, it may well succeed in doing so. If it did not, the attractions of new investment would steadily decline. A managerially controlled company might contemplate reducing dividends per share as the capital was being watered. But it could not embark on this course for long without not only destroying the possibility of new equity issues, but also destroying the earnings basis for new fixed interest securities. Thus it too would have to raise prices and profit margins, or see its investment slashed.

An increase in margins and prices is not itself a cause of continuing inflation if monetary demand is held to some planned course. But the rise in profits in relation to wages means that wider share ownership has been paid for in part by forced savings. Employees who did not wish to save in this way would, if left to themselves, be able to sell their holdings in the market. To the extent that the employee share units really did represent redistribution and not just forced saving, there would be a case for some restrictions on the rate at which they could be sold off in the market.

The method of restriction proposed in the original plan is, however, over-cumbersome and restrictive. A rolling forward of withdrawal rights year by year is envisaged, and all withdrawals would have to be financed from accumulated dividend income or unspecified company cash contributions. These restrictions would make the scheme pretty unpopular; and the property rights would be of an inferior and restricted kind. It would be much better to let the units be marketable, but to place a limit on the rate of realisation in the initial few years.

Nevertheless, unless the restrictions were so severe as to make the workers' equity units nothing more than a variable social security entitlement, some employees would be pretty efficient at disposing pretty quickly of any share bundles they were given (an experience amply confirmed by the ICI and similar experiments), while others would save, or 'play the market' and accumulate fairly large nest eggs. This is just an illustration of the point made long ago in David Hume's *Enquiry Concerning the Principles of Morals*, that, even if possessions were rendered 'ever so equal, men's different degrees of art, care and industry will immediately break that equality'.

An equal spread of property rights is thus an unattainable idea. It might, however, be possible to reach an economic and social equilibrium, with the tendency of wealth to concentrate offset by some watering of capital to provide fresh employee shares each year and a more sensible system of taxing wealth and inheritance.

Job Rights — An Alternative Approach (June 1976)

The weakest aspect of the popular case for the free market has been the bias in favour of change and the impatience with those who lose from it. Individualist economics, properly understood, seeks neither to facilitate nor to prevent change, but to provide a framework in which people can make up their own minds. If we are looking for a corrective, the best place to start is with the principle derived from Pareto, which states that we can only say that a change is for the better if no one is made worse off as a result: or more realistically that the gainers can afford to compensate the losers so that the latter are prepared to accept the change. The Pareto principle belongs to the world of theoretical economics; but it is in fact a political judgement, and one that is preferable to the ultra-democratic principle that the interest of the majority should always prevail.

If protecting the losers from change meant a nursemaid state and discretionary government intervention whenever anyone claimed to be worse off, the Pareto principle would be thoroughly in conflict with personal liberty. But it can be given a different interpretation. Protection of people's existing positions could take the form of a contractual right, of which they could not be deprived without their consent. What I am proposing is something far more radical than anything that Tony Benn has ever proposed, although entirely compatible with a market economy. It is the option, for workers who want them, of *property rights in jobs*. A worker possessing such a property right would be entitled to stay until retiring age. If, on the other hand, he wished to leave, he could sell his job entitlement at market value to any qualified person wishing to take his place.

This is a more far-reaching idea than redundancy compensation (which ranged up to £2,400 in 1976, to which the Government made a contribution of 40 per cent). The latter is determined by past contributions and statutory provisions. There is no relation between redundancy pay and the value of the disappearing job compared with the next-best alternative, or with the costs, risks and anxieties of searching for that alternative. Under a job rights contract an employee could not be made redundant unless he had voluntarily agreed to go in return for an acceptable cash payment.

A closer approach is the scheme being developed by the *Financial Times* under which the employer guarantees to make post-tax earnings of redundant employees up to their previous level, after taking into account social security payments, official training grants and other schemes, and earnings in a new job. But job rights would go further still. An employee would be able to stay on in his previous employment, or receive his former pay in lieu of work, if he did not wish to move to an alternative employment. An employer taking on a new recruit under such a contract would have to reckon that he is committed to providing him with work until retirement, or compensating him appropriately.

Industrially, the establishment of property rights in jobs would recognise that restrictive practices and overmanning are a form of insurance against people who are displaced by up-to-date working methods not being able to find alternative work offering comparable pay and conditions. Such practices, however irrational for the whole economy, are not necessarily irrational for the individual worker. Property rights in jobs provide them with the insurance in alternative form. They are a generalisation of the valid element in productivity deals. Jobs with property rights attaching to them could still be abolished, but only on the payment of mutually agreed sums in compensation. Property rights in jobs would be a genuine Social Contract, but with individual workers rather than with union leaders.

The argument for a market in job rights is in some way comparable to the standard economic argument that a cartel will do less harm if there is a market in quotas and import restrictions, and if the licences are auctioned and then made transferable, than it would otherwise do. The biggest difficulty of job rights is that contracts of employment would have to be complex, and to spell out a great many conditions at present unspecified. They would have, for instance, to specify how the going wage at which the contract operated would be determined, as well as working conditions and range of tasks, together with arbitration machinery for settling disputes. Otherwise employers could induce people to leave voluntarily by offering unattractive terms, and unions could insist on real wages which made property rights prohibitively expensive.

My proposal has been touched off by the Japanese system of permanent employment, but is by no means an exact replica. Japanese experience suggests that it is possible to spell out the conditions for job security without misunderstanding. Large Japanese companies have offered lifetime employment for several decades, and the system has been no more than slightly dented by the 1975 recession. An employee has to accept postings to a different branch or activity within his corporation within the same area but he is not discharged for refusing to change his residence.

The Japanese worker cannot, however, sell his job rights; and a worker who leaves his firm loses a valuable asset. His difficulties are further increased by the seniority system under which he would have to start low down on the ladder in a new employment. My suggestion, by contrast, is that a departing employee could sell his job entitlement to a newcomer; and this feature would remove the undesirable feudal aspects of the Japanese system. If the newcomer were a younger person, the job right he purchased would expire before his own retirement age. It would be open to him to negotiate an extension with the employer.

An employer who wanted to reduce his labour force might, with a job rights system, offer a price for voluntary redundancies and see how many workers came forward. He would have to pay more per head if he wanted a thousand than if he wanted a hundred redundancies. This is reasonable because when redundancies are small they will be concentrated on those who have only a marginal preference for their present employment, but as the number rises they will affect people who regard their job loss as a serious hardship. (There would have to be safeguards against collusion to overstate the true value of job rights to employees.)

Guaranteed employment probably covers no more than 30 per cent of the Japanese labour force. The self-employed, agricultural workers and employees of small firms are excluded. The large firms operate with a buffer of 10–15 per cent of temporary employees who can be hired or discharged according to trading conditions. Sub-contractors who do not offer job security are also deliberately maintained in existence. There is no need to copy all these Japanese features slavishly. But the existence of some non-guaranteed jobs is probably a condition of the guarantee system operating successfully in a free society. Pay and conditions in the non-guaranteed sector would provide at least a reference point in interpreting guaranteed contracts.

Property rights in jobs would be expensive because the flexibility of employers in varying their labour force would be reduced; and this would mean a lower level of real wages, compatible with normal employment, than would otherwise be possible. Provision would be required for employers who were not financially able to carry out their obligation to provide continuing employment. A variety of approaches would be possible, including perhaps compulsory insurance by employers in respect of protected jobs. Compensation for dismissed workers could be a prior charge on firms' assets, as back payment of wages is already under the Employment Protection Act.

The point that cannot be sufficiently emphasised is that property rights are not a soft option or an easy way for market economists to appeal to the Left. On the contrary, they would be expensive. Employers offering such contracts would have to make more far-reaching commitments than at present; if they miscalculated future demand, they would either have to pay workers who were not fully occupied or diversify into other activities to avoid manpower wastage, or pay workers to go away. The flexibility of employers in varying their labour force would be reduced; and this would raise employment costs. Thus, the level of real take-home pay they could afford to pay would be less than under 'hire-and-fire' procedures. The insurance premia or any ultimate government guarantee would also be a financial expression of the cost of the system. The argument is that some workers would be willing to pay a price in lower real wages for job security.

There is no reason to suppose that everyone would want guaranteed jobs. In Japan such jobs tend to carry better, not worse, wages – despite the cost of the guarantee. This is because the contracts are offered to the more skilled and reliable workers. But there is no reason why, in this country, there should not be some high-quality jobs that are specially well paid because no property rights attach to them, or some relatively low-paid guaranteed jobs for workers without any very marketable skills who want some insurance for the future. (I do not imagine that people will work side by side in the same assembly line on a variety of different contracts. The division would probably be at first by firms, or major groups within firms; but eventually toleration of differences in employment contracts at lower levels might spread.)

There is no right or wrong way of deciding on the many possible variants of job guarantees. For instance, many Japanese firms have a retiring age of fifty-five. Most employees stay on longer, but not as of right; and they may be demoted to different posts and lower pay. A higher retiring age would be more expensive to employers and would therefore be associated with lower real wages over the lifespan of the contract. Ideally, one would like to see a spectrum of alternative contracts associated with varying wage levels among different enterprises and perhaps even within the larger firms.

Dual labour markets, with a core of secure jobs and a surrounding fringe of more volatile employment for less qualified or less stable workers, are disliked by sociologists and radical economists because they involve different treatment for different people. I think it would be possible to enlarge the range of options so that we had more of a multiple than a dual labour market. But there would still be a sharp contrast between the two ends of the spectrum.

What the critics fail to realise is that the existence of a variety of labour markets enables people who could not gain a secure job on standard terms to price themselves into employment. The people involved are not always the less able; they may prefer a more volatile pattern of earnings and employment to the obligations of a conventional 'good job'. The attempt to enforce uniform conditions is likely to force onto social security, or into illegal and undeclared employment, many people who could have found work on a freer labour market. A multiple labour market enables square holes to be devised for square pegs.

The Employment Protection Act, in its present form, provides the worst of all worlds. It does not provide genuine job security, as employers can in the last resort make workers redundant against their will. On the other hand, so many hurdles are erected, both against general redundancies and against laying off individuals, that employers will think several times before taking on workers.

At least three things went wrong with the post-1974 Labour Government's approach. It is one thing to take workers on a contractual basis; it is quite another to superimpose half-hearted job security on enterprises that have been built upon traditional principles and are faced with an unexpected impediment to their operations.

Secondly, the Government and TUC have not taken aboard the fact that job security, like other improvements in conditions, involves an addition to labour costs, and thus reduces the level of real take home pay that is compatible with full employment. Indeed, from the beginning, the Government failed to bring home to people that excessive real wages – not just money wages – can price people out of jobs; and that if the available real wage is taken in one form, it cannot be taken in another.

Thirdly, conservatives and collectivists alike find it extremely difficult to take account of the great diversity of human desires, abilities and situations. Running through the Employment Protection Act is an attempt to produce a broadly similar regime of workers' rights in all enterprises; and this is even more true of much current thinking on workers' participation and industrial democracy. The basic mistake of the Act is not the increase in employee rights, but the attempt to enforce a uniform regime for all major enterprises. Indeed, the provision under Schedule 11 for preventing employers from offering terms and conditions less favourable than those prevailing for comparable workers in the same district narrows the range of options open to both sides, and if effective will be a certain recipe for unemployment.

The job rights proposal is worth pursuing for its own sake. But it would also serve as a *quid pro quo* when the problem of strike threat power comes to be tackled, as one day it will have to be, after the illusions of incomes policy have worn away.

Most of the discussion that preceded Harold Wilson's 1969 attempt to reform trade union law and the abortive Conservative Industrial

Relations Act of 1971 concentrated on abuses to be removed, and carefully avoided the question of whether the strike threat system, even if operated under the Queensberry rules, was itself the fundamental threat to stability.

Fortunately, strike threat power is not possessed in this extreme form by most unions. It is obviously not held by most white-collar workers; it is not even held by most engineers. There is, of course, no hard and fast dividing line; but effective blackmail power is probably concentrated in no more than 5–15 per cent of the working population at most. There is no right to strike in the armed forces, and few people would advocate it there. Why should not some 5–15 per cent of the economy be categorised as outside the strike threat area? In contrast to the armed forces, workers would still have the right to withdraw their labour individually, but not collectively. Strikes were illegal in a few key sectors such as water, sewage and power *before* the Conservative Industrial Relations Act of 1971; and I am merely suggesting the restoration of the earlier position and an extension of the list. On choosing or changing a job, a worker would have to weigh up the disadvantages of the absence of the strike weapon in these sectors with the compensating advantages of the better pay and conditions necessary to recruit enough people to these sectors.

A limit of this kind is probably a condition for the continuation of the independent collective bargaining system in the remainder of the economy. The alternative is a change in the functions of union leaders from that of being workers' representatives to being disciplinary instruments of government, Soviet-style, as the more ardent supporters of pay pacts would like.

A limitation of the right to strike in key industries is logically separable from property rights in jobs. Why weaken the case for either measure – whose political appeal lies in rather different directions – by coupling them together? This difference of appeal is the heart of the proposed bargain. If you are thinking of curtailing trade unionists' rights in some directions, you should think of extending them in others so that the bargain seems worthwhile, if not to trade union leaders, to the workers themselves. The one measure for which people might be prepared to rethink the hallowed right-to-strike doctrine for a few key sectors is an alleviation of the job anxieties which loom so large in British consciousness.

The trade-off would operate at an individual, and not just national political level. Just as job rights are a cost to an employer (private or state), which reduces the real wage he can offer a worker of given skill and reliability, so a no-strike contract is a benefit which enables him to afford higher wages.

Thus, both employers and employees would be able to choose among four basic kinds of contracts, with any number of individual variations:

1 no job security and full right to strike;
2 no job security and no right to strike;
3 job security and full right to strike;
4 job security and no right to strike.

The fourth type of arrangement corresponds to what used to be known as the civil service principle. It might ultimately be prescribed by statute for a few essential industries, although it is conceivable that we should get there by negotiation. Elsewhere there would be the full menu of choice. Obviously, not all employers would offer all four kinds of contract; many might only offer one.

Many concerns in industry and commerce would be able to offer their permanent employees job security without limiting the right to strike. But there would be a strong case for variations in both directions. The existence of non-secured jobs would provide some essential flexibility, as well as help workers who would otherwise be difficult to place. At the other extreme, I do not see why an employer, even outside some of the essential services, should not offer some or all of his workers, whether or not they have guaranteed employment, specially good wages and terms in return for a no-strike undertaking.

It should be possible to proceed a long way through amendment of the Employment Protection and Redundancy Payments Acts and related legislation. In any essential services where the right to strike is withdrawn by Parliament, job security should be established forthwith for career employees. For the remainder of the working population, job rights would be just a possible option. To begin with, the State should confine itself to financial encouragement, for example by making available its redundancy contributions and perhaps also the equivalent of unemployment pay to employers who themselves bear the cost of retaining workers who, under conventional arrangements, would be declared redundant. What is required is not just an anti-recession expedient such as the Temporary Employment Subsidy, but long-term support for job security contracts. Clearly, a great deal of case law will be required to prevent abuse; but we cannot argue about detail until there is some support for the principle itself.

As far as the no strike type of contract is concerned, it would be best to proceed on an experimental basis with groups who wished to work in this way. The first need is to bring such contracts from the reaches of the unthinkable into the reaches of the possible. It will be necessary to ensure that there are at least no legal obstacles to such contracts; and perhaps in the end to make them legally enforceable. After the new approach has been in operation for some while, the national law relating to strikes should be examined, with special reference to the essential services.

Two recurrent objections have been voiced in discussion to the suggestions in this article. The first runs: 'Is not the jobs rights proposal something like the dock labour scheme, under which dockers cannot be sacked without being paid large sums in compensation?' It is not in fact exactly like it, because the compensation sums in the docks are not related to the market value of the jobs, and rights to the latter are not transferable. But even if the similarity were closer, this would not be a fatal objection. There is much to be said in favour of a permanent employment option to remove insecurity from dock work. The objection to the scheme is that the terms on which such employment is available do not reflect the market value of dockers' services, or even the industrial power of that union, but the political influence of the T & G W Union on national policy. The valid objection is to these abuses, not to the dock scheme as such.

The other objection is: 'How can you make sure that no-strike contracts are enforced?' Making either union leaders or individual strikers liable for breach of contract would keep the matter in civil courts. But if someone keeps throwing the question back by asking 'Why should workers obey the courts?' there is eventually no answer. How do you prevent strikes in the Army when the ultimate sanction is the troops themselves? All law, and the use of force in its implementation, depends ultimately on opinion.

The object of these suggestions is to open up possibilities of progress based on consent, both at a national level and through an extension of freely negotiated contracts. This is potentially a superior approach to the steamroller use of a parliamentary majority, and to corporate state deals with a handful of unions and business leaders.

Postscript

[The above suggestions are all designed in various ways to break down class divisions, by enabling all citizens who want to do so to participate in the rights and obligations of a decentralised market economy. Their prospects have been badly – I hope not irreparably –

damaged by government attempts to promote the particular sectional interests of union officials by a variety of measures. Although these measures were sparked off by Labour's social contracts, so anxious were politicians of all parties to woo the TUC that it was highly uncertain whether a change of government would affect fundamentals.

Many overheads and impediments have been imposed on the recruitment of labour – equal pay, fair wage provisions, an employers' national insurance tax, laws against unfair dismissals, redundancy compensation, etc. – yet workers do not have the security envisaged in the job rights proposal. To bring in that proposal would require not only an overhaul of recent Acts of Parliament, but a belated attempt to bring home to unions the trade-off between real wages, other conditions of work and employment security.

Similarly, so many burdens have been placed on the private equity-holder – taxation of the paper capital gains due to inflation and taxes of up to 97 per cent on incomes that can be negative in real terms, a severe Capital Transfer Tax and the threat of a wealth tax – that one could not just bring in proposals to water capital by means of an employee's equity. As it is, the lack of an effective real yield on new investment is a powerful disincentive to capital formation, especially of the riskier variety. The whole package would have to be unscrambled and put together differently if a worthwhile employee status in nationwide share trusts were to strengthen rather than weaken a mixed economy.

As for a transformation of all major firms into workers' co-ops: as I feared, those who liked the common ownership aspect of the Jay proposals were completely uninterested in the restoration of a competitive labour market, while those who were impressed by Jay's analysis of monopolistic union bargaining and the case he made for free markets refused to take the co-operative aspect seriously. The free market camp had no time for the Bullock proposals on industrial democracy, which were likely to lead to union control of British industry; while many supporters of industrial democracy were prepared to take them as a basis for discussion. Wrongly so, in my view. Not only were the interests of the workers automatically identified with unions – worker-directors were to be appointed wholly through union channels – but the role of shareholders was in effect to be abolished; and equity-owners were to become simply owners of a particular class of debt. Thus no one would be left with an interest in maximising the yield on capital. This is much inferior either to workers' shares or to industrial co-ops proper, in which the equity interest is vested in the members. Hence the control of companies is likely to fall into the hands of a self-perpetuating management–union oligarchy.]

References

Dore, R., *British Factory – Japanese Factory* (Allen & Unwin, 1973).

Jay, Peter, *Employment, Inflation and Politics* (Institute of Economic Affairs, 1976).

Patrick, H. and Rosovsky, H., (eds), *Asia's New Giant* (Brookings Institution, Washington, 1976).

Peacock, Alan, 'The Political Economy of the Dispersive Revolution', *Scottish Journal of Political Economy* (November 1976).

PART IV

Economics and Democracy

21 What's Wrong with Economics?

The Market for Economic Witchdoctors

Theologians, philosophers, art critics, meteorologists, cosmologists and geneticists often disagree ferociously among themselves. Yet few would want to dispute their credentials for that reason. Why then do disagreements among economists give rise to so much public indignation? One reason is perhaps unduly flattering to economists. It is the widespread wishful belief that there exists, away from the clamour of party politics, an impartial expert answer to difficult problems of public policy – a belief that is often held by party politicians themselves. Patients have a similar attitude to doctors, who often disagree as much as economists. But medical practitioners keep their divergencies out of the newspapers, especially where individual patients are concerned.

Professional economists often play up to the 'impartial expert' view of their role by a clamorous insistence that their subject is, or should be, a science – an insistence that in no way prevents them from engaging in gladiatorial combat in front of the public with a ferocity that makes ordinary party politics seem like a children's game.

The formal way of proceeding would be to discuss whether there is or can be such a thing as positive economics – concerned only with what does happen or could happen in specified circumstances. The next stage would be to examine the value judgements that have to be introduced before policy conclusions can be drawn. An examination of economic controversies in the media or before parliamentary committees suggests, however, that this demarcation is far from easy to make. An alternative starting point is to apply elementary economic analysis to the problem, in other words to examine the market for economic controversies.

The first clue to understanding is that economists do not exist mainly to promote enlightenment, to discover how the economy works or for other such vague and worthy purposes. Like other producers, economists survive and prosper by studying the market and supplying what it appears to want.

At the academic level the main market is, of course, for learned papers. The contribution of such papers to economic understanding is one criterion by which they are judged. But it is not the only one, and it is a very elusive and intangible quality to assess. More important in practice tends to be 'professional competence'. This is something rather different, involving the sophistication of the statistical and mathematical methods used, knowledge of, and references to, the previous literature, internal consistency and so on. It is much more important for a paper to be 'competent' than for it to be right or enlightening.

Things could hardly be any different. When economists consisted of a small band of gentlemen scholars, as they did in the great age of David Hume, Adam Smith and Ricardo (and to a lesser extent up to the eve of the Second World War), it was possible to put great weight on general insight, and to allow room for a great variety of methods and approaches. With the explosive growth of the profession since the end of the Second World War and the need to fill hundreds of new teaching posts, an emphasis on technical competence in the narrow sense was probably the only way of keeping any sort of watch on standards; indeed, British economists have still to work out of their system a partially justified inferiority complex in relation to American professional techniques.

There is, however, one aspect of the market that is relevant both to the really ambitious academic aspirant and to the top-level economist pontificating before a parliamentary committee or a television screen. This is the well-known process of 'product differentiation'. At the academic level prizes are to be gained by slightly differentiating one's theories and methods from those of other economists, while staying within the professional canons mentioned above. At the level of public debate the effects are more serious. For there is no doubt that leading economists can make a great, if superficial, impact by differentiating their advice as much as possible from that of their colleagues, and putting the emphasis on those points that they believe to be original rather than on the common elements on which most economists agree. This was symbolised by a cocktail party in Washington where one economist present remarked: 'I have got some really smashing evidence to present to Congress tomorrow', but refused to discuss its nature in case he was pre-empted by someone else.

It is easy enough to state the ideal qualities that should be exhibited in public pronouncements by an economist. He should first emphasise the areas and topics on which there is some consensus, then go on to the areas of disagreement, explaining as far as possible how far these are about cause-and-effect relationships and how far they involve differing judgements about political goals. At the end of such an exposition he might then tentatively offer his own contribution to the unresolved issues. Yet there is extremely little chance of this ideal being realised. (Nor can one claim that economic commentators have followed it any more than academics have.) Apart from anything else, it is simply not what the market wants. Three distinguished economists, Friedman, Samuelson and Krause, gave evidence on the same day in September 1971 to a US congressional committee on foreign trade and currency issues. There was an overlap of about 75–90 per cent both in their analyses and in their policy recommendations; and the three economists concerned did not particularly try to emphasise their differences. Yet the inevitably brief public reports concentrated almost entirely on the minor issue of whether or not a small 'cosmetic' increase in the dollar price of gold would be a good thing. After all, it was this that constituted the news value of the hearings. (At that time the dollar was no longer convertible into gold; nor was any other major currency. But there was still an official gold price for the dollar, which was way below the market price and subsequently abandoned.)

There is a deep seated ambivalence in public attitudes towards economists. While people delight in ridiculing them for their disagreements, they are also entertained by 'original', 'provocative' and controversial viewpoints; and a high price and some prestige can be gained by meeting this public demand. The key to understanding many economic pronouncements is that they belong at least as much to the entertainment as the information industry.

The original name of the subject 'political economy' throws doubt on whether it can ever be entirely neutral politically in the sense demanded by some critics. But there is one kind of bias that is clearly undesirable. This is where economists make partisan points designed to provide ammunition not for their political beliefs but for the political party they favour – sometimes in opposition to their own more basic beliefs. This was particularly noticeable in the United States in 1971, for instance, when some pro-Republican economists defended the Nixon wage and price controls, while Democrat economists searched around for tiny niggling points of criticism – despite the fact that President Nixon moved much further in their direction than a

Democrat president would have dared at the time. Bias of this kind is easy to dress up in respectable statistical form. But, again, simple condemnation is of little help. The market demand, when politicians consult economists, is partly for debating ammunition or for loaded prognoses of the movement of the economy.

Some economists steer admirably clear of anything resembling partisan debating points but succumb to temptation of a different sort. They are tempted to fall in with the latest fashion and to advocate, for instance, incomes policies or the replacement of reserve currencies by paper units. But there is also a sophisticated market for those who are prepared deliberately to go against fashion and deride what they believe to be conventional wisdom.

Unfortunately, economists of this latter brand are apt to change their opinions with such rapidity that any layman who tries to base himself on their pronouncements would soon feel bewildered and shell-shocked. Indeed, one is often struck by the way in which the severest academic critics of the journalistic approach outdo all the journalists. Again, however, they are providing a service for which there is a definite demand.

Of course, not all the difficulties of economics can be attributed to the characteristics of the market or to confusions of presentation. There are major differences on some of the most basic questions of how the economy works. Would a much higher level of demand (with or without an incomes policy) lead to a virtuous circle of growth and lower prices, to growth alone or simply to an explosive and unsustainable situation culminating in 'go–stop' and less growth rather than more? You can find learned pieces of econometrics to justify all these incompatible positions.

Technical economics has indeed remarkably little to say about the causes of the 'wealth of nations' – and therefore about major questions such as Britain's decision to join the EEC. At the anniversary dinner of the Political Economy Club in 1973, Lord Robbins demonstrated that many contemporary arguments were already current in the early nineteenth century, and it is a myth to assume that they will be quickly resolved – any more by the importation of sociology today than by the importation of techniques from the physical sciences, from which so much was hoped, in the 1930s.

Back to Political Economy

A sense of perspective and of humour should enable us to cope with most of the anxieties about the status of economic arguments and those who take part in them. There are, however, two nagging doubts about professional economics as a discipline applied to policy into which it is necessary to go a little further.

It was one of the strong points of eighteenth-century political economy, as developed by David Hume and Adam Smith, that it started with human beings as they were rather than as some moralists thought they ought to be. The two thinkers were themselves moralists; but they accepted the legitimacy of self-interest, and they believed that the way to reconcile this with the general good was to devise a suitable framework of rules in which self-interest was allowed to operate. A twentieth-century representative of this tradition – and hardly a right-wing Conservative – was Bertrand Russell, who declared: 'If men were actuated by self-interest, which they are not – except in the case of a few saints – the whole human race would co-operate. There would be no more wars, no more armies, no more navies, no more atom bombs. . . .'

'Self-interest', even of the enlightened variety, is not perhaps the most felicitous term. The main assertion of the classical liberal is that the pursuit of *self-chosen* goals within an appropriate framework of rules is compatible with public harmony. These goals can be altruistic, aesthetic, religious or of any other variety. In the economic sphere it is rational for an altruistic businessman to work for high profits, along with his competitors – and perhaps to put even more effort into the process. His altruism will show itself in what he *does* with his gains rather than in his refraining from making them.

Nevertheless, the basic inclination of the early political economists to take human beings as they found them, and to seek rules that did not depend on a fundamental 'change of heart', was very much their strong point. One may wonder how this approach developed into modern economics. This is a subject widely regarded as doubly unreal in assuming the possibility of a model world, yet one populated by un-attractively consistent and cold-blooded people, always reacting in a predictable way to any given stimulus.

The transformation just caricatured was the natural result of the search for rigour and the growing professionalisation of the subject at the academic level. Effort was devoted to asking what were the con-ditions under which the market process achieved not merely a rough harmony, but an *optimum* allocation of resources. Not surprisingly, these were found most unlikely to occur. One need only mention the existence of large spillover effects from many activities (such as private motoring) or unregulated urban development – in other words, costs and benefits imposed on others, which are not taken into account in an unregulated market. Nor is there anything in the least bit optimal about the distribution of income and capital brought about by the combination of market forces and people's differing initial endowments. These are only the most blatant cases. The mere existence of 'economies of scale', or even the need for taxes on income or commodities, would prevent the optimum from being achieved. A little imagination – and mathematics – can always produce new and more subtle elements of fallibility in the working of the 'invisible hand'. The result was a concentration of interest on how an ideal market would work and on a set of interventionist policy prescriptions for dealing with the numerous departures from it likely to occur in the real world. This viewpoint has been labelled by critics the 'Nirvana' approach and is known more neutrally as 'static welfare theory'.

It would be Luddite to decry the search for greater rigour. It is surely better that government intervention should be based on research rather than on ignorance. But unfortunately this more rigorous approach was achieved at a price. For it tended to assume that the relevant information about people's tastes and behaviour, about production techniques and so on, was (a) known to policy-makers, and (b) either unchanging, or changing in a predictable way. These are assumptions into which anyone is likely to be drawn who attempts to express economic relations in simple mathematical form and who attempts to make economic forecasts.

This approach has the defect of assuming away the main problems of economic policy. No human being or central institution (or computer) can hope to have the information – most of it is not easily reducible to statistical form – to work out an ideal distribution of resources or even a 'second best' one. The role of the market is not to bring about an 'optimum' but to act as a signalling device to enable information scattered among millions of people to be diffused through the community and to be used as a guide to action. Like all signalling systems, the market is of course capable of improvement.

There are in fact some promising developments in political economy which aim to remedy the defects of the Nirvana approach. Most of these have come from across the Atlantic (often building on foundations laid by Austrian economists, who do not always receive their due acknowledgement). These new approaches are only now beginning to penetrate into the United Kingdom, where they are still largely a closed book to many economic practitioners skilled in their own subject. Even in the United States they are not yet in the mainstream of teaching or of practice.

The one transatlantic development that has penetrated British consciousness has the unfortunate label, 'monetarism'; and it is largely misunderstood either as a technical proposition about banking policy or as the view that 'only money matters'. This is almost the opposite of the true monetarist position, which was expressed by John Stuart Mill when he wrote that 'There cannot be intrinsically a more insignificant thing in the economy of society than money .... Like many other kinds of machinery, it only exerts a distinct and independent influence of its own when it gets out of order.'

There has been more than enough about such questions in previous chapters, and I would prefer to concentrate here on other transatlantic developments. There are at least five others of outstanding interest.

1   One of the most important for practical affairs is the analysis of markets as a *discovery procedure* in a world where tastes and techniques are changing and information scarce and expensive. This has immediate applications to labour markets and to the analysis of unemployment which are not revealed by either the conventional 'demand management' (or 'macro') approach employed at the Treasury or its critics in most of the public economic debate.

2   A second development is the analysis of *property rights* and the effects of their different allocations on the use of resources. It is worth emphasising that nearly all the adverse 'externalities', which are so often cited as arguments for political intervention, arise from the absence of clearly defined exclusive property rights or from the transaction costs of certain kinds of contracts. It is because no one owns the air space, pleasant vistas or the ocean bed that market disciplines do not apply, and exploiters and destroyers can escape without paying a price. Where the public authorities do in some sense 'own' resources such as the nation's road space, they inflict untold harm by not behaving like owners and instead allowing 'free', and therefore wasteful, use of scarce assets. It is not property rights but their absence that is antisocial. None of this implies, however, that the existing distribution of property rights is right.

3   The third important development relates to the economics of benevolence and charity, which has emphasised the distinction between *privately chosen* and *selfish* aims. The latter are in no way required for the successful functioning of markets, contrary to popular belief and some of the writings of the early economists.

4   A fourth contribution is the application of the theory of com-

petition to the political market and to the struggle for votes and powers, as well as to the functions of state bureaucracy. Much British thinking on economic policy is rendered worse than valueless by a sharp contrast between the faults of *real*-world markets and the actions of some non-existing and improbable *ideal*, benevolent and omniscient government. Real-world markets, with all their faults, have to be compared with real-world politicians, civil servants, pressure groups and experts.

5   The fifth and to my mind most interesting trend transcends academic demarcation lines and is the work either of philosophers with a special interest in political economy, or of economists using their tools to tackle wider subjects. It aims to throw light on questions such as the 'just' distribution of property rights (if there is such a thing), the permissible or required redistribution of income, the legitimacy of the coercion implied by majority voting and the tax and legislative power of the State.

The last two areas of study are of course intertwined and will be discussed further in the final chapters of this book. A preliminary result of this new thinking is to induce a little caution about the improvements that government is likely to bring – a caution, which unlike the old *laissez-faire* is in no way based on an idealised view of the private market place. A more far-reaching moral – easier to state than to observe – is that there is little point in preaching enlightened economic policies without asking: Who will carry them out, and under which incentives? Ultimately all reform is constitutional reform.

The Forecasting Delusion

But before we can move on to these matters there is one delusion that needs to be taken seriously. This is the identification of economic study in the public mind – and still more in the minds of politicians, officials and businessmen – with forecasts; and in particular with forecasts of the course of the whole economy of this country or even of the world. It would come as a surprise to many Whitehall officials and company chairmen to learn that the majority of economists have never made such a global forecast in their lives and are none the worse for that.

Nothing has done more to discredit serious economic analysis than its identification with the set of guesses about output, employment, prices, the balance of payments and so on which British chancellors have so often felt obliged to make, and which immediately became the subject of agonised debate among rival forecasting teams. When predictions of this kind are rendered ludicrous by events (e.g. the 'world dollar shortage' which turned into a glut, the supposed ability of sanctions to destroy the Rhodesian economy within 'weeks rather than months', or the unexpected runaway rise in unemployment in the winter of 1971–2,) the gibe about economic witchdoctors seems all too justified. Unfortunately, the cause of rational analysis of any kind also. receives a body-blow.

The fundamental error springs from the mistaken identification of scientific method with prophecies about the future. It is not the task of the social sciences to engage in historical prophecy. The view that it is has been aptly labelled 'historicism' by Sir Karl Popper. (Historicism has been exploded in its 'scientific Marxist' version; the new-style Marxists take their inspiration from the younger Marx and not from the arid prophetic economics of *Das Kapital*.) But it is not generally appreciated that even the more mundane concerns of present-day economic punditry suffer from a milder form of the historicist distortion.

Like many distortions, historicism has its origin in a correct observation. This is that the physical sciences, which social studies have for so long tried to emulate, have predictive power. But what this argument overlooks is that scientific predictions are conditional. They assert that certain changes, such as an increase to a certain point of the temperature of water in a kettle, will, granted certain other conditions — for example a given atmospheric pressure — lead to a state that we know as 'boiling'. But they cannot tell us whether the required conditions will be fulfilled.

Historical prophecies are *unconditional* scientific predictions. They can be derived from valid scientific theories if, and only if, they can be combined with correct assertions that the required conditions are in fact fulfilled. Sir Karl Popper, who has emphasised this crucial distinction, has pointed out that the requirements for successful long-term prophecies can be fulfilled only for systems that are 'well isolated, stationary, and recurrent'. This happens to be approximately true of the solar system, which is why predictions of events such as eclipses of the sun are possible many years ahead. But contrary to popular belief such systems are not typical even of the physical world; and certainly not of the rapidly changing society of human beings.

One must be careful not to overstate the case. There are certain features of business cycles (or, more accurately nowadays, official policy cycles) that tend to be moderately repetitive and only partially dependent on unpredictable changes in, say, the state of technology or the political colouring of governments. There is an analogy with the cycle of monarchy, oligarchy, democracy and tyranny observed by the ancient Greek writers which had some very modest predictive value as a scientific hypothesis.

It follows from this that attempts to forecast the short-term business cycle are less open to objection than the more ambitious attempts to forecast social changes at the turn of the century. There would be something to be said for starting with a theory of the typical business or policy cycle, and then asking in what respects the present cycle is likely to differ from the past. The second part of such an exercise would have to be impressinistic and subjective. The typical economic forecast is not, however, much like this. It is full-bloodedly historicist, in that it assumes that we have both sufficiently tested theories and enough knowledge of present and future conditions to made a determinate forecast. The criticism is not avoided in attaching an (almost wholly subjective) 'range of error' to these forecasts. Either the range of error is ignored in practice, or it is found to be so large that the forecasts are useless for policy purposes. It would, for example, have been little comfort to ministers caught by surprise by the alarming increase of unemployment in the politically traumatic winter of 1971–2 before the Heath–Barber boom to be told that the delay in the unexpected economic upturn was well within the margin of error.

What, after all, were the topics with which the great economists from Adam Smith to Keynes concerned themselves? The main questions that Keynes sought to answer were not what would happen to the economy in 1937 or 1938 (although he was not above a little bit of journalism on the subject); his principal contribution to thought consisted in trying to discover what were the circumstances in which a private enterprise system would fail to provide reasonably full employment and what institutional changes might make such failures less likely. Earlier on he had asked the same question about the types of situation liable to lead to runaway inflation; and at the end of his life he was concerned with devising an international monetary system that would discourage recourse to trade restrictions, competitive devaluations and other unneighbourly behaviour.

None of this is meant as an attack on the use of statistical or econometric methods. But these will be more scientific – as far as the social sciences can be scientific – if they confine themselves to *conditional hypotheses*. It is, for example, very useful to examine (without prejudging the question) whether a systematic relationship can be observed between index of primary product prices, on the one hand,

and the rate of domestically generated inflations and deviations of production from trend in the industrial countries, on the other. But an attempt to forecast world commodity prices over the next twelve months is a different matter. It involves assumptions about what domestic costs and prices in the industrial countries will actually do and the rate at which their output will grow. A conditional hypothesis can also reasonably assume average world weather conditions, and either no political disturbances, or none that is untypical of the period in which the hypothesis is supposed to hold; and there are a great many other things implicitly assumed to be given in conditional scientific predictions which are not given in the real world.

It is a wise principle to look for the elements of value as well as of error in methods of thought that are being criticised. There are such elements in the economic forecasting models. One of the main benefits from forcing someone to forecast, say, the national income and the balance of payments next year is that it imposes some consistency check on his separate individual beliefs. We cannot say what will happen. but a good forecasting model might enable one to say that certain events are impossible − or impossible without developments that have had no precedent.

The correct role for forecasting models is thus as one of many backroom research tools. But they do need to be displaced from the central position they have come to occupy in the thinking about the economy; and they are pretty worthless as a way of briefing ministers on their way into Cabinet meetings. A disadvantage of current orthodoxy is that many economists have acquired a vested interest in the existence of stable, discoverable numerical relationships between phenomena such as incomes and consumption, or short-run changes in the money supply and the price level, or exports and international price relativities, to name only a few. One cannot rule out the successful discovery of relationships of this kind; but, equally, one cannot guarantee it. Scientific method can still be applied to predict certain general features of an interacting system even in the absence of specific numerical relationships. Such procedures are commonplace, for example, in biology and linguistics.

Specific predictions are useful when they can be obtained. But even if they cannot be, some good generalisations are a good deal better than nothing. Indeed, the most important advice that needs to be given often involves extremely elementary economics of a 'first-year' kind. It can for example be asserted with considerable confidence that a country cannot have a balance of payments problem if there is no convertibility of its currency into gold or other international assets, and if the authorities do not attempt to peg its rates in terms of any other national currency. But it may not be possible to predict – within a useful margin of accuracy – the numerical value of the exchange rates that will emerge between the dollar and other currencies once convertibility is suspended.

Again, however, the clue is to, look at the market. If economic advice concentrated on such elementary home truths, the need for employing large numbers of specialist advisers might be called into question. On the other hand, economic forecasting looks like a highly technical service, which permanent secretaries could hardly provide for themselves with the aid of a scribbling pad. No matter how often forecasts go wrong, the moral that is drawn is that one should continue to work to improve them.

One of the greatest difficulties of accepting the anti-historicist's view is that it means admitting that we know less about the future than some people, especially those in authority, would like. Characteristically, it is just the type of politician that is most scathing about official economic forecasts who asks me over the lunch table: 'What do you think will happen to prices next winter?' – as if I, or anyone else, had some mysterious intuition that could tell him the answer within a range of accuracy that would in any way be useful.

The real art of policy analysis is to work out the appropriate response to an extremely wide range of contingencies that are liable to occur. This could take two forms. One is the formal analysis of a great many contingencies with the aid of decision trees and other tools. I suspect, however, that these would turn out to be largely parade ground exercises, at least for major problems of economic steering. Second, and more promising, would be to work out broad rules which would as far as possible put the economy on an automatic pilot and minimise discretionary intervention. Such rules could never be entirely mechanistic, as they would always call for interpretation; and during any period of difficulty there will be a transitional stage before the rules can again be fully applied. Thus either approach to living with an unknown future is a great deal more difficult than proclaiming the rival merits of different exercises in historical prophecy. But it is also a great deal more worthwhile.

Value Judgements

Finally, a word about the intrusion of political considerations into economic analysis. Economists who engage in partisan point scoring have little claim on our respect, but this does not mean that they can or should exclude political considerations from their serious work. Where the investigations of an economist lead him to certain political conclusions he has every right and even duty to promulgate them. Nor should he be deterred by fear of introducing 'value judgements'. Many apparent value judgements are susceptible to further analysis.

There is a strong but questionable emphasis in much modern academic writing on a strict distinction between 'positive' social science – which is supposed to have no policy implications – and personal 'value judgements'. The distinction was worth making to protect scholarly standards; but it has reached the point where it is doing more harm than good.

Admittedly, no 'ought' judgement can be logically inferred from an 'is' statement; but it is extremely difficult to distinguish between the two kinds of statement in actual language. Most generalisations in the social sciences are a subtle blend of positive assertion and value judgements. Assertions about 'efficiency', 'cost', 'consumer wants', 'harmony', 'real income', 'economic welfare', 'unemployment' or even demand for reserve currencies' usually embody both value judgements and generalisations about the world in a mixture that is very difficult to disentangle. All the above terms – of which 'efficiency' is the most frequent – occur in objective tests administered to beginners in economics. It is unconvincing for orthodox economists to assert their scientific virginity when challenged by critics. They would do better to be less defensive, to accept that certain value judgements are involved in their own doctrines, and to come out into the open in their defence.

It is often supposed that, because value judgements cannot be scientifically established, rational discussion of them is impossible. They are usually assumed to emanate mysteriously from governments, or electorates, or the individual economist himself. The ultimate reason why we can argue fruitfully about many value judgements has been given by Professor A. K. Sen. Value judgements can be divided into two types, 'basic' and 'non-basic'. A basic judgement is one that applies in all conceivable circumstances. If circumstances can be envisaged where it would not apply, it is non-basic. Take the statement, 'Men and women should be allowed to dress as they like.' This may appear an ultra-liberal basic judgement. But if the person who utters it flinches when asked, 'Even if it turned out that mini-skirts caused cancer in the eye of the beholder?' then it is non-basic.

The fundamental point is that, while it can sometimes be shown that a particular judgement is non-basic, there is no way of demonstrating that a judgement is basic. In Sen's words, 'No one would have occasion to consider all conceivable factual circumstances and to decide whether in any of the cases he would change the judgement or not.' Where we have not had to face a concrete choice, we may simply not know what our real values are.

The approach of moving to and fro between principles to case studies and back again is probably the best way of proceeding in these matters, and it is used implicitly even by writers who claim to be following other methods. The best that one can hope for from such studies is not rigid rules, but some conscious presumptions, guidelines and maxims which may be better than the unconscious ones that guide those who vainly suppose that they are 'examining each issue on its merits'.

References and Further Reading

One of the few textbooks that take into account the role of markets as a discovery procedure, the existence of altruistic motives and the importance of property rights is: A. A. Alchian and W. R. Allen, *University Economics* (Prentice-Hall International Paperback Edition, London, 1974).

On historicism and scientific method, see Sir Karl Popper, *The Poverty of Historicism*, 2nd edn (Routledge, 1960).

A concise statement of Popper's views can be found in 'Prediction and Prophecy in the Social Sciences', *Conjectures and Refutations*, 4th edn (Routledge, 1974).

For a critique of the view that economics consists in the discovery of stable numerical relationships, see the first two chapters of: F. A. Hayek, *Studies in Philosophy, Politics and Economy* (Routledge, 1967). See also I. Kirzner, *Competition and Entrepreneurship* (Free Press, New York, 1973).

On value judgements, see A. K. Sen, *Collective Choice and Social Welfare* (Oliver and Boyd, 1970).

On property rights, see E. Furubotn and S. Pejovich (eds), *The Economics of Property Rights* (Ballinger, Cambridge, Mass., 1974). See also A. Alchian *et al*, *The Economics of Charity*, (Institute of Economic Affairs, 1974).

22 The Defects of the Political Market Place

On from Adam Smith

What is unique about Adam Smith's *Wealth of Nations*, the bicentenary of which was celebrated in 1976? It is sheer myth to regard Adam Smith as the first major economic writer. The position is often attributed to Aristotle, and there are several other claimants. He may, however, be entitled to the more doubtful honour of being the first academic economist – the first great writer on the subject whose contributions arose from his work as a university professor.

Nor was Smith even the only eighteenth-century economist with a claim to immortality. A very large contribution was also made by Smith's older Scottish contemporary, David Hume. Although primarily a philosopher, Hume's few short economic essays are way ahead of much late twentieth-century discussion. It was Hume who exposed the absurdity of governments' balance of payments obsessions, then expressed as the fear that 'all their gold and silver may leave them'. He was undoubtedly far ahead of Smith in his understanding of money, prices and fluctuations in output and employment – what today is called macroeconomics. The heart of the matter is expressed in Hume's statement: 'Money, when increasing, gives encouragement to industry, during the interval between the increase of money and the rise of the prices.' After this, Keynes and Milton Friedman alike are merely footnotes. But it is only in the late twentieth century, when people have rediscovered his doctrines through hard experience, that Hume's claims have even begun to be recognised; and for the purpose of this chapter we had better stay with Smith.

The influence of Smith is partly a matter of doctrinal history. The contributions of succeeding economists such as Ricardo, Malthus and even Marx were to a large extent elaborations or criticisms of Smith; and it is possible for historians to trace back to him some of the key theories of late nineteenth-century economists. But there is also a more popular reason for the unique place of the *Wealth of Nations*. During most of the two centuries since publication, it was the one book on the subject that all economists and many educated laymen – from statemen to ministers of religion – would have read or looked at. They would have been attracted by its blend of theory and observation enlivened occasionally by caustic Scottish comment. But above all they knew that their followers were also likely to refer to it, and it therefore served as a common frame of reference for serious discussion. There is no comparable volume that serves such a function today – just one minor aspect of the disintegration of Eliot's 'common culture' of shared assumptions.

Smith is often portrayed as an optimistic believer in the limitless benefits of competitive private enterprise. But although this picture is purveyed both by the more mindless economic interventionists and the more unsophisticated free market propagandists, it is an absurd distortion. Smith was one of the authors of the labour theory of value taken over by Marx; and some scholars even find a somewhat obscure doctrine of 'exploitation' in his work. He also made an unfortunate distinction, which has reappeared among contemporary economic planners, between productive and non-productive labour. The latter included the activities of 'churchmen, lawyers, physicians, men of letters, players, buffoons, musicians, opera singers' and so on.

All this is – dare one say? – not very serious. Much more important is the highly pessimistic model of economic development lurking inside the *Wealth of Nations* and unknown to most of Smith's popular detractors and admirers alike.　For in fact, Smith foreshadowed Malthus and the ecologists in asserting a tendency for population growth to drive down wages to subsistence. Prosperity was a temporary interlude in the movement towards a stationary state, such as the China of his day, and all we could hope to do was to prolong this interlude.

This pessimistic model remains a logical possibility; but one that did not seem in accordance with events as living standards rose in the nineteenth and twentieth centuries. It is, alas, far too early to be sure whether this period of increased wellbeing will prove a refutation of Smith's long-run theory or simply the interlude to which he referred.

The *Wealth of Nations* is of course better known mainly for two other doctrines: the division of labour (which is limited by the extent of the market), and the Invisible Hand, which explains how the self-interest of the butcher, the brewer and the baker can be channelled to provide us with our dinner, so that we do not have to rely on their benevolence alone. From these two principles, Smith derived his arguments for free trade, characteristically qualified by the cautious observation that defence was of more importance than opulence.

Smith was neither a supporter of crude *laissez-faire* nor a spokesman for the business class. It was he who made the celebrated observation about merchants never sitting down 'even for merriment or diversion' without some conspiracy against the public emerging. Less well-known is that he already had a very good idea of the qualifications to the case for free markets – even when these were highly competitive – and of the nature of the intervention that might be appropriate. He was one of the first to expound the theory of collective goods, which the market will not provide because there is no way of charging all those who benefit. The stock examples in his day were bridges and lighthouses, but his analysis can be extended to anti-pollution and many other areas. His principle is that the State, instead of trying to make business decisions, should do those things that no one else will do.

Seen in this way – and ignoring the more speculative stationary state theories – Smith's doctrine held promise of a long line of continuous development as an aid to enlightened policy. A comparison of the differing assessments made of his *Wealth of Nations* at fifty-year intervals – 1826, 1876, 1926 and 1976 – is very helpful here. There were no celebrations to mark the golden jubilee of the *Wealth of Nations* in 1826. The Political Economy Club had just been formed to support the principles of free trade and a gradual start had been made in dismantling protection. But not even the economists were in favour of dismantling all protective duties instantly.

The high noon of Adam Smith's influence coincided with the centenary of the *Wealth of Nations* in 1876. Gladstone took the chair at a commemorative dinner; Gladstone's former chancellor, Robert Lowe, gave a highly complacent account of the success of free trade; and the French finance minister came over for the occasion. As Stanley Jevons complained, 'the statesmen had mostly their own way' and cared little what economists had to say. The livelier of these were worried that Smith's ideas had fossilised into a dogma. Their concern was directed partly at the unthinking dogma of *laissez-faire*, but also at shortcomings in Smith's analysis.

The next celebration, in 1926, seems to have been oddly unsatisfactory. The year of the general strike was not one in which economists' services were in great demand; and they had been left alone to develop their analysis. Smith now appeared as the foundation of a structure that others had much improved. The political message was very unclear. As Keynes said, 'We see but indistinctly what were once the clearest and most distinguishable instruments which have ever instructed political mankind.'

If the bicentenary had occurred, say, in the early 1960s, there might well have been a mood of renewed complacency. Keynes's own doctrines on money and employment would have been regarded as supplying one part of what was missing in Adam Smith. The modern theory of welfare economics would have been used as a guide to areas of likely market failure, such as transport or urban planning, where intervention was required; and a so-called political judgement would have been made on fiscal redistribution. With the aid of these crutches Smith's Invisible Hand could have been rehabilitated for the remaining areas of activity. Indeed, Anthony Crosland's *Future of Socialism* was very much along these lines.

By 1976, the actual year of the bicentenary, it was no longer possible to approach economic policy in such an optimistic spirit. Most of the modern refinements of economic analysis have not in fact helped to guide government into beneficent lines, and we now approach Smith in a different spirit. Simply to point to departures from some mathematical ideal shown by real-world markets gets us nowhere at all without an examination of the political and governmental instruments at our disposal. We can no longer suppose that economic planning will be carried out by omniscient but benevolent dictators; and we must examine the political and bureaucratic market, the knowledge available to those who work in it, and the incentives that influence it.

The Vote Motive Versus the Profit Motive

One of the earliest British ventures into the economics of the political market place did not come all that long after Adam Smith. It was undertaken by James Mill (1773–1836) – the father of John Stuart Mill – who tried to prove that, under universal franchise, rulers would be forced by their own self-interest to provide the best possible form of government. This attempt was the subject of a devastating essay by Macaulay, who concluded that such a study was a 'poor employment for a grown man', although it 'certainly hurts the health less than hard drinking and the fortune less than high play; it is not much more laughable than phrenology, and is immeasurably more humane than cockfighting'.

Unfortunately, instead of trying to improve their political analysis to make it less vulnerable to this sort of ridicule, most subsequent British economists implicitly assumed that the defects of real-world markets could be put right by ideally wise and benevolent government. The inventory of unsold economic prescriptions has therefore grown. The connection between the actions taken by governments and the textbook recommendations has, indeed, become more and more tenuous. Optimal subsidies, for instance, would not create butter mountains or wine lakes.

The next breakthrough came more than a century after Mill's death when the Austro-American economist Joseph Schumpeter began to analyse the political system as a market place in which entrepreneurs bid for the citizen's role instead of for the consumer's dollar. The economics of politics (or the theory of public choice, as it is sometimes called) has since become a flourishing if not yet very widely practised study in the United States. But with some honourable exceptions most British economists and officials did not appear, at least until recently, even to have heard of it, and if it was brought to their notice treated the notion as an amusing joke. When I suggested to one Treasury official that public expenditure control should pay attention to the motives of those in charge of spending programmes, he replied that unfortunately he was not well up on psychoanalysis.

It is a measure of the backwater state of so much British political economy that a short introductory book entitled *The Vote Motive* by Professor Gordon Tullock of Virginia, published in 1976, came as such a novelty. The basic assumption behind the 'economics of politics' with which this book deals is that politicians and bureaucrats try to serve their own interest just as businessmen or trade unionists do. The economics of politics tries to compare the likely defects of real-world governments with real-world markets, instead of assuming perfection on either side.

An initial difficulty is that there is no single goal that politicians and bureaucrats try to pursue in the way that, in the conventional economic textbooks, businessmen and wage-earners are supposed to pursue money gains. In the special case of elections it is normally assumed that politicans are seeking votes rather than money.

The vote-maximising assumption leads to what Professor Tullock calls the 'median voter theorem' and what political writers already know as 'fight for the centre'. If views on a particular issue can be arranged along the spectrum with more people in the middle than at the extremes, then both main political parties will end up taking midway positions very similar to each other's. In a system with three parties or more, this proposition will not apply to the parties themselves, but will apply to the policies of a government that receives a majority in the legislature. Moreover, these middle-of-the-road policies are supposed, in Tullock's words, to inflict 'the least disaggregate dissatisfaction upon society as a whole'.

Stated thus boldly, the conclusion seems both obvious and complacent, and Macaulay's ghost would chuckle at the word 'theorem'. But the interesting aspects are the conditions when it fails to hold; and to discover them it does help to set out clearly the assumptions and reasoning, a point that Macaulay, who detested mathematics, never really grasped.

One qualification is that the model – and, by extension, conventional democratic politics – is best suited to tackling problems that can be presented in one-dimensional form, for example whether to have a little less or a little more of some activity. The democratic adversary contest is quite well suited to reflecting changing public moods on how much should be spent on rubbish collection, education or the health service, but not to whether the services should or should not be provided by the State. It can cope quite well with marginal changes in defence expenditure, but much less well with questions as to whether the Vietnam War should be waged or not. Schumpeter – who, unlike the formal model-builders who followed him, would have had nothing to fear from Macaulay – always emphasised that the democratic method would not work successfully if there were deep-seated cleavages on fundamentals.

One particular distortion of the democratic process comes from bureaucracy. Officials are not bidding for votes; nor are they (normally) selling their services for money in any direct way. The best approximation to the bureaucrat's objective is that he tries to maximise the size of his 'bureau'. The larger the department, the greater the prestige, and probably the salaries, of those who run it. And the larger the budget, the greater the opportunities for benefits in kind, such as an attractive office, a leisurely pace for work and other amenities.

The great advantage of the bureaucrat is that he is much better informed on the details of his operations than the parliamentarian, who is not well placed to discover the true minimum costs of providing a service. The bureaucrat is helped by the special interest groups – whether farmers, council workers or schoolteachers – who can bring vociferous pressure to bear for an expansion of his services. The number of people working for central and local government services is also now so large that their votes can be crucial in an election.

The classic technique of the bureaucrat when asked to make 'cuts' is to suggest savings of a deliberately unpopular kind. When a permanent secretary of the American Political Science Association was asked for economies he immediately offered to reduce the staff concerned with journal subscriptions rather than the more amorphous activities which members really wanted to reduce. A more dramatic example was when the US Federal Customs Service suggested laying off every customs inspector while keeping all the rest of the staff. There were also at one time suggestions that the US Immigration Service was investing resources in office staff at the expense of inspectors, to make it necessary for Congress to increase its budget. Are these cases all that much more blatant than the British public expenditure 'cuts' concentrated almost entirely on capital investment and transfer payments and not involving any major reduction of public sector payrolls?

The formal analysis suggests that, in the extreme case of bureaucratic exploitation of political ignorance, expenditure on a service will be so large that the excess cost of it will outweigh all the public benefit (in jargon, the bureaucrats will have captured all the consumer surplus). Some consequences follow, which are not so obvious. The human dislike of hard work will reduce the quality of service, but may also reduce the effort to exploit political ignorance. The citizen may in fact be better off with lazy civil servants than with capable, diligent ones.

The whole Armstrong–Heath approach of setting up large super-departments to prevent overlapping and rationalise functions was based on the wise and benevolent despot approach. From an 'economics of politics' point of view, wasteful duplication may be a positive benefit because it creates some competition between public agencies and yields more information about true costs. A fragmented police force which allows comparisons between cities is preferable to the integrated national force which the social engineer might prefer. Experiments with private tendering for publicly financed services, such as fire protection in Arizona, act in the same direction.

There is, however, a fundamental defect of the political market place quite apart from bureaucratic distortion. The political market cannot provide different collective services or different policies to suit different tastes. In the private market we can, subject to our personal budget constraint, make our own decisions about how much of a service, and of what kind, to buy. A collective choice on the other hand has to be made for everyone centrally. We cannot make our own individual choices about how much it is worth paying in tax for police protection, or how much excess unemployment to accept to reduce the rate of inflation, or whether to bear the cost of an incomes policy. Thus even where the 'median voters theory' applies, most voters will still receive too much or too little, or the wrong kind of, service. Common policies are enforced on those who dissent.

This takes one to the most controversial part of the economics of politics. In the US Congress, there is explicit logrolling in which votes for, say, a dam for one district are traded for a harbour or road in another. And it is well known that legislators may overcome their dislike for certain defence policies if the contracts are placed in the right districts. Such 'pork barrel' politics are less overt in the United Kingdom, but take place in more gentlemanly fashion in Cabinet, party or interdepartmental committees, in which politicians and officials trade support for each other's projects.

Professor Tullock regards logrolling, so far from being a scandal, as an improvement in the political process. For it does enable intensity of preferences to be taken into account in a way that would be impossible if voting on each issue were conducted in isolation from voting on every other issue. Are there not, however, too many pork barrel projects? The excesses arise, according to some of the new school of analysts, not from logrolling as such, but from the voting rules chosen. The horizontal axis in Figure 18 represents the minimum percentage of votes required to pass a measure. The line marked 'external costs' shows the costs imposed on the people who do not benefit, but who have to pay for it.

In the case of a unanimity requirement such external costs would be zero. But contrary to popular belief, measures would still get passed provided that total benefits to society exceeded costs, owing to the operation of logrolling. The real disadvantage of unanimity is the very heavy costs of a different kind, namely bargaining costs (including that of dealing with the bluff of the last person whose vote is needed). The best voting rule is that which minimises the total external and bargaining costs. This need not be the conventional 51 per cent majority. Professor Tullock advocates a two-thirds majority for most legislation, a recommendation that is controversial even among public choice analysts.

Are proposals for reinforced majorities merely reactionary attempts to help the privileged? Remember that a Conservative prime minister would need a two-thirds majority to repeal the Capital Transfer Tax, to stop compulsory comprehensives or change Labour's union legislation. Such requirement would surely have prevented many of the

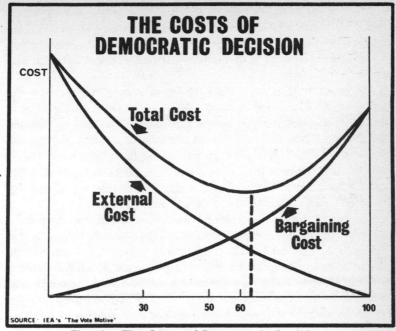

Fig 18.   The Costs of Democratic Decision

about-turns and policy reversals of the last few decades.

It is unlikely, however, that a government of one main party could wean away the votes of even a few MPs of the other side under our present highly regimented two-party system, however much it modified its proposals. Reinforced majorities would work only if there were either a loosening of party discipline or electoral reform which allowed more political groups to be represented.

There are many problems still to be tackled. Representative democracy tends to give concentrated sectional interests a disproportionate influence relative to dispersed taxpayer or consumer concerns; it is not certain how far changed voting rules would overcome this. A still more important problem is that the bidding process is liable to whip up unrealistic expectations; and one would like to know how serious a threat to democracy this is and how any self-corrective processes can be strengthened. (A few speculations of my own are to be found in the next chapter.) The gap between elections, voter ignorance and the representative process itself all give political leaders more influence than the 'median voter theorem' would suggest. This set of problems is not really tackled by the formal American models, which tend to assume a high degree of voter rationality on policy; and there is much to be said for going back to Schumpeter's own assumption that electorates vote for leaders rather than policies, and judge, as best they can, by results.

All these problems are within the 'economics of politics'. But the fundamental objection that many people will have is that politics is both more and less than the assertion of self-interest. Men and women rise above self-interest in the pursuit of visions and ideals, and they fall below it under the influence of myths, images, hatred and envy. This is true; but it is also true that non-economic elements such as solidarity, ritual, convention or inherited mores play a large role in a supposedly economic matter such as Britain's low growth rate.

Viewed as a study of the rational pursuit of self-interest, economics can never be the whole explanation of any kind of behaviour. But it is high time the political market place was examined in economic terms instead of in terms of the benevolent despot model which has hitherto been the practice. Such an examination might lead to the conclusion that, far from being morally superior to a self-interested bid for citizens' votes, the British system does not even achieve as much as that.

Because of the winner-take-all system, with its tendency to one-party dominance, the partisan element is too strong. This is because, whenever the electorate is tired of a ruling party, it has effectively only one alternative. This provides scope for party activists, who derive an unusually high personal utility from political activity, to impose views that are neither enlightened nor in keeping with popular feeling. Before discussing how the political system might utilise higher motives or the electorate become more far-sighted, it would be better to remove this particular distortion of the political market place, which not merely enhances the role of party activists but forces party leaders to speak the language of these activists and adapt themselves to their mental world.

References

Collison Black, R. D., 'Smith's Contribution in Historical Perspective' in T. Wilson and A. S. Skinner (eds), *The Market and the State* (Oxford University Press, 1976).

Tullock, G., *The Vote Motive* (Institute of Economic Affairs, 1976).

23 The Politics of Excessive Expectations (1974)

The Conjecture

The conjecture to be discussed in this chapter is that liberal representative democracy suffers from internal tensions, which are likely to increase in time, and that, on present indications, the system is likely to pass away within the lifetime of people now adult.

This idea has now become commonplace; and any interest it has must lie in the supporting argument. It may help to avoid misunderstanding if I emphasise right at the beginning that there is no such thing as historical inevitability. The point of saying that a house is on fire is to alert the fire brigade, not to sit back and enjoy the blaze. If my reasoning has any elements of validity, it may help to suggest either what can be done to improve the prospects for our type of democracy or, if that cannot be saved, what can be done to ensure that any successor form of government does the minimum of damage to more fundamental values.

In my own case the values that serve as a yardstick are those of an open society, where a large weight is put on both freedom of speech and freedom to choose one's own way of life, in which no group is oppressed or denied the means of subsistence, and in which the use of force and the infliction of pain (whether or not dignified by the name of punishment) is reduced to the feasible minimum. I mention these cliché simply as a reminder of the more basic ends that any political system should serve. On balance, democracy has advanced them; but there is nothing necessary or invariable about the connection.

Two endemic threats to liberal representative democracy are: (a) the generation of excessive expectations; and (b) the disruptive effects of the pursuit of group self-interest in the market place.

These two threats are in an obvious sense of the word 'economic'. I do not wish to underplay other kinds of threat, such as those arising from the clash of irreconcilable nationalisms or from other

247

manifestations of the herd impulse and the self-destructive impulse. But sufficient unto one essay is the evil discussed therein. Any dangers that I have neglected will — unfortunately — serve to strengthen the argument.

Nor is it part of my thesis that even in the economic sphere people are guided purely by self-interest or by the pursuit of self-chosen ends. Such an assumption is the best starting-off ground for dealing with human beings in their dealings *in normal times* outside the circle of their family and close friends. But people are also interested in their own role and status and in the moral legitimacy of the prevailing order. The changes that have taken place in what is acceptable here — to be discussed later in the chapter — have, however, served to aggravate rather than ameliorate the economic threats.

The two of these threats mentioned, excessive expectations and the disruptive pursuit of group self-interest, have different origins. Excessive expectations are generated by the democratic aspects of the system. The disruptive effects of group self-interest arise from elementary economic logic and are not directly connected with the political structure.

Nevertheless, the 'liberal' aspect of liberal representative democracy is important as an inhibition on tackling the group pursuit of market power. Some 'people's democracies', and some trigger-happy military dictatorships (by no means all), have shown that they can deal, at a price, with coercive power of rival groups. But it has yet to be shown that a society where legislation can be enforced only if it enjoys at least the tacit long-run acceptance of all major groups, including those on the losing side, can do so. The omens are not good.

There are clear interrelations between the two problems — the pursuit of group self-interest and the generation of excessive expectations in the political market place. Producer groups, of which the trade unions are an outstanding but by no means unique example, have not in the past made use of their full potential power, but have tended to make increasing use of it as time has passed. It is commonplace to observe that the size of group demands depends on members' expectations; but these in turn have been fanned by the competitive wooing of the electorate. Moreover, as already implied, liberal democracy inhibits governments from tackling coercive groups by an abnegation of the full-employment commitment, or by the effective restriction of union monopoly power, or by the enforcement of an 'incomes policy'.

A formula that may link the two problems is that an *excessive burden is placed on the 'sharing out' function of government.* This function may be defined as the activities of the public authorities in influencing the allocation of resources, both through taxation and expenditure policies and through direct intervention in the market place. The growth of expectations imposes demands for different kinds of public spending and intervention which are incompatible both with each other and with the tax burden that people are willing to bear. At the same time, in their pursuits of 'full employment' without currency collapse, governments are tempted to intervene directly in the determination of pre-tax incomes. But these attempts come to grief when they come up against the demands of different groups for incompatible relative shares.

The tensions described here are at work in most countries, but they need not have the same outcome in different places. The fact that they are particularly acute in the United Kingdom, which provides the case material for this study, is shown by the use of the label 'English sickness' when they turn up elsewhere. The question is left open in this chapter whether the denouement will be more favourable to liberal democracy in some other countries than in the United Kingdom. The greater tradition of stability in the British case has to be balanced against the greater severity of the pressures. But the view is taken here that the stresses are those endemic to democracy everywhere and were already visible before the world oil crisis of 1973–4, which of course made them more difficult to bear.

The Political Market Place

To carry the analysis further, it is necessary to put forward some view, inevitably brief and oversimplified, of the nature of liberal representative democracy.

The 'liberal' part of the label refers to the standard civil liberties of expression, association and assembly, together with the generally accepted constraints upon the degree of coercion that the forces of government can impose upon dissidents. I have in mind not some ideal free or open society, but the degree of tolerance and personal freedom that Western countries normally expect to achieve, lapses from which give rise to criticism and anxiety.

A good deal more needs to be said about the 'representative democracy' aspects of the system. My starting-off point is the theory of Joseph Schumpeter in his book of the 1940s, *Capitalism, Socialism and Democracy*. Schumpeter defined democracy as an 'institutional arrangement for arriving at political decisions in which individuals acquire the power to decide by means of a competitive struggle for the people's votes'. There is a link between the 'liberal' and the 'democratic' aspects of the system thus defined, but it is a loose one. If rival political teams are to compete, a minimal freedom of debate is required; and, once freedom has acquired a toehold in the party political arena, it tends to spread to wider areas. Yet it is essential to remember the distinction between the two aspects. The link is loose enough to allow persecution of unpopular minorities and widespread restraints upon freedom of action in systems with unfettered elections and majority decisions. Indeed, such repressive actions have been common in democracies – though less widespread (in modern times at least) than in undemocratic regimes.

The point of Schumpeter's theory becomes clear when we compare it with the popular theory which assumes that electors have definite beliefs about policy, represented by political parties which are expected to implement them. Edmund Burke defined a political party as a group of men who intend to promote the public welfare upon some principles upon which they are all agreed. In subsequent forms of the popular theory, parties were actually expected to formulate their policies in response to the desires of their mass membership. Such models of democracy received a body blow when nineteenth-century writers such as Michels, Mosca and Pareto showed that no mass democracy could or did work in this way. Policies were formulated by small groups within political parties or the civil service; and what was done often had very little relation to professed ideologies. These sceptical conclusions were confirmed very much later by sophisticated opinion studies pioneered by the 'Michigan School' of American political scientists, which showed that most voters were largely oblivious of most policy debates in the legislature and the press. The strongest claim that can be made on behalf of voters' awareness is that they do have a rough general impression of the stands of the main parties on a few of the headline issues when these are sufficiently simple.

The lesson of most studies of electoral choice is that changes in political allegiance are more performance-related than issue-related. Voters attempt to judge success in the pursuit of generally agreed objectives, such as peace or prosperity, rather than to evaluate rival objectives or alternative policies for achieving agreed objectives. The studies show that, not merely do voters not use the labels 'left' or 'right'; they do not think in such terms at all. To the extent that most people think in terms of issues, their attitudes are largely atomistic. On many issues on which the official positions of the parties are sharply divided, the proportion of people supporting different policies bears almost no relation to partisan allegiance. Clusters of 'ideologies', linking together opinions on different issues among the politically interested minority, are almost completely absent among the mass electorate. Such refusal to conform to stereotype is due not to nonconformist heresy, but much more often to basic ignorance of the simplest facts taken for granted even in the most popular of newspapers or television programmes. Voters simplify the problems of choice by shifting attention from policies to consequences; beliefs about the latter are formed by 'simple inferences from who is or was in power'.

Schumpeter's achievement was to show that representative democracy could work and need not be a fraud, despite these features. The best way to think of politicians, he maintained, was neither as ideologues nor as spokesmen, but as entrepreneurs who deal in votes just as oilmen deal in oil. The principles or policy platforms that characterise a political party may be important for its success at a moment, but they have no deeper or more permanent significance than the particular brand lines that a department store finds it expedient to carry this month but may well want to change next spring or autumn. Different department stores will feel more at home with different kinds of merchandise, but all will alter their lines in trial and error fashion in a bid to win public support. More deep-seated divergences are to be viewed as pathological symptoms.

Like all good theories, this is an unrealistic simplification. But it is neither as cynical nor as shocking as it appears at first sight. It is the political equivalent of Adam Smith's doctrine that it is not from the benevolence of the butcher, the brewer or the baker that we expect our dinner, but from their regard to their own interest. In politics as in economics, the pursuit of self-interest may, contrary to what unreflective moralists suppose, serve to promote the welfare of one's fellow citizens.

The competitive theory can explain why the policies of the leadership of the main parties are likely to resemble each other far more than partisan enthusiasts would like, and why a party's policies may change so as to become almost unrecognisable in a very few years. It also explains the role of political leadership. The fact that most electors have at best, as Schumpeter put it, an 'indeterminate bundle of vague impulses loosely playing about given slogans and mistaken impressions' is not fatal if the job of the elector is to choose between competing teams. Policy formulation is on this model a task for politicians and officials; if the electorate does not like the result, it does not buy it again.

Neither economic nor political markets produce ideal results. This is not a condemnation. Some of the defects of democracy have become familiar platitudes. One, so obvious that it is often overlooked, is the wastage of governmental energies. Prime ministers and their principal colleagues are involved in a never-ending contest, which goes on in an only slightly less acute form between elections. Both their opponents and their own followers have to be watched carefully if the leaders are to remain in the saddle. A very small fraction of a prime minister's time is available for thinking about policy, or even for plain reflection.

Good political tactics do not always produce good policies. Because every issue is seen in the context of a constant partisan struggle, it becomes distorted. Short-run ends, such as keeping the mortgage rate down, prevail over longer-term aims, such as producing a sensible housing or credit policy. Whether or not advertising or other mass media men are employed, their approach comes to dominate. In other words, emotive catch-phrases and reiterated slogans or assertions count most in the public arena. The trouble is not so much that or-dinary voters – who do not and cannot rule – think in these terms, but that the political professionals come to do so as well.

There is also the problem of product quality. The attitudes and abilities that make for a good candidate are not necessarily those of a good MP; and a good MP is not necessarily a good minister. Above all, there is the danger that the political process may repel men who could make a success of anything else. In view of all these problems, Schumpter was among the many writers who were sure that poli-ticians could not run the economy – from which he did *not* draw the conclusion that socialism was impossible, for reasons to be discussed later.

Other defects have emerged from the subsequent work on the com-petitive model. There is the possible oppression of a minority by a bare majority, or of the majority by a coalition of minorities with strong views on particular issues. Special interest groups are likely to prevail over more general interests, because of the concentration of the former and the dispersion of the latter. The beneficial impact of any one protectionist or restrictionist measure on an individual via his professional or geographical interest is far greater than any loss he may bear along with fifty or sixty million other citizens.

Pressure group politics of the old-fashioned logrolling type (as dis-tinct from withdrawing an essential service from the market place and using coercion to keep out substitute supplies) is, however, unlikely to be fatal to the success of democracy. Casual historical observation suggests that democracies can carry on almost indefinitely subsidizing prestige high-technology activities such as aerospace, protecting inefficient farmers, imposing tariffs and quotas, encouraging union restrictive practices, rigging interest rates for favoured groups, 'supporting' key prices – from air or cab fares to beef and beetroot – preserving monopoly rights for state industries and carrying out hosts of similar welfare-reducing actions, without producing catastrophic results or even preventing a considerable advance in living standards.

Excessive Expectations

Schumpeter's own criterion for the success of a political system was fairly modest. By success he did not mean achieving an ideal, optimum performance or anything of that kind, but simply a political system that could reproduce itself without creating conditions that led to resort to undemocratic methods, or – which he took to be equivalent – that all major interests would in the long run abide by the results of the democratic process.

He himself was non-committal on democracy's prospects. But his own analysis provides plenty of grounds for expecting a trend towards excessive expectations, which could prove fatal. Unlike his more formal successors who have elaborated on his competitive model, he did not hesitate to draw on the analysis of crowd psychology. People in a crowd are apt to exhibit a reduced sense of responsibility and a lower level of energy and thought than the same individuals in their private or business life. A crowd need not mean a screaming mob in a sultry city. It can just as easily be a television audience, or an electorate, or a committee of generals in their sixties. Even supposedly individual demands are not the outcome of rational deliberation about the best means of satisfying inherent desires but can be artificially generated by advertising or propaganda.

These anti-rational or non-rational influences are less important in personal, business or professional life than in political behaviour. Frequently repeated experience in everyday life, as well as personal responsibility, exert a rationalising influence. The picture of the prettiest girl that ever lived will in the long run prove powerless to maintain the sales of a bad cigarette. Failure to take this on board accounts for the vast overemphasis by Galbraith on the powers of a large firm to manipulate consumer demand.

The rationalising influence of personal experience can be extended to hobbies, relations with friends, the affairs of a small township or a small social group. It might also influence views on public policy where personal pecuniary matters are at stake. But here the influence acts mainly in favour of influencing short-run rationality and short-run aims. Schumpeter's most telling comparison is that of the attitude of the lawyer to his brief with the same lawyer's attitude to political statements in his newspaper. In the first instance he has not only the competence, but also the stimulus, to master the material. In the latter he is 'not all there' morally or intellectually. Without the pressures that come from personal responsibility, masses of information and education will not help, and he 'will not apply the canons of criticism he knows so well how to handle' in his own sphere. For most people the great political issues are 'sub-hobbies' to which they devote less attention than to bridge; and there is little check either on dark urges or on bursts of general indignation.

The more modern 'economic' analysis of rational political behaviour also leads to the conclusion that it is irrational to be rational, because of the information and other costs involved. This is highlighted by the problem of the *voting paradox*, that is the problem of finding a self-interested motive for voting when the probability of any one vote determining the outcome is vanishingly small. Its importance is not the literal one of explaining why most electors vote. The cost of so doing is extremely small; and a sense of public duty, emotional satisfaction or a blown-up sense of self-importance can be called in aid. The validity of the phenomenon to which it refers can be seen by the way in which the slightest increase in the cost of voting influences the turnout. A US presidential commission, for example, called in aid such extremely simple practices as voting on a Sunday to explain part of the difference between turnouts of 80–92 per cent in German and Italian national elections and US presidential turnouts of little more than 60 per cent. In the United Kingdom, Labour party leaders, who face the greatest risk of abstention, have been known to protest against the possible appearance on polling night of popular television serials.

The main point is that, if a self-interested citizen has little or no incentive to vote, he has even less to make a detailed study of facts, controversies and policies. Any short cut, such as taking on trust views of the party one generally supports, or going by television impressions, will be quite rationally undertaken to avoid time-consuming study, which would in any case hardly be feasible over more than a very tiny range. Given the likely extent of individual influence, it is perfectly reasonable to regard political programmes as show business, to be watched only if they are entertaining.

Nor is such reasoning applicable just to non-political citizens. An individual MP has such a small chance of influencing his party's policy that it is rational for him to use short-cut methods, such as following a particular leader or faction within his party, on all except a handful of issues of which he has made a speciality. It is on these lines that one can best explain the role of stereotyped packages of ideas or ideologies. A politician, civil servant or academic who has neither the time nor the incentive to study every subject in depth can reasonably ask: 'From what stable does this particular idea come?' It may be better than going by pure hunch.

These considerations would not themselves be a threat to democracy if they simply led to the wrong result in particular elections or in particular policy decisions. The basic trouble is *the lack of a budget constraint among voters*. This means that errors are biased in a particular direction. In their own private lives, people know that more of one thing means less of something else, on a given income and capital. They know that they can improve the tradeoffs, such as that between take-home pay and leisure, by a careful choice of residence. But they also know that such improvements are not unlimited and cost effort to find. In the absence of such knowledge in the political sphere, electorates tend to expect too much from government action at too little cost, e.g. a painless improvement in economic growth or reduction in inflation, and they tend both to praise and blame governments for things which are largely outside their control. The impetus to consistency, without the discipline and responsibility of personal experience, is not strong.

The temptation to encourage false expectations among the electorate becomes overwhelming to politicians. The opposition parties are bound to promise to do better and the government party must join in the auction – explaining away the past and outbidding its rivals for the future, whether by general hints or detailed promises. Voters may indeed be cynical about promises. Yet citizens' demands for government action and their attribution to it of responsibility for their own or the nation's past performance are altogether excessive.

The analogy with commercial advertisements, which promise to fulfil all our daydreams if we buy 'getaway' petrol or the right type of underwear, is inescapable; the difference is the absence of the immediate and personal corrective experience. The elector cannot compare experimentally a wide range of different governments and policies and examine their effects in isolation from other disturbing influences. Moreover, the normal competitive processes tend to bring to the top within each party leaders who genuinely believe that they can improve the tradeoffs more than is actually possible – usually by some form of minor improvement in machinery of administration. The obvious British examples were Harold Wilson and Edward Heath, both of whom attached disproportionate weight to Whitehall reorganisation, both in their initial plans while in opposition and in their first years of power. Such attitudes are perfectly compatible with a great deal of apparent tough talking but do not suit the sceptic or realist who actually knows the score.

The expectations that are relevant are not all the wants and demands that people make of life, but only those expectations that they expect the political process to underwrite. These expectations can be shown *ex ante* in positive if vaguely formulated demands, and *ex post* in the attribution of blame for events and developments. A report by the Survey Research Unit of the Social Science Research Council showed that 67 per cent of respondents felt in 1973 that their standard of living was below the one to which they were entitled. The average respondent felt that he was entitled to a standard of living 20 per cent more than he actually had. But there was a large spread round this average. The most modest aspirations were held by 'the rich, the very poor and the elderly'. Most other sections felt that they needed an extra £8 or £9 a week (in end-1973 pounds). The behaviour of politicians in the year subsequent to the survey showed that they were very sensitive to such aspirations. Although they called for 'sacrifices' on account of inflation and oil crises, they were extremely reluctant to take any measures that might reduce consumption. Indeed, the subsequent action of the Labour Government in freezing the rents of council tenants, from whom it expected to draw a large vote, and of the Conservatives in promising '$9\frac{1}{2}$ per cent mortgages' at a time of rapidly rising prices, showed that they were still in the game of whipping up expectations among different groups.

I am not pretending, of course, to offer a complete theory of political expectations, which are determined by innumerable forces apart from competitive vote-bidding. The spread of information about other people's life-styles through the media and advertising, so that they look like attainable ideals rather than fantasies, is frequently cited. The breakdown of traditional ideas of hierarchy, to be discussed below, is another obvious influence. It has also been suggested that expectations tend to be low during protracted periods of economic hardship, as they were in the depression of the 1930s; the gap between expectation and reality is greater during periods of prosperity and advance, and perhaps greatest of all when expectations are frustrated by a sudden and unexpected check to progress. The main point to stress is that democracy, viewed as a process of political competition, itself imparts a systematic upward bias to expectations and compounds the other influences at work.

Is it possible that the gap between expectations and performance will ultimately prove self-correcting as public credibility becomes eroded? There are certainly periods of masochistic reaction in which parties vie with each other in promising hard times ahead. The periodic revulsions towards 'sweat, toil and tears' are, however, no more rational than the conventional outbidding. Each person is concerned that others should bear their proper share of sacrifice and that 'less essential' activities should be cut down to size. It is still likely that, if we could add up the demands by different people for their own groups and their own favoured section of public expenditure, the result would far exceed the resources available.

It is interesting, too, that moves away from excessive promises have so far taken the form only of hesitation about promising a larger cake. The outbidding continues on promises about distribution. Unfortunately, neither promises of redistribution from politicians nor demands for it from the electorate carry with them a knowledge of how much there is to redistribute, let alone a consensus on a just distribution.

The elector tends, because he has no yardstick in his everyday life against which to measure consistency, to favour all worthy objects at the same time: more of the national income for the old and sick, the lower paid, the skilled craftsman, for those doing important professional work, the mortgagee, the ratepayer and so on. The one group that people always think too well paid are the politicians, from whom omnipotence and omniscience are expected.

Nor are distribution and growth *per se* the only spheres in which excessive demands are made from the political process. The US administration is expected to prevent pollution without increasing transportation or energy costs, to protect forests and lower timber prices – and in general to protect the environment – without paying any obvious price. What has gone is the tacit belief in limiting the role of political decision: and this is likely to put a burden on democratic procedures which they are not designed to bear. The usefulness of inflationary finance as a short-term method of postponing political choice between incompatible objectives has long been known. By running a budget deficit, financed by excess money creation and rationalised by some fashionable economic theory, government is able for a time to increase some expenditures without curtailing others or increasing taxes overtly. (The citizen of course pays through the 'tax' that inflation levies on the value of his nominal income and monetary assets.) But enormously important though it may be, inflation is but a particular case of the consequences of inconsistent expectations and demands.

The Rivalry of Coercive Groups

It has already been suggested that the pursuit of group self interest through coercive means in the market place is a much more serious threat to democracy than the traditional logrolling among legislators and ministers. The most obvious form of this is the conflict of different groups of trade unionists − ostensibly with the government or employers, but in reality with each other − for shares of the national product. This rivalry induces more and more sections of the population, including those who have previously relied on individualistic efforts, into militant trade unionist attitudes in self-defence.

The direct effect of unions is not, as is popularly believed, to cause a continuing inflation. This cannot happen without an accompanying expansion of monetary demand. The contribution of unions to inflation is indirect. First, if a sufficient number of trade unionists make *increased* use of their monopoly power, this leads to a loss of jobs for their members, and also for other people, to the extent that more purchasing power is absorbed in the purchase of the output of the strongly unionised sector. As those displaced will be slow to accept reduced real wages or to price themselves into other (and in their eyes inferior) jobs, the net result will be an increase in the unemployment total. Inflation comes into the picture when governments expand the money supply and increase their budget deficits in an attempt to mop up the unemployment by pushing more spending money into the economy. But this by its nature can be, at best, of only temporary assistance. For unless the stronger unions are indefinitely fooled by the 'money illusion', they will demand and receive further wage increases to restore the differentials that their original settlements were intended to achieve. This in turn will threaten unemployment and tempt or force governments into a further expansion of monetary demand and a repetition of the earlier process. As the spiral proceeds, the result is not inflation, but accelerating inflation. In the last analysis the authorities have to choose between accepting an indefinite increase in the rate of inflation and abandoning full employment to the extent necessary to break the collective wage-push power of the unions.

Even in the absence of such a politico-economic spiral, there is a second way in which the unions can make the control of inflation prohibitively difficult. Let us assume that the rate of inflation has reached, for reasons unconnected with the unions, a level that has become politically, socially and commercially intolerable. To move to a lower rate will require a slowdown in the growth of spending brought about through tighter fiscal and monetary policies. How far and how soon this slowdown is reflected in smaller rises in money incomes and prices, and how far it is wasted in increased unemployment, will depend on the extent to which unions resist the forces of the labour market and price their members out of jobs.

Union monopolies differ in an important way from other organised groups. A business monopoly, or cartel with market power, will hold its output below competitive levels for the sake of higher prices. A farmers' association will try to achieve the same effect by political lobbying. But none of these will normally withdraw output from the market until representatives of the public sign an agreement to pay more. This is a quasi-political power or threat, different in many ways from the textbook monopoly. Of course, there have been collective boycotts and even a resort to violence in business history, especially in the United States in the late nineteenth century, but nothing as extended in scale or as pervasive throughout the economy as the effects of union power in the context of a commitment to full employment.

The conventional answer is that a voluntary or statutory 'incomes policy' could modify collective bargaining enough to prevent governments from being faced with such impossible choices. Now even if a long-term statutory incomes policy could resolve this dilemma, it is unenforceable for any extended period if democracy is to remain 'liberal' and violent means of coercion are not to be employed on dissenting groups. (Indeed, if public opinion is in this sense 'liberal', then it is unenforceable so long as democracy of any sort prevails.) Thus the only sort of incomes policy that could help would be a voluntary one, or at least a statutory one that enjoyed the 'full-hearted consent' of those affected by it. Apart from brief emergency freezes, the main problem posed by such a policy is one of relativities, as every schoolboy knows.

Agreement on such relativities is extremely unlikely on any self interested basis. The basic difficulty is that the benefits from restraint in the use of group market power are 'public goods'. They consist of things such as price stability, fuller employment or faster economic growth, which are thinly diffused among the whole population, while the costs are incurred by the group that exercises restraint. It is therefore in the interest of each union group that other unions should show restraint while it exploits its own monopoly power to the full. For it is clear to any particular union leader that most of the gains from price stability and fuller employment spill over to members of other unions and the general public, while the costs of settling for less than he could obtain are highly concentrated among his own members. The chances that an example of restraint by one will be followed by others is so small that his best bet is to pursue his members' own interests. If the leadership of a union is prepared to look beyond the (fairly short-term) self-interest of its own members, it is likely eventually to be thrown out of office. One does not have to look for 'reds under the bed'. The 'militant moderates' will do the job; and rationally so from the members' point of view.

It is uncertain whether the unions are unique in the role they exercise. A possible comparison is the fivefold increase in the oil price made by the OPEC countries in 1973–4. If this was a once-for-all event, the analogy does not hold. For however severe the initial disruption, it could not push the world monetary authorities into policies of continuously accelerating inflation. If, on the other hand, there are going to be further attempts by producers to raise the price of oil (relative to other commodities) by withholding supplies, or if similar cartels are to be formed among other primary producers, and if in turn industrial workers are going to strike in an attempt to preserve their relative share of world income, then the analogy will hold and the problem becomes the wider one of the explosive potentialities of certain means of pursuing group interest. On present evidence, however, the problem focuses on union power in an environment of high labour demand.

Indeed, the difficulties that unions pose for anti-inflationary policy are but the surface manifestations of a much more fundamental threat posed by the rivalry of coercive groups; that is, that they are likely to have non-negotiable demands for more than a country's whole output. Such demands risk straining to breaking point the 'sharing out' function of democratic society. The paradox that the freedom of individuals to form associations can itself threaten individual freedom was noted by A. V. Dicey as early as 1905. What is true for freedom, is also true in the economic field. While the individual pursuit of self-interest within a framework of rules and conventions is compatible with the successful functioning of a market economy, the group pursuit of self-interest may be inherently unstable. Even if the government could in the circumstances still pursue a non-inflationary monetary policy, the conflicts and instability would still be there. Indeed, a non-inflationary policy would bring them more quickly into the open, which is one reason why it is so rarely pursued.

It is sometimes asserted that the explosive potentialities from the collective pursuit of self-interest are due to the new vulnerability of a modern economy to group action which did not previously exist. But it is often forgotten that as long ago as 17 July 1914 Lloyd George declared that, if the threats of the Irish Rebellion and the Triple Industrial Alliance were to materialise, 'the situation will be the gravest with which any government has had to deal for centuries'. Ernest Bevin subsequently said of these events: 'It was a period which, if the war had not broken out, would have, I believe, seen one of the greatest revolts the world would ever have seen.'

The Vanishing Heritage

The mention of earlier alarms brings us to one of the main problems facing the analysis so far presented. This is why the tensions endemic to democracy did not emerge much earlier than they have. We have no lack of warnings about the self-destructive tendencies of democracy dating back well into the nineteenth century. Bagehot's Introduction to the second edition of *The English Constitution*, written after the 1867 Reform Bill, is full of gloomy forebodings about the effects of enfranchising an ignorant and greedy electorate, and full of fury with Disraeli for having sold the pass. While preparing this essay, I came across a remarkable address given by the historian J. A. Froude to the 'Liberty and Property Defence League' in 1887. Some of the passages could have been reproduced without alteration in the political and fiscal debates of recent years.

Writing in the aftermath of the Third Reform Bill, Froude warned:

> It is one man one vote. And as the poor and the ignorant are the majority, I think it is perfectly certain – and it is only consistent with all one has ever heard or read of human nature – that those who have the power will use it to bring about what they consider to be a more equitable distribution of the good things of this world.

Some egalitarians will claim that this quotation gives the game away and that all the doom-mongering from Bagehot and Froude down to the present day simply reflects the fear of the rich and the powerful that they will lose their favoured position. The attribution of a motive does not, however, make the content of the warnings groundless. If 'a more equitable division' were an unproblematic and costless operation, we could afford to dismiss the warnings. But there are both historical and logical reasons for agreeing with Froude, that the result of attempts to bring about such a division has always been and always will be: 'factions and quarrels, confiscation and civil disturbances, and the convulsions of war . . . and finally an end to liberty'.

A good insight into the forces by which liberal democracy has so far protected itself against the tensions proclaimed by the doom-mongers can be obtained by going back to Schumpeter and re-examining some of the conditions he set for the effective working of the system. The most important was that *'the effective range of political decision should not be extended too far'*. Most issues are too complex to be decided by a competitive vote-seeking process. Although Parliament may vote on such issues and ministers may introduce legislation, their actions are purely formal, as the real decisions will have been made elsewhere. This applies not only to issues such as the permissible size of the Budget deficit or official operations in the foreign exchange market but to as fundamental a matter as the criminal code, which would otherwise be at the mercy of alternating fits of vindictiveness and sentimentality.

Schumpeter makes a very firm distinction between extending the area of state authority and extending the area of political decision. The former can be done by means of agencies whose heads are not appointed by competition for votes and who do not have to please the electorate in any direct or immediate sense. Apart from the permanent civil service, there are many special agencies whose non-political nature is constantly stressed both by themselves and by the government of the day. Perhaps the most interesting historical example is the pre-1914 Bank of England which made key economic policy decisions at its own discretion. There are numerous regulatory agencies in the United States which, if they are influenced by anyone, are influenced by the industries they are supposed to regulate. In Britain we have long had experience of organisations such as the BBC, the University Grants Committee and the Morrisonian public corporation. It is no coincidence that bodies such as the Prices and Incomes Board, the Pay and Prices Board and *ad hoc* committees presided over by judges have been used to extend state control into the most sensitive areas of economic life.

Another vital condition put forward by Schumpeter for the success of a competitive vote-bidding system was *tolerance and democratic self-control*. All groups must be willing to accept legislation on the statute book. Political warfare must be kept within certain limits; and this involves the Cabinet and shadow cabinet being followed by their supporters and not being pushed from behind. Political action is to be left to politicians without too much back-seat driving, let alone direct action. We cannot expect to see these conditions met unless the main interests are agreed on the broad structure of society. If the electorate is divided into two or more deeply hostile camps, or there are rival ideals on which no compromise is possible, these restraints will cease to function and democracy may wither.

A further requirement was *the existence of a well-trained bureaucracy* – not the powerless eunuch of constitutional mythology, but a group with their own principles not merely of procedure, but in a more subtle sense of policy as well, deciding on their own promotions and enjoying security of tenure. Many people would say that we have such a class, which has been responsible for our major postwar blunders and for preventing both Labour and Conservative governments from implementing distinctive policies of their own, and that this has led to a proliferation of ideas for introducing irregulars, outsiders, ministerial *cabinets*, 'think tanks' and so on, the results of which have been – to put it mildly – not spectacular.

The reason why an entrenched bureaucracy is so essential is precisely because politicians are professionals at dealing in votes but amateurs both in administration and in policy-making, with a strong tendency (already discussed) to take refuge in the world of the advertising slogan and the media headline; in other words, the alleged orthodoxy and lack of imagination of the bureaucrat is part of the price of having a democratic system at all.

But without the fulfilment of the earlier conditions – a limit on the area of political decision and a sufficient agreement on the broad structure of society to enable groups to accept legislation with which they disagree – such a professional bureaucracy will not function effectively and its morale and effectiveness will be undermined, as they manifestly have been in the United Kingdom since the mid-1960s. Evidence for the frustrations felt by senior civil servants is the plaintive demand frequently made in conversation (and hinted at in the Queen's Speech of March 1974) that certain officials should be assigned the job of advising the opposition, so that it does not come to office so ill-prepared. (One very prominent official not long ago observed privately that he would like to be on holiday for the first two years after every change of government!)

Mass electorates were able to accept the Schumpeter conditions of self-restraint for a surprisingly long period partly because they were slow to realise their power. The lack of incentives for the voter to inform himself has already been emphasised. There were also a series of *ad hoc* events such as the First World War, which produced an external threat and a patriotic myth to override sectional conflicts, and the Great Depression, which weakened the market power of the trade unions.

But just as important was an ethic, which took a long time to erode, which limited the demands on the sharing-out functions of the State. As Kristol has emphasised, personal success was seen by nineteenth-century defenders of capitalism as having a firm connection with 'duty performed'. In a society 'still permeated by a Puritan ethic', it

> was agreed that there was a strong correlation between certain personal virtues – frugality, industry, sobriety, reliability, piety – and the way in which power, privilege and property were distributed. And this correlation was taken to be the sign of a just society, not merely a free one. Samuel Smiles or Horatio Alger would have regarded Professor Hayek's writings [divorcing reward from merit] as slanderous of his fellow Christians, blasphemous of God, and ultimately subversive of the social order.

The point that Kristol does not bring out sufficiently is that the public morality of early capitalist bourgeois society was a transitional one. On its own grounds it could not hope to stand up to serious analysis. Luck was even then as important as merit in the gaining of awards, and merit was inherently a subjective concept in the eye of the beholder. Hayek is right not to base his defence of a market economy upon it. Early capitalist civilisation was living on the moral heritage of the feudal system under which each man had a superior to whom he owed obligations and from whom he received protection in a 'great chain of duties'. A medieval king was expected to 'do justice and to render each his due'. It was not a matter of what the king thought a subject ought to have, or what the subject thought best for himself, but what belonged to him according to custom, which in turn was supported by theological sanction.

For a long time capitalist civilisation was able to live on this feudal legacy, and the aura of legitimacy was transferred from the feudal lord to the employer, from the medieval hierarchy of position to that derived from the luck of the market place. But this feudal legacy was bound to be extinguished by the torchlight of secular and rationalistic inquiry, which was itself so closely associated with the rise of capitalism. The personal qualities of the middle-class leaders did not help to kindle that affection for the social order that is probably necessary if it is not to be blamed for the inevitable tribulations and disappointments of most people's lives. Modern politicians and business chiefs lack the glamour of an aristocracy. With neither the trappings of tradition nor the heroic qualities of great war leaders or generals, they cannot excite the identification or hero worship that previously reconciled people to much greater differences of wealth and position than exist today. Moreover, the 'fairer' the process of selection, the less the governing classes are differentiated by special clothes or accents, the more they will be resented. At most they are tolerated on the strict condition that they bring results; and we have seen that expectations here tend to be excessive.

Schumpeter himself had some half-hearted hopes that the degree of institutional consensus and agreement on fundamentals required for the working of democracy might be restored under 'socialism'. For one thing, the issue of capitalism versus socialism would be out of the way, and there would be no more argument about profits, dividends, private ownership of capital or gains from rising land values. Moreover, the twentieth-century development of non-political agencies made socialism possible and perhaps compatible with democracy. By 'socialism' he had in mind the old-fashioned definition of collective control over the means of production – roughly the 'Clause 4' conception. But the condition of success was that democratic politics was *not* extended to economic affairs. Beyond setting the rules in the most general way possible, it was essential that politicians resist the temptation to interfere with the activities of the managers of state enterprises and regulatory boards. (He had in mind a form of market socialism.) Indeed, Schumpeter remarked that at long last managers would be able to do their jobs without guilt feelings and with more freedom not only from interfering politicians but also from fussing committees of consumers, demands for workers' control and all other demands for 'participation'.

We do not, however, need to follow out these paradoxes, because the type of collectivism now in vogue among all parties concerns not only ownership of productive assets but also, and more important, relative incomes. The popular desire is to transfer from the private to the public sphere the determination of who gets how much; and to make this determination not on the basis of market values, nor on egalitarian principles, nor some compromise between them, but by a revival of the medieval notion of the just wage – a doctrine sometimes miscalled 'fairness'. This is to be done, moreover, without benefit of the feudal relationships and scholastic theology which enabled an earlier age to attach a meaning to such concepts.

It is hardly conceivable that anything as sensitive as the determination of relative awards will be left to bodies enjoying the degree of autonomy of the pre-1914 Bank of England or the nationalised industries before their finances and freedom were undermined by prices and incomes policy. Reference has already been made to bodies such as the Pay Board which may occasionally provide politicians with a useful fig leaf. But if pre-tax incomes are to be determined, or even heavily influenced, by state authority, elected politicians will want – quite rightly – to have the last word; and their decisions are bound to figure prominently in the competitive struggle for votes – again rightly so. Thus currently fashionable doctrines, so far from providing a solvent for the tensions of democracy, seem likely to make them worse.

The Argument So Far

It might at this stage be worth giving a provisional summary of the argument of this chapter. Democratic political practice is best regarded neither as a method of popular participation in government nor as a means of putting into effect the people's will, but mainly as a competition for power by means of votes among competing teams. But, even when viewed in this relatively unambitious light, it is subject to endemic and growing weaknesses. The two principal ones analysed in the preceding pages are the generation of excessive expectations among voters by the processes of political competition and the disruptive effects arising from the pursuit of self-interest by rival coercive groups. These weaknesses have become more important than they were before because of the lack of any widely shared belief in the legitimacy of the present order, which might have held them in check. Nor, on the other hand, is there any commonly held conception of any feasible alternative social order in which democracy might operate in the future.

The diagnosis, if true, has grave consequences not only for democracy and freedom of action but also for intellectual freedom and freedom of speech. This was originally defended by its great expositors from Milton to Mill as a means towards the discovery of truth. But let us suppose, in line with much modern thinking, that there is no absolute truth on fundamentals of morals and politics or, if there is, that it cannot easily be found. A free society will then produce, in de Jouvenel's words, not a convergence but a divergence with 'less and less agreement on the general rules of social life, with each sect seeking to make its respective principles the criterion'.

If the divergences are strongly felt and far-reaching, de Jouvenel points to three consequences that will follow. First, the laws must be tightly enforced to prevent society tearing itself apart. To do this requires a repressive force since citizens are not united by any belief, not even belief in legality. But, secondly, 'laws which are at stake in embittered public conflicts do not inspire much respect, even among those who execute them.' It would, therefore, be tempting to entrust the making of laws to some authority outside the public arena. Even this, however, would not be enough. For 'institutions cannot maintain themselves in being forever without consent.' The third temptation would, therefore, be to strike at disorder at its source, and for the rulers to do their best to prevent the dispersion and clash of opinion — e.g. expel Solzhenitsyn from the polity — thereby reducing the need to rely on police repression.

It is by such reasoning that de Jouvenel convincingly explains the link between Hobbes's extreme individualism — in which no one desire can be regarded as higher or better than any other — and his ultimate authoritarianism. But any number of other big names have traced in only slightly differing forms the path from extreme individualism to the extinction of freedom. There was Dostoevsky's parable of the grand inquisitor, or Rousseau's insistence on silence on the part of philosophers in his ideal democratic society.

The Mirage of Social Justice

It should by this time be obvious that a resolution of the problems of liberal democracy is unlikely on a basis relying entirely on self-interest or private interest (which need not be selfish in the vulgar sense). Can any other motives be brought in which would both make members of economic groups refrain from exercising their full market power and induce electors to reduce the excessive and incompatible demands they make on government services? Is it possible to create or evolve a consensus, so far missing, on a legitimate social order which would appeal to people's sense of justice and persuade them to moderate their pursuit of private interest, both in the ballot box and in their other collective activities?

The problems discussed would clearly be a good deal easier if there was some consensus on how goods, status and power should be shared out. The common view that the basis of consent at present missing could be supplied by the pursuit of 'social justice' or 'fairness' is in all probability fallacious. At its most primitive level such thinking assumes that 'social justice' and 'fairness' are natural qualities such as redness or hardness, which are either present or not. Some more sophisticated exponents of this approach realise that subjective nature of such concepts and try to seek a *de facto* consensus. But there is in fact little agreement on what *ought* to determine relative income levels, let alone wider matters of power, opportunity, prestige or influence. As a leading sociologist, John Goldthorpe, has written, 'Given the diversity of moral positions that are tenable in the existing state of public opinion, virtually any occupational group seeking a pay increase is likely to be able to find some legitimization for pressing its case.' Hence the proliferation of incompatible criteria: rewarding skill, overcoming labour shortages, helping the lower paid, preserving traditional differentials and so on.

There are two logically tenable ways of looking at the distribution of resources. One is to envisage a pie, to be divided up by a central authority. From this point of view, the natural principle of division is equality and departures from it have to be justified. The other is to emphasize that, in Nozick's words,

> we are not in the position of children who have been given some portions of pie .... There is no central distribution. What each person gets, he gets from others who give it to him in exchange for something, or as a gift. In a free society, diverse persons control different resources, and new holdings arise out of the voluntary exchange and actions of persons .... The total result is the product of many individual decisions.

Provided that the initial holdings were justly acquired, there can be no question of social injustice or wrongful distribution – although there may still be a desire to help the worst off for humanitarian reasons.

The two approaches may be called the entitlement theory and the pie theory. The weakness of the entitlement theory is that the very content of property rights and the rules governing their transfer, as well as their physical protection, are the results of collectively enforced rules and decisins, which we are at liberty to change. As Froude put it, 'Without the State there would be no such thing as property. The State guarantees to each individual what he has earned ... and fixes the conditions on which this protection will be granted.' The weakness of the pie theory is that there is no fixed sum to go round, that individuals add to the pie by their activities (the success of which may be very imperfectly correlated with effort, let alone merit) and that it is by no means obvious that others should treat the results as part of a common pool. Both theories have elements of validity, but there is no obvious compromise between them that is likely to be cither logically or emotionally satisfying.

The equality suggested by the pie theory is, of course, notoriously difficult to define. Is it to be equality in relation to individuals or families, or needs? Is someone with greater capacity for happiness to be given more, as in some versions of utilitarianism, or less, to compensate for his inborne advantage? The complications are endless; and they are multiplied enormously once we abandon absolutes and talk about 'more equality' or 'less equality'. The essential point has however been well stated by de Jouvenel: 'Every allocation of reward [that is founded] on equality under a certain aspect, will be hierarchical and contrary to equality under another aspect.'

Most popular discussions of relativities, 'national job evaluation' and similar notions are based on neither the pie nor the entitlement theory but on the very slippery idea of reward according to moral merit. The argument against this has been well stated by Hayek, who points out that, even if all inherited wealth or differences in educational opportunity could be abolished, there would still be no inherent moral value attaching to the resulting distribution of income and wealth:

> The inborn as well as the acquired gifts of a person clearly have a value to his fellows which does not depend on any credit due to him for possessing them. There is little a man can do to alter the fact that his special talents are very common or exceedingly rare. A good mind or a fine voice, a beautiful face or a skilful hand, a ready wit or an attractive personality are in a large measure as independent of a person's efforts as the opportunities or experiences he has had. In all these instances the value which a person's capacities or services have for us and for which he is recompensed has little relation to anything that we can call moral merit or deserts.

Hayek argues that no man possesses the ability to determine conclusively the merits of another. To assess merit presupposes that a man has acted in accordance with some accepted rule of conduct and that someone else can judge how much effort and pain this has cost him. Often, of course, a highly meritorious attempt may be a complete failure, while a valuable human achievement will be due to luck or favourable circumstances. To decide on merit 'presupposes that we can judge whether people have made such use of their opportunities as they ought to have made, and how much effort of will or self-denial it had cost them and how much of their achievement is due to circumstances'. This is impossible in a free society or probably at all. (Moreover, only a fanatical ascetic would wish to encourage a maximum of merit in this sense. It is more rational for people 'to achieve a maximum of usefulness at a minimum of pain and sacrifice and therefore a minimum of merit.')

Indeed, it is one of the advantages of a market economy enjoying basic bourgeois liberties that a man's livelihood does not depend on other people's valuation of his merit. It is sufficient that he should be able to perform some work or sell a service for which there is a demand. Hayek concedes that as an organisation grows larger it will become inevitable that ascertainable merit in the eyes of managers (or some conventional seniority structure) should determine rewards. But so long as there is no one single organisation with a comprehensive scale of merit, but a multiplicity of competing organisations with different practices (as well as smaller organisations and a self-employed sector), an individual still has a wide degree of freedom of choice.

Hayek is, however, wrong to suppose that all policies for redistribution of income and wealth inevitably involve assessing merit, measuring need or aiming to achieve equality of reward – whatever the latter would mean. There is another position. This is to accept the rankings of the actual or a reformed market but to use fiscal means to narrow differentials so that the game is played for smaller stakes. What is then needed is a view on the *general shape* of a tolerable distribution which does not involve a moralistic evaluation of any person or occupation.

One of the interests of Professor John Rawls's theory of justice is that, although he agrees with Hayek that reward based on supposed merit is neither desirable nor feasible, he nevertheless believes that the concept of social justice can be given a definite meaning. Rawls attempts to introduce an element of impartiality into the assessment of distribution by means of the 'veil of ignorance'. The idea is to work out the principles on which 'free and rational persons concerned to further their own interests' would desire their community to be run if they did not know their own social or economic place, the market value of their own talents and many other key features of their real situation. A wealthy man might like to establish principles that minimise taxes for welfare purposes; a poor man might espouse principles of an opposite kind. If one excludes knowledge of one's own actual situation, there is some chance of working out the principles on a disinterested basis.

The Rawls theory is the most ambitious and serious modern attempt to construct a theory of social justice which attempts neither to assess merit nor to aim at complete equality but nevertheless seeks to provide criteria for state action in the field of income distribution and elsewhere. The 'maximin' principle, in which inequalities are justified if and only if they are to the advantage of the least well off, is at bottom a sophisticated version of the pie theory designed to take into account the effects of slicing on the size of the pie.

Yet, at least according to my reading of the critical literature, it has not succeeded. The basic flaw in the argument is the belief that a thought process under the 'veil of ignorance' must yield a unique result, and the consequent attempt to erect a dubious system of orderings and priorities which has kept the academic industry fully employed, if not 'overheated'. The 'veil of ignorance' is a very useful device for narrowing the range of disagreement, despite the imaginative leap required; but it cannot eliminate differences in subjective preferences. The varying hypothetical distributions which different people would support under the 'veil of ignorance' would reveal differences in attitudes to uncertainty. Someone with a taste for gambling would be interested in seeing that there were some really big incomes, just in case he came out lucky. One might hazard the guess that, if they were ignorant of their own position in the income distribution, most people would be concerned to 'level up' at the bottom so that there was no longer a depressed minority to which they might be consigned. Attitudes would, however, still differ a great deal towards the number and height of the summits at the upper end of the income distributions. Rawls himself agrees that, even if his principles are accepted, there is much room for disagreement about the range of social and economic inequalities which they actually justify.

Apart from the purely logical difficulties, it is doubtful if the Rawls scheme would ever have much popular appeal. A criticism that would probably be echoed by non-philosophers and non-economists, if they were following the discussion at all, is that, starting off as it does from calculations of rational self-interest, the Rawls theory contains very little 'justice' in the sense in which that word is normally used. Irving Kristol has pointed to the huge gap between Hayek's concept of a 'free society', in which we do not claim that position and reward depend on merit or work, and the traditional defences of capitalism, which asserted that they did. But the contrast is equally great with a social democracy of the Rawls type based purely on what 'free and rational persons' might contract to do in their own self-interest.

Thus, if it is true that people do have, as Kristol argues, an emotional yearning for some quasi-theological justification for differences in position, power or well-being; if the rational arguments for accepting a system that does not aim at complete distributive justice are too abstract or sophisticated to command assent; and if there is an emotional void that cannot be met merely by rising incomes and humanitarian redistribution unrelated to 'merit', then the outlook for liberal democracy is a poor one.

Further Perspectives

One obvious gap in the preceding pages has been any specific scenario by which liberal democracy might disappear; and I have deliberately avoided discussing questions such as: 'Could the army become a political agency?' or 'What form might a middle-class revolt take?' The view that the present situation is unsustainable does not itself imply anything about the process of change or the nature of any new system.

There is no need to suppose that there will be an overnight coup; there could be a gradual process of disintegration of traditional political authority and the growth of new sources of power. Indeed, a continuation of present trends might lead to a situation where nothing remained of liberal democracy but its label. Nor need we assume that a new system will be repressive but efficient. It is just as easy to imagine a combination of pockets of anarchy combined with petty despotism, in which many of the amenities of life and the rule of law are absent, but in which there are many things which we will be prevented from doing or saying. Nor can we say whether the union problem will be tackled by right-wing authoritarian measures or by the unions themselves becoming the agents of repression in a People's Democracy. Let us not forget too that authoritarian regimes have their own weaknesses — above all those arising from the lack of effective criticism; and nothing that has been said in this paper implies that they will provide a stable solution. Above all, diagnosis is not historical prophecy. My conjecture about democracy could be forestalled by events or by preventive action. This is, after all, the point of making it.

To point to weaknesses, tensions and dangers does not mean that we must succumb to them.

It would be presumptious to add a 'blueprint for salvation' as a tailpiece or afterthought. In any case, the key to a more hopeful future lies in understanding rather than in blueprints. The most popular nostrum in the United Kingdom at the time of writing is a coalition or 'government of national unity'. Its advantage would be that it might do something about the generation of excessive expectations. If the leaders of the main parties shared responsibility, it would be difficult to pretend that all national difficulties sprang from the 'other side' being in power and that all would be well if there were a change of government. Those outside the coalition would be more likely to represent fundamentally different policies; and there would be no need for mainstream politicians to denigrate everything that goes on in the country for the half of the time that they are not in power.

The big disadvantage of a coalition is that it would tend to represent the conventional wisdom and wishful thinking of the hour, which would be even more difficult to displace than it is at present. Moreover,

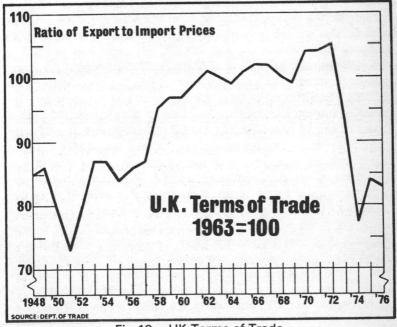

Fig 19. UK Terms of Trade

the process of outbidding could be eventually started up again by outside 'extremists', and disillusionment against all conventional
politicians could eventually increase further. But there are occasions
when it is worth buying time, and I would stick to the judgement I
made in 1968 that 'an experimental interval of coalition would be
desirable'. Some of the same considerations apply to a minority
government depending on a (perhaps shifting) House of Commons
coalition. The advantage of such an experiment do, however, depend
on it being fairly broadly based and would apply in much smaller
degree to a pure Con–Lib or Lab–Lib arrangement.

Nor, while on the subject of buying time, should one overlook the
possibility of a change of economic luck. A favourable combination of
events such as improved terms of trade, followed by good fortune from
North Sea oil, would provide a better climate for the 'sharing out'
functions of government than the last few years, in which expectations
of growth have suffered a nasty jolt and economic policy has looked
like a zero-sum game between different sections.

Yet it would be folly to depend on such once-for-all palliatives to do
more than postpone the tendency of liberal democracy to generate un-
fulfillable expectations or the tensions arising from the pursuit of group
self-interest. As the tensions spring from attitudes, it is in the realm of
attitudes that a more enduring solvent will have to be found. Even an
authoritarian government would be ultimately dependent on opinion,
although perhaps the opinion of fewer or different people. As David
Hume remarked, 'The governors have nothing to support them but
opinion. The Sultan of Egypt or the Emperor of Rome might drive his
harmless subjects like brute beasts, against their sentiments and inclination; but he must at least have led his mamelukes or praetorian
bands like men by their opinion.' It is, of course, not an easy matter to
say in complex societies whose opinion counts and to what extent.

There is one tempting blind alley to avoid. Some philosophic conservatives trace the source of the contemporary malaise to the abandonment of the belief in absolute values and look back with nostalgia
to the time when no one supposed that ordinary people were the best
judges of their own happiness but it was taken for granted that such
knowledge was available to a metaphysical, religious or political élite.
Now, even if this is true as a diagnosis, it offers little hope of cure. For
myths cannot hope to serve a social purpose if people know that they
are myths and seek to preserve them in a utilitarian spirit. If God does
not exist, He cannot be invented.

Many of our present tensions would become much less important in the unlikely event of a genuine revulsion against materialism or the 'consumer society'. Modern technology does make it possible to reduce the obsession with procuring ever more material products without having to submit to a life of ascetic poverty. It is unfortunate that the leadership among those who talk of an 'Alternative Society' should have been taken over by intolerant and envious political revolutionaries and that those most concerned with freedom, personal relations and the devising of new life styles for *themselves* should have lost ground. Perhaps the 'nice guys' who merely want to 'opt out' are bound to lose; but it would help if the forces of authority distinguished between the Angry Brigade and the left-wing student fascists on the one hand, and those primarily concerned to 'do their own thing' on the other.

Differences in status, because they lie in the eye of the beholder, are potentially both more disruptive and more emollient than material differences. If there is general agreement on what the top status positions are, combined with an intense desire to be at the top and a resentment of the way that it is recruited, then a great deal of tension can be predicted. By contrast, a society in which manual workers, professional and white-collar workers all regarded themselves as the true aristocrats would be good for people's self-respect. While not everyone can occupy the top income brackets, it would be possible for most people to value highly the activities that they themselves do; and the greater the range of human qualities that is admired, the less there need be feelings of inferiority. There is no exact or necessary correspondence between income or position in the productive process and either self-esteem or esteem in the eyes of others. But this is an area where opinion is all-important, and Marxists who insist on a one-dimensional model of satisfaction both help to make it true and increase the sum of human misery.

The ultimate sin of the politicians, the academics and the media has been their obsession with interpersonal and intergroup comparisons. This is seen in concepts such as 'relative deprivation' in sociology, 'inequality' (a loaded way of describing differences) and 'interdependent utilities' in economics, and 'equal freedom' in political philosophy. It is no use saying that resentment and envy of the possessions and achievements of others, and strong views about people's life-styles, simply exist whether the liberal individualist likes it or not. The attitudes in question are influenced by what is said and written; and the contribution of too many of our communicators is to focus all attention on relativities to the exclusion of absolutes. Moreover, their object in so doing is not to stir up personal rivalry and emulation, which add to the interests and joys, as well as the unhappiness, of life; it is to emphasise differences while asserting that they should not be there. The result is to reinforce the type of envious self-defeating attitudes revealed by the UK Survey Research Unit, in which 80 per cent of those questioned said they would rather receive an extra £4 a week in common with everyone else than receive an extra £5, if everyone else's income were to rise by the still higher sum of £6.

If comparisons are always with other people, and never with past achievements, the hope of progress is at an end; and what the pessimistic theologians have failed to do will have been achieved by the secular egalitarians. If we look at definite things, such as treatment of children, the level of nutrition, health, housing or consumption of the poorest, or the efficiency and humanity of the penal system, improvement is possible. In the realm of intangibles such as self-respect and regard for others, improvement is more difficult but can still be envisaged; and this also applies to the reduction of coercion in human affairs. But if all that matters is whether other people are better or worse off than oneself in these respects, then human history is a zero-sum game. Even if the principle of diminishing marginal utility is misapplied to assert that the gains of those who moved up are greater than the losses of those who move down, then all advance stops when equality has been reached; and, as has already been pointed out, the definition of that state is far from obvious and likely to cause extreme acrimony, with most people feeling that they have been treated less equally than others.

Quite apart from these conceptual difficulties, there is no reason to suppose that any target reduction in 'inequality' (or even in the share of property income) would supply a basis of consent to the social or economic structure. Indeed, the more that policy concentrates on eliminating disparities and differentials, the greater the sense of outrage likely to be engendered by those that remain. Moreover, the smaller the financial contrast between the mass of wage- and salary-earners and the wealthy minority, the greater the attention that is likely to be paid to relativities among workers. As it is, 90 per cent of consumer spending comes from wages, salaries and social security payments, and the annual wage round is to a large extent a contest between different groups of workers for relative shares. It is one of the defects of the present preoccupation with differentials, whether from a desire to establish an 'incomes policy' or from a wish to iron out 'inequality', that each group becomes much more keenly aware of what other groups are obtaining and more critical of the basis of comparison, which can always be made in more than one way; and this increases rather than diminishes the ferocity of the struggle.

The ideal of equality has had a noble role in human history. It has served to assert that all men and women are entitled to respect, and to rally people against oppression. But it has now turned sour. Liberal democracy will not be saved by detailed policy programmes which will soon be overtaken by events. It could yet be saved if contemporary egalitarianism were to lose its hold over the intelligentsia. But this will happen only if those who recognise it for the disease it has become are prepared to come out in the open and have uncongenial labels placed upon them.

References

Abrams, Mark, 'This Britain: A Contented Nation?', *New Society* (21 February 1974).

Bagehot, W., *The English Constitution*, with introduction by R. H. S. Crossman (Fontana edition, 1963).

Brittan, Samuel, *Left or Right: The Bogus Dilemma* (Secker and Warburg, 1968).

Brittan, Samuel, *Steering the Economy* (Penguin, 1971).

Butler, David and Stokes, Donald, *Political Change in Britain: Forces Shaping Electoral Choice* (Penguin, 1971 and subsequent editions).

Campbell, Angus, Converse, Philip E., Miller, Warren E. and Stokes, Donald E., *The American Voter* (Wiley, New York, 1960).

de Jouvenel, Bertrand, *Sovereignty* (Chicago: University of Chicago Press, 1957).

Dicey, A. V., *Law and Public Opinion in England* (Macmillan, 1963), pp. 152-8.

Froude, J. A., *Address to the Liberty and Property Defence League* (Liberty and Property Defence League, 1887).

Goldthorpe, John, 'Social Inequality and Social Integration in Modern Britain', in D. Wedderburn (ed.), *Poverty, Inequality and Class Structure* (Cambridge University Press, 1974).

Hayek, F. A., *The Constitution of Liberty* (Routledge, 1960).

Hayek, F. A., *The Mirage of Social Justice* (Routledge, 1976).

Hume, David, *Essay on the First Principles of Government* (oxford University Press, 1963).

Jay, Peter, *Wincott Memorial Lecture* (Institute of Economic Affairs, 1976).

Kristol, Irving, 'When Virtue Loses Her Loveliness' in Irving Kristol and Daniel Bell (eds), *Capitalism Today* (Mentor Books, New York, 1971).

Nozick, Robert, *Anarchy, State and Utopia* (Blackwell, Oxford, 1974).

'Psychological and Administrative Barriers to Voting', *Report of the President's Commission on Registration and Voting Partiipation*, Edward Dreyer and Walter A. Rosenbaum (eds), (US Government Printing Office, Washington, DC, 1963); reprinted in *Political Opinion and Electoral Behaviour: Essays and Studies* (Wadsworth, Belmont, California, 1966).

Rawls, John, *A Theory of Justice* (Clarendon Press, Oxford, 1972).

Runciman, W. G., *Relative Deprivation and Social Justice: a Study of Attitudes to Social Inequalities in Twentieth Century England* (Routledge, 1966).

Schumpeter, Joseph A., *Capitalism, Socialism and Democracy*, 4th edn (Allen & Unwin, 1952).

24 Inflation and Democracy (1977)

Inflation is a monetary disease. But this does not take us far without some further analysis of the forces which lie behind excessive injections of money into the economic system. It is doubtful if a completely general explanation, valid in all conditions, can be given. The aim of this chapter is to explore the links which may exist between the democratic form of government and inflationary policies. Some tentative reasons are given at the end for supposing that the present acute inflationary disorders may be transitional and could subside in time; but the underlying tensions of which they are symptoms will not necessarily subside and could express themselves in other, and even more unpleasant, forms. I have no illusions that I have been able to write in an entirely value-free manner, but the purpose of this chapter is diagnosis, not prescription. It should be obvious that the last thing I should favour is a preventive authoritarian regime. Quite apart from the cure being worse than the disease, a dictatorship can hardly be a remedy for contradictory policies which arise from the lack of checks on the aspirations of existing elected governments.

It will be helpful to set out first a few reasons why inflation may be tempting to a ruler pursuing his own interests without consitutional checks, before examining how the introduction of modern representative democracy affects the picture.

The Inflation Tax

Inflation has many aspects; but one thing which it is always and everywhere is a tax. At the very least it is a tax on holders of money. The revenue from the inflation tax is not unlimited. In the simple case when all money is issued by the government, and there is no economic growth, the value of the tax revenue from a continuing rate of inflation, to which everyone has adjusted, is equal to the inflation rate multiplied by the real value of outstanding money balances. (The existence of a fractional reserve banking system dilutes the gain to the government). As the rate of inflation increases, individuals and traders will hold a smaller and smaller fraction of their income in the form of cash balances. At the point where any further increase in the inflation rate is fully offset by a fall in the real value of cash balances, the revenue from inflation is at a maximum.

The revenue-maximizing rate of inflation clearly depends on how fast the demand for real cash balances falls off as inflation rises. This will vary according to the type of society, its state of development and its own monetary history. The range might vary according to estimates collected by Milton Friedman from 5 to 50 per cent. This might suggest a rationale for 'Latin American' rages of inflation; but it would also suggest that hyperinflation would not normally pay the rulers of a country, quite apart from the damage to trade and the risk of total destruction to the currency.

It is not, however, wise for the most selfish ruler to maximise the yield of the inflation tax in isolation from conventional taxes. For if there are limits to the share of its resources that a population will tolerate being taken for collective use, then the higher the inflation tax the greater will be the resistance to other forms of levy.

There is a further cost of inflationary finance that is rarely mentioned. Excess monetary expansion will yield inflationary revenue only to the extent that people can be induced to continue holding the currency in question despite the fact of its deterioration. There is no law of the universe saying that a particular currency must be used either for debt settlement or as a unit of account. People will withstand a surprising amount of debasement for the sake of dealing with the known and familiar. But, beyond some degree of debasement, citizens have to be forced to use their own currency by legal-tender laws and exchange control.

Temporary Gains

The discussion so far assumes a long-established and anticipated inflation to which all adjustments have long ago been made. Some of the largest 'gains' come, however, from the act of moving from one inflation rate to a higher one. One of the most important, as David Laidler has pointed out is the reduction in the real value, not merely of cash balances, but of fixed-interest government debt. This is a once-for-all, but permanent, effect. For even if nominal interest rates adjust to the new rate of inflation, holders of previously-issued government debt will never see their gains recouped. The trick can be tried a number of times, but not indefinitely. For if it is repeated too often the likelihood of a rising rate of inflation (i.e. an accelerating increase in the price level) will be reflected in the supply price of loanable funds.

Another governmental 'gain', known as fiscal drag, comes from taxes which are levied on nominal income. Realistically, there will always be some pressure to adjust thresholds and tax bands to inflation; and the revenue gain will depend on the adjustment lag. The latter is probably greatest when there is a sudden rise in inflation rate above that to which government and citizens have already been accustomed. Revenue gains, however, fall off and become negative once the erosion in the real value of direct taxes during the interval for collection exceeds the gains from fiscal drag. This is estimated to occur in Britain at present at about a 30 per cent inflation rate.

But there are many taxes whose real yield falls off with the rate of inflation. These include specific duties on goods, poll taxes and land taxes. Such imposts have historically been more important than income tax or even *ad valorem* indirect taxes; and there has probably been more strife and bloodshed arising from attempts to adjust such specific levies to the changed value of money than on any other fiscal issue. Conflicts have ranged from the Peasants' Revolt of the fourteenth century to the 1977 British parliamentary skirmishes over petrol duty.

But perhaps the most tempting, although ephemeral, benefit from inflating at above the long term revenue-maximising rate is simply the familiar time lag between the initial monetary expansion and its ultimate effects. Again, the more frequently rulers try to take advantage of time lags, the shorter the lags become. The specific exploitation of time lags in modern full-employment policies will be discussed below when we come to consider how democracy affects the tempation to inflate.

It will be noticed that many of the self-interested arguments for governments *not* attempting to obtain the maximum theoretical inflationary revenue, such as the adverse effect on the willingness of people to pay other taxes or to hold the national currency, are of a long-term nature. The arguments for inflating at above the ruler's steady-state optimum, such as the exploitation of time lags or the impoverishment of rentiers, are of a short-term or once-for-all nature. It follows from this that highly inflationary policies are characteristic-ally a response to stress, when the pressures on government are to finance a sudden increase in expenditure at all costs. The characteristic stress that led sovereigns to debase in the past was that of expensive wars.

The Role of Democracy

The discussion so far has implicitly regarded the rulers as a separate body from the mass of the population, with different and perhaps conflicting interests. Democracy, however, is supposed to reduce or eliminate this conflict. There are at least two different ways of looking at democracy. There is the classical ideal of 'government of the people by the people for the people'. There is the alternative interpretation, promulgated by Schumpeter in 1942, of democracy as a system whereby rulers are chosen by means of competitive bidding for people's votes. Politicians attempt to maximise votes just as businessmen attempt to maximise profits. (Elements of the idea can be found as far back as James Mill). On this interpretation the machinery for bringing about an identity of interest between rulers and ruled is akin to that of the invisible hand in the commercial market place; and, like the invisible hand, is subject to numerous imperfections and distortions.

The Schumpeter vote-bidding approach is more realistic for the purposes of this chapter. Just as the theory of business competition can be adapted to deal with modified objectives, such as growth subject to a profit constraint, so voting theory can be modified to take in – for instance – ideological objectives subject to a vote constraint.

At first glance, a democratic system ought to be less inflationary than other systems. For it is no longer a question of attempting to extract the last ounce of revenue from an unwilling population by force or trickery. Public expenditure is now supposed to express popular wishes on the amount and composition of that part of their spending which citizens consider can best be carried out collectively; and the tax burden is distributed in a way that has at least majority consent.

Indeed there is no inflation bias in the simpler formal models of the operation of the 'vote motive'. These tend to follow the elementary competitive market models of the textbooks in assuming that information is freely available and that the only object of entrepreneurial activity is to satisfy known wants.

The omission of information and search costs is much more serious in the political than in the commerical market place. Political entrepreneurs are under similar temptations to commercial ones to whip up expectations for their products – indeed more so to the extent that the issue is whether to be in or out of office rather than to effect marginal changes in sales. But, on the buyers' side of the market, the corrective force of direct and clear-cut personal experience is lacking. The route from a voting decision to a change in a citizen's own circumstance is complex and debatable. Indeed he does not have any personal incentive to acquire information about it because of the negligible probability of his own vote determining the outcome – a consideration which had led some American theorists to discover a paradox in why people vote at all. (The fact that they do shows that a narrowly self-interested view of political behaviour is over-simplified. But the smallness of the cost of voting and the way in which even minor inconveniences reduce turnout, suggest that the approach still embodies a useful simplification.) Above all the cost of a political decision is borne by people other than the voter. A customer buying a suit or a washing machine has to bear the cost himself. A vote for a candidate who offers to introduce or extend a particular public service, or to redistribute income in a certain way, or to favour a certain trade, usually assumes that others will bear the cost. This is realistic, as the gains of any particular policy are normally heavily concentrated among a minority while the tax and other costs are more widely spread amoung the electorate.

The bias of excessive expectation in democracy has a particular form. The benefits of specific programmes are heavily concentrated among minorities, who do have an incentive to keep informed and to organize. On the other hand, the costs are widely distributed among the bulk of the population for whom the loss is unlikely to be a decisive factor in casting their votes. The familiar example is that of a subsidy or tariff which benefits a few producers in large measure, but whose cost to each consumer or taxpayer is small. The minority can be quite a large one, ranging from home buyers to trade union activists; but their incentives to organize and inform themselves are still relatively greater than those of the population at large.

Does this mean that public expenditure will always be excessive because the tax cost of each item is spread thinly over most voters? Not quite. For general programmes which benefit the whole nation rather than specific interest groups will also suffer from the dispersion of interest. It thus seems that pure public goods, whether defence, environmental protection or public health regulation, are likely to be under-provided, whereas help for specific groups will be over-provided. But even this conclusion needs to be qualified. For if the providers of a public service are at all numerous or powerful, they will themselves form a group of concentrated beneficiaries with politial power. Such arguments help to explain the military-industrial complex in the United States, and the allegedly excessive number of educational and municipal bureaucrats in Britain. The public is not necessarily over-provided with the final product, whether defence or education; but it is likely to be over-provided with personnel in these fields in the way elaborated by modern theories of bureaucracy such as those of Downs and Niskanen.

Yet the taxpayer is not as powerless as a case-by-case examination of the political market would suggest. (As in other markets, a partial equilibrium approach can be misleading.) The taxpayer's gains from cutting down in any one item of expenditure may be very modest compared with the impact on the beneficiaries. But if one puts together a large number of programmes, the tax savings assume a large size. Thus attacks on public spending in general will always be more popular than attacks on any particular spending. The periodic economy drives, sometimes but not always associated with electoral change, can be regarded as counter-offensive by those who bear the cost of a combination of programmes. Such attacks will pay best politically, if their progenitors are as vague as possible about where the axe will fall beforehand; and *ex post* if they make across-the-board cuts, together with a few more severe attacks on very small and politically defenceless spending beneficiaries. It will not pay to attract opposition by a selective attack on major programmes such as council housing, even if they are not achieving their stated purposes. It is better to avoid threatening large groups more than necessary by adopting the approach: 'All these programmes are good, but we have to trim all back a little because we can't afford them.'

Inflation and the Vote Motive

It is because expenditure curbs and taxes are both unpopular that the temptation to inflationary finance arises in a democracy. But this temptation could hardly occur without the existence of lags in the inflationary process. If monetary expansion led to the immediate levying of the full inflation tax, it would be no more attractive than straightforward taxes of similar import. The existence of lags also provides scope for controversy about causal relationships, which in turn adds a crucial element of uncertainty.

The inflationary time lag occurs because monetary expansion can give output and employment a short-term boost of a Keynesian kind. If there were never such a boost, there would be an immediate cost to all government spending, whether financed by taxes, borrowing from the public, or monetary expansion; and in the latter case the inflation tax would have to be paid straight away.

If tax rates are difficult to vary in the short run, it might be rational to meet a sudden emergency or temporary bulge in spending through the inflation tax, even if there were no lags in its operation and no electoral myopia. The characteristic examples of such emergencies are major wars, which usually involve some inflation, even on the part of constitutional regimes normally committed to sound money – Britain in the Napoleonic Wars, the United States in the Civil War and most countries participating in World War I are examples.

Of course the short-term boost to output and employment is often the direct object of monetary and fiscal expansion, and not merely a way of financing particular spending projects; and an examination of full-employment policies is thus the best way to the root of the temptations and limitations of inflationary finance in contemporary democracies.

The Political Trade Cycle

A sizeable academic literature now exists on the political trade cycle; one particularly clear formulation is that of William Nordhaus. For the mechanism to work, three assumptions have to be made.

(i) It is possible to boost output and employment, at least for a while, by a monetary or fiscal stimulus, but at the cost of a higher eventual rate of inflation.

(ii) There is a lag between the effects of a monetary or fiscal boost on real activity and its inflationary consequences. Thus, in the run-up to an election, it is possible to have the benefits without all the costs of inflationary finance.

(iii) The electorate's memory is subject to fairly rapid decay, so that the incumbents lose less from high unemployment early on in the period of office than they gain from low unemployment nearer polling date. In addition voters have imperfect foresight so that they do not give full weight to the likely post-election consequences of policies.

The classic electoral cycle is then one in which employment and activity are at their peak around the election date. Then soon after the election there is a severe retrenchment with the object of getting the increase in unemployment over as quickly as possible. There would then be a fall in unemployment up to the next election. The exact pattern of the inflation rate (or of currency crises) would depend on the lags; the peak rate would be reached after or in between elections.

Nordhaus finds evidence of an electoral cycle in some, but not all, democratic countries. But the cases where the theory does not fit are as interesting as where it does. The classic examples of Presidents either not stimulating the US economy before elections, or doing so by controversially small amounts, were Eisenhower in 1960 and Ford in 1976. In Britain the main comparable example was Roy Jenkins in 1969–70, which was followed by Labour's surprise loss of the 1970 election.

David Butler and Donald Stokes found that there was a very close relation between unemployment and the government's perceived ability to handle the British economy between the end of World War II and the mid-1960s. In the United States, however, the economic variable that relates most closely to Administration popularity is the growth of real disposable income per capita in the year of the election (cf. Fair, cited by Robert Gordon). It may be that in Britain in 1958–68, unemployment, which had a strong cyclical movement, happened to be a good index of economic conditions generally – better than any direct index of spending power. But once unemployment experienced a secular shift to a higher rate – it settled on a plateau in 1968–70 – the old relationship disintegrated.

In the American case Fair has calculated that strict adherence to vote-maximising policy would require a temporary spurt in the growth rate to 20 per cent before each Presidential election – with an enormous recession afterwards. If this policy had been rigorously followed, the electorate would surely have been bound to see through it and it would have long ceased to work. It is only because manipulation is irregular and sparingly used, that the election cycle has lasted as long as it has.

Long-Run Stability

The political trade cycle can do only a limited amount of damage if it leads merely to oscillations in the inflation rate. The important question is whether there is any tendency to an upward drift, or even eventual explosions, over a run of such cycles. The crucial point is the tendency for the trade-off between unemployment and inflation to deteriorate and the Phillips curve to drift upwards. The simple Phillips curve PP′ shown in Figure 20 assumes that people are fooled by higher money rewards; that is in conditions of excess demand they will be fobbed off with a higher rate of money payment. But this cannot last indefinitely. Once workers realize they are being paid in shrunken pounds or dollars in a labour market tight enough for them to obtain real increases, they will insist on still larger wage gains to offset inflation. Thus excess demand leads not merely to inflation but to accelerating inflation (strictly an accelerating price level and increasing inflation). Thus at any level of unemployment below some sustainable level wages and prices will increase indefinitely.

In the long run then there is no trade-off between unemployment and inflation. Demand management cannot reduce unemployment below a sustainable minimum determined by the real forces of the labour market. The only long-run choice is the rate of inflation that will accompany the sustainable unemployment rate. In other words the long-term Phillips curve is a vertical line.

There has been some debate on whether this is so, or whether the long-term Phillips curve is merely steeper than the short-term one. On the other hand there are those who argue that high inflation rates are eventually deleterious to employment. For convenience the long-run Phillips curve is shown on the diagram as a vertical line; but it would merely have to be steeper than the short-term one to give rise to an upward drift of both inflation and unemployment and a loss of political support.[2]

In the figure, the sloping straight line PP' is a segment of a Phillips curve drawn for a period of zero inflationary expectations and a given mark-up on wage costs. The curved line running through E concave to the origin represents combinations of unemployment and inflation to which voters are indifferent. There is a whole series of such curves; and the ones nearest the origin give the government the greatest popularity, as they provide the most favourable combinations of unemployment and inflation.

At the start of the story the government is on the curve $V = 60$, signifying that it has 60 per cent of total votes (assuming for simplicity a two-party system). The government moves along the Phillips curve until it has reached the most favourable voters' indifference curve, here shown at E, where unemployment is OM, and inflation is OW. The Goodhart–Bhansali study of 1970 suggested that voters' optimum position in the decade from 1958 was at 200–250,000 unemployed (about 1 per cent), then associated with a price inflation of 5 per cent.

But unfortunately this is not a stable long-term position. Over a run of political cycles the short-term Phillips curve will drift upwards. The government will still do its best to get on the most favourable indifference curve; but as it moves towards the right-hand corner along the electoral path ED, unemployment, inflation and its own support will all deteriorate. A long-term equilibrium is possible – if it

Fig 20. Government Popularity and Deteriorating Inflation/Unemployment
Tradeoff

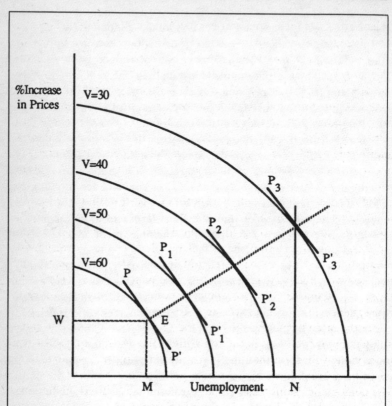

Key:

Curved lines represent combinations of unemployment and inflation to which voters
are indifferent, and are labelled according to proportion of votes (V) gained by
government.

Straight lines PP′, $P_1 P'_1$, etc. are segments of short-term Phillips curve giving tradeoffs between unemployment and inflation at successive intervals of time (assuming
constant proportional mark-up on wages).

Vertical line from N represents long-run Phillips curve showing no trade-off.

ON represents sustainable rate of unemployment.

ED represents 'election path'.

is possible at all – only where the long-term Phillips curve (here shown by the vertical line up from N) is reached. Then unemployment will be at the sustainable level ON.

Although illustrative only, the figure does bring home that in the best of circumstances, democratic myopia and economic time lags will land the economy with an excessive rate of inflation. Unemployment will end up at ON in any case; but will be approached along the path ED, which will take the economy to the higher rates of inflation in the top right of the diagram. It would have been possible to have combined the sustainable unemployment rate with low inflation, or even price stability, and pleased more voters, if the government had settled for ON in the first place, and concentrated on long-run improvements in the working of the labour market to reduce unemployment, and forgone the temporary benefits of a short-term stimulus.

But this is by no means all. The point of long-run balance is one of much lower voter support for the government than at the beginning of the story – some 30 per cent in the illustration. If this merely leads to an alternation of governments, it may be tolerable. But governments may not be content to be voted out in this way and believe, not necessarily correctly, that they have found policies which will enable them to stimulate the economy without the usual inflationary consequences, i.e. to improve the short-term or long-term trade-off.

But the more serious point is that the combination of inflation rates and unemployment rate in the top right of the diagram may provoke more violent reaction than the mere change of party, and that there could be a breakdown in the whole political and economic system. The democratic doom thesis is that the sustainable rate of unemployment is beyond the limits of political tolerance and will lead to the abandonment of democracy and/or the present type of mixed economy.

If we combine the short-term political cycle with the long-term deterioration of the trade-off between unemployment and inflation, we reach the following account. Each stimulus takes the economy to a fresh inflationary height; and the subsequent check to demand raises the unemployment rate while administering only a limited and temporary check to the inflation rate, which resumes its upward drift once governments have become sufficiently worried about unemployment to restimulate demand. The model can be made more realistic by not insisting that *every* cycle reaches fresh inflationary heights, and instead looking for the upward trend over a succession of several

cycles – even that could produce the explosion so vividly foreseen in
Peter Jay's writings as early as 1974. All that one needs to generate
this model is an employment target above the sustainable level and
governmental determination to pursue it by fiscal and monetary
expansion. The explosion will occur whether the gap between
governmental aims and the sustainable rate is due to union monopoly,
as in the Jay version, or to a governmental objective which is too
ambitious in relation to other policies. The danger has been vividly
described by Goodhart:

> If we cannot shift the natural rate of unemployment down to a more
> acceptable level by a prices-and-incomes policy [sic!] nor make the
> existing, possibly fixed natural rate of unemployment more accept-
> able, the economies of the West will remain faced with an internal
> contradiction which may well serve to destroy the democratic,
> capitalist structure of their existing system.

The Role of the Unions

There are many other issues to be considered, above all union
influence. For all the pulp forests that have been consumed in
discussing this question, no one knows how large a role union power
has played in generating the dilemmas discussed in the last section.
Even among those who accept that monetary expansion is a necessary
and sufficient condition for a prolonged major inflation – and the
evidence here is overwhelming – there is still every conceivable shade
of opinion on the extent to which union behaviour has impelled the
monetary authorities to inflationary action.

Flemming has mentioned two ways in which unions may raise the
sustainable unemployment level. First, changes in the pattern of
union power – or in the use made of that power – must be added to
changes in taste and technology as influences which bring about
frictional unemployment. Secondly unions reduce wage flexibility and
thereby throw more of the burden of adjustment to change onto
output and employment. Against this must be offset the positive role
of unions in reducing transaction costs by bargaining on behalf of their
members and disseminating information.

These are all 'micro' effects. Much more controversial is the
possibility of most or all unions acting together in a concerted wage
push. Strict neo-classical economists are highly suspicious of its
likelihood. This is because in their view unions (like all other
economic agents) are already exerting their maximum degree of
monopoly power ('everyone maximizes'). But there is a great deal to

suggest that many unions normally operate with an unused margin of monopoly power. The electricity-generating workers – as we are constantly reminded in the press – are in a position to raise their relative wages by a combination of the strike threat and denial of entry to competitive workers willing to train. Let us assume that the power workers did try to maximize their monopoly wage bill and insisted on £500,000 per head per annum at the expense of somewhat smaller electricity consumption. If the power workers did secure such rises, the other groups would hardly let the position stand. The miners, sewer workers, dustmen and many others would all be able to take action to recover at least some of their relative position; professional groups might surprise people by showing the degree of monopoly power they possess if they chose to use it. There is thus a large conventional element in the balance of the labour market between different unions, which incorporates a mixture of historically determined and free market relativities, together with traditional ideas of status. It is a balance of forces, vulnerable to disturbance, rather than an equilibrium in a narrow market sense.

On this interpretation wage-push would arise if some or all unions, acting either in concert, or in response to common signals, tried to make more use of their monopoly power. This could be represented as an upward shift of the short term Phillips curves shown on the chart. A great deal depends on whether the underlying aim is an increase in real or money wages. In the former case nothing will prevent workers being priced out of jobs and thus bringing about an increase in the sustainable unemployment rate, irrespective of whether monetary policy is very rigid or highly accommodating. If the union aim, on the other hand, is simply an increase in money wages, a monetary injection would maintain employment at the previously sustainable rate at the expense of the higher price level.

To admit the possibility of union wage-push does not mean that one should throw in the towel and abandon any economic explanation. A sudden shock to previous existing real income expectations, such as the fivefold oil price increase of 1973–4, can trigger off such wage-push. An increase in money wages is, as Flemming points out, a funny objective. But in the uncertainty which follows such events unions may put in large money wage claims to insure against adverse price movements without being too specific about real wage objectives. Unrealistic real income aims on an economy-wide scale are likely to be transitional, as eventually some learning will occur. Moreover this learning is easier when a once-for-all contraction of real incomes is in the past and growth is once more possible, and it is simply a matter of not catching up with lost time. If the check to world growth since 1973 proves, however, more fundamental than the loss of a few years increased output – whether because of physical resource constraints or the increasing role of positional goods (cf. Fred Hirsch) – then the learning process could take a great deal longer, and both wage-push and electoral pressures on governments will be that much more intensive. My own suspicion is that the more fundamental limits to growth will make themselves felt gradually and that world output will continue to grow over the next few cycles even if at a reduced rate.

The increase in world inflation rates began in the late 1960s, well before the oil price explosion. The difficulty with a wage-push explanation is that no one has explained why there should have been an internationally synchronized increase in the use of union monopoly power during the period. An alternative explanation is available in terms of the inflationary turn taken in the US policies – partly due to deficit finance for the Vietnam war – and the currency link of other countries with the dollar.

The most important macro effect union power may be one not so far mentioned explicitly. It may slow down the reaction of wages to a reduction in the growth of monetary demand. (In other words it will flatten the slope of the short-term Phillips curve to the right of the point of balance, the curve then becoming kinked.) This means that the transitional increase in unemployment involved in any attempt to reduce the inflation rate will be higher. Thus inflation will tend to be a one-way street. Any shock or policy error will tend to increase the rate, which will not fall back to its old level before the next shock.

Democracy comes in as an inhibition on methods which might otherwise be attempted for curbing the power of unions to force the authorities to finance inflation – on pain of pricing workers out of jobs. Just as democracy whips up expectations, it reduces the means available for fulfilling these expectations. There is first the difficulty of persuading the electorate that the normal process of collective bargaining backed by the strike threat can be inimical both to the general standard of living and to the stability of the social system. An even greater inhibition is that of enforcing by tolerable methods legislation designed to curb coercive union practices which are used to prevent undercutting ('blacklegging'). One should not underrate changes in sentiment that come with time; but trade unionists' instincts of fraternity have up to now been too strong to be overcome by peaceful methods of law enforcement.

It is a delusion to suppose that incomes policy offers a way of coping with union market power by means of consent. This is a question which I have discussed at length elsewhere. Briefly, an incomes policy will always founder on the rock of relativities and differentials; and there is no such thing as a fair or scientific assessment of relativities. An *a priori* case can be made for a short-term emergency freeze or ceiling as a shock to expectations; but in practice such shock tactics have been accompanied by such other measures, and presented in such misleading ways, that they have done more harm than good to both inflation and employment.

The End of the Gold Standard

There is even now, however, a missing element. Democratic pressures for government spending and full employment policies, even combined with union factors, could not have brought the recent rise in inflation rates without a parallel erosion of institutional monetary constraints. With fixed rules of budget balancing, and gold-standard restrictions on the creation of money, an attempt to satisfy too many competing demands would lead to high government spending and correspondingly high taxation. The budget might balance at too high a level; but the size of the tax burden would provide a built-in constraint against indefinite expansion.

The necessary condition for the political overload on democracy to take inflationary form was, as Karl Brunner has emphasized, the disappearance of the gold-standard rules. The disappearance was gradual. The first element to disappear was the convertibility of the privately-held domestic currency into gold in the 1920s. This loosened the link between the domestic money supply and the gold stock. The next stage, which also had its roots in the 1920s, but did not become *de jure* until Bretton Woods, was the transformation of the gold into a dollar standard. Most countries used dollars to settle imbalances in official transactions. Domestic monetary policies were limited by the need to maintain dollar convertibility; and only the United States was required to supply gold to other national monetary institutions. A further looseness was the adjustable peg mechanism, which enabled other countries to follow monetary policies partially independent of the United States. The constraints on the United States weakened once it became clear that gold convertibility was available only on the understanding that the option was not widely exercised; but the United States was not finally free to determine its own monetary policy until the formal end of gold convertibility in 1971; and it was not until early 1973 that most of the world went onto a floating system which removed even the temporary constraint of the adjustable peg and the link with the US inflation rate. Each of the successive steps appeared logical on its own merits; but the end result has placed the entire burden of checking inflation on the democratic self-restraint on which Schumpeter laid so much emphasis.

The sheer physical limitations of the gold supply in relation to world economic activity might in any case have made it difficult to maintain the pre-1914 form of the gold standard. The inverted pyramid of paper money, bank deposits and credit instruments standing on the base might have been extended further. The low physical cost of paper money and bank deposits, compared to mining gold, would have provided an incentive for such extension. But the paper and credit element could not be stretched excessively without making the gold base increasingly fictional and also making the system highly crisis-prone, as the interwar years showed. An alternative line of argument is that the system could have been made to work through periodic changes in the dollar price of gold. But quite apart from all the problems of whether other countries would have found the dollar link attractive in such circumstances, a politically set gold price has none of the automatic qualities of the orthodox gold standard: a system revised on these lines would have just been a series of discretionary dollar devaluations – a series of step debasements in place of the continuous ones which take place today.

The speculative reasoning of the age also contributed to the erosion of the role of gold. Whether the object of monetary policy is a stable price level or (as in the later writings of Keynes) to facilitate employment, it seemed absurd to tie the quality of money in a loose and unpredictable way to the physical supply of a particular metal. It was surely more rational to have a paper money the quantity of which could be controlled by governments in the light of requirements; and differences between national objectives could be reconciled by floating exchange rates.

Such arguments were – and remain – valid in their own terms. The trouble was that they presupposed that governments were Benthamite dictatorships rigorously devoted to some economist's conception of the public interest, rather than flesh-and-blood human beings subject to the push and pull of a highly imperfect political market place. But there is unlikely to be a solution through returning to some version of the gold standard. For myths have social value only when people do not realize they are myths. Once it is realized that the money does not depend on the gold backing for value, but only on its acceptability and quantity – and that the gold base is merely a device for limiting that quantity – then it is difficult to see governments again accepting gold convertibility at a fixed rate as an overriding aim for which real short-term sacrifices have to be made.

Unbalanced Budgets

The undermining of the gold standard went hand in hand with the overthrow of another moralistic constraint on monetary expansion – the balanced budget doctrine. Here again the traditional form of the doctrine had little logical basis. A Gladstonian budget covered mostly current government spending or non-revenue earning infrastructure investment, and it was a comparatively simple matter to say whether the budget was balanced or not. With the vast increase on the capital expenditure and lending side, the growth of expenditure by public bodies outside central government, and the complications of interest payments in an inflationary period, there are dozens of different balances which could now be used; and even if all agreed on a definition, it would still be far from obvious that the optimal size is zero. Again the balanced budget was but a myth or convention which provided a rough and ready built-in safeguard against monetary over-expansion.

The new philosophy which replaced the old restraints was that of demand management labelled (justifiably or not) 'Keynesian economics'. The doctrine, stated in its full rigour, holds that neither the money supply nor the budget balance is an independent objective of policy, but both are instruments for achieving a target pressure of real demand (measured by the ratio of actual output to assumed capacity output), itself geared to a specific employment objective. The demand management doctrine reigned for so long, partly because of the intellectual atrophy of the defenders of the old orthodoxy. So long as the main danger was seen as one of inflation (normally assumed to be within the 2 to 7 per cent 'creeping' range) rather than accelerating inflation, it was possible for the demand managers to say that some inflation was a price worth paying for full employment; and the argument was further confused by the poorness of fit in many countries of the old Phillips curve and its tendency to shift its position. There was also the vain hope that incomes policies would enable high demand targets to be set without inflationary consequences.

But it would be wrong to exaggerate doctrinal influences. Countries were not able to pursue full employment policies *à outrance* so long as there was some inhibition against large or frequent devaluation against the dollar. Paradoxically, monetary growth seems to have been more restricted in the 1950s and early 1960s by apparently irrational balance-of-payments fetishes than in the subsequent period when monetarism has been more fashionable. In the United States, the demand management philosophy never took full hold until the Kennedy–Johnson Administration of the 1960s; and no one knows what effect the ideological change would have had without the Vietnam War and the temptation to try to finance it without raising its full cost in taxes. Outside Britain and Northern Europe the Keynesian approach to deficits and monetary policy never really caught on; but Keynesian forecasting methods did; and these – together with the toleration of international bodies – enabled governments to live with their bad conscience when running deficits, France being a frequent case in point.

The Full Employment Era

The analysis so far still has important gaps. It does not explain why so many countries were able to maintain successful employment policies for up to twenty or thirty years after World War II, while also keeping the rate of inflation down to a creeping level. The tendency to explosive inflation began only with the late 1960s.

There is no shortage of explanations after the event, but we still do not know which are correct. There are any number of hypotheses about why the sustainable rate of unemployment should have risen. One of the most popular is the sharp increase in the ratio of unemployment benefit to average earnings in many countries, especially when tax, travel and benefits in kind are taken into account. Another explanation is in terms of structural changes, such as a decline in relative demand for unskilled labour at conventional wage ratios, or the disturbances to the pattern of industrial demand following the oil price explosion. Other hypotheses are in terms of government controls, which hold down the rate of return on capital; but such controls have in almost all cases been a response to an acceleration in inflation, which has already occurred for some other reason. A different category of explanation is in terms of money illusion persisting for several decades at steady and moderate rates of inflation, which meant that trade unions and probably other groups settled for lower real rewards than they could have obtained in the prevailing state of demand; but once the increased inflation rates of the later 1960s had shattered the earlier expectations, money illusion was punctured very quickly and will not now be easy to recreate.

Changes in Prospect

Does the above analysis, based on a combination of the imperfections of the political process and economic time lags, lead inexorably to ever higher inflation rates? Some caution is in order, if only because predictions based on extrapolations of the immediately previous decade have so often proved erroneous. The key to the doomsday machine is that Keynesian stimulation does increase output and employment in the short run, but only prices in the longer run. The process has been analysed by academic monetarists in their accounts of the 'expectations-augmented Phillips curve'.

But it is a common experience in analysis economic change that no sooner has a particular relationship been established by analysis of past data and no sooner has it come into use among economists, then it breaks down – an example of the familiar interrelation between the observer and the observed. In short, once a monetarist diagnosis is publicly accepted in however crude and bowdlerized form, monetary expansion ceases to provide even a temporary stimulus to activity. This would be an inference from the theory of rational expectations; but it can be seen in all sorts of specific ways. An announcement of a series of high monthly monetary aggregates soon leads to a fall in government bond prices and thus to a rise in interest rates. This discourages investment both directly and via its effects on confidence; while any increase in inflationary expectations among wage bargainers soon leads to more inflation and less growth for any particular monetary stance.

While academic debate has been proceeding about whether there is no long-run trade-off between employment and price stability, or merely an uncomfortably steep one, actual events have overtaken the arguments; and high inflation has brought lower employment – either because of greater uncertainty, the difficulties of coping with high nominal interest rates and fluctuating asset values, or through government attempts to suppress the inflationary symptoms. Some of these perverse effects could prove as transitional as the employment-creating effects proved to be; but at least the route to high employment through taking risks with inflation can be seen to be well and truly closed.

Above all there is the fact that in any open economy the main immediate impact of monetary expansion is on the exchange rate. The effect has become much more rapid than it used to be, both because the temporary prop of the exchange rate peg has been removed and because monetary expansion itself leads to expectations of depreciation which defeat most efforts by the authorities to hold up the rate. An exchange depreciation is not only a force for inflation, but may also have a *contractionary* effect on real activity. A depreciation raises the domestic price level – directly and quickly for imports, through competitive forces for internationally-traded goods, and gradually through shifts in activity in the case of non-traded goods. As a result the real value of a given money supply falls, an effect which was obscured in the days of the (very occasionally) adjustable peg and accommodating monetary policy. The adverse effects are directly visible via real disposable income, interest rates, consumer confidence, asset values and many other channels. These may well outweigh any temporary boost from export profits, a stimulus which industrialists tend increasingly to write off in advance.

A similar process of disillusion with inflationary finance may be occurring on the union side. Much recent inflation can best be understood as an attempt to persuade powerful groups that they have won more than they really have, while disguising their real losses from others by means of a general depreciation of the monetary unit. Once this process is seen through, bargaining may be expected to be increasingly in real terms. This could aggravate inflation if there were large money wage settlements combined with the wrong sort of indexation clauses, such as the Italian *scala mobile,* and monetary policy financed the result. But there is at least a chance that unions will cease to demand or even welcome such monetary policies, and the struggle will become an open one about real shares and the distribution of unemployment resulting from given real claims. The relative mildness of British TUC calls for 'reflation' in the deepest of postwar recessions may be a pointer towards things to come.

It would be wrong to exaggerate. Western economic leaders have not so much lost their faith in monetary stimulation, as in its domestic variety. Demand expansion brought about via exports and world trade (or in some eyes through protection) is regarded as being much less dangerous – exactly why would make an interesting digression. The upshot is that governments are calling upon each other to expand demand, while being reluctant to do so themselves; but one must never rule out the perverse possibilities of international co-operation.

A look at the record may help. There has basically been one change of gear – from the prewar assumption of stable prices (with deviations in a deflationary direction) to the postwar expectations of upward creep. International evidence for inflationary acceleration is confined to two cycles, 1966–71 and 1971–5. This has been insufficient to establish a secure secular trend towards accelerating inflation. The Vietnam war and the magnification and concentration in a short time span by OPEC of the inevitable oil price increases, aggravated these two cycles. There may not be comparable bad luck next time; and there is more caution about monetary policies on the world scene – despite the desire for mutual stimulation – than when President Nixon proclaimed he was a Keynesian and when there was a general consensus about a supposed shortage not merely of conditional liquidity but of international reserves.

A return to price stability or the postwar rate of creeping inflation is not being predicted. Nor is it being asserted that inflation will be below the 1965–75 average in future cycles. The rigidities of the established methods of wage and price determination may well remain; and there could still be a tendency for outside shocks to give upward boosts to the inflation rate, not easily reversed.

The residual effect of the full employment commitment may thus be to underwrite part at least of the levels of inflationary expectations brought about by such shocks. But this is not quite the same as the remorseless doomsday machine produced by the pursuit of unattainable full employment goals heedless of the monetary cost. It was on the basis of such a diagnosis that Professor Michael Parkin – almost the only writer in this area to contribute to knowledge by making a falsifiable prediction – asserted at the beginning of 1975 that world governments and central banks would react to the developing recession by pressing monetary and fiscal accelerators 'as hard as possible'. As a result 1976 was going to be a year 'of rapid real growth and falling unemployment', and 1977 'a year with inflation rates into the 20s and 30s rather than the mere teens'.

Tensions Still Present

Although the threat of runaway inflation may recede, this does not mean that economic dangers to democracy would then be over. On the contrary, the tensions which gave rise to inflation could show themselves in other, and perhaps more dangerous forms. The disappearance of inflation as a temporary solvent would bring certain tensions into the open. The rivalry of coercive producer groups with incompatible real demands on the national product could appear more serious once they came out into the open and were no longer disguised as a mere wage-price spiral. Professor Colin Crouch has stressed the role of inflation in enabling governments to postpone a resolution of interest group rivalries. The period when it was possible to drown relativity changes or the lack of them by a general rise in the price level might therefore come to appear the hallmark if not of a golden at least of a silver age. Similarly, the disappearance of 'reflation' and rapid 'growth' will make it more difficult for governments to appear to reconcile conflicting promises to different groups, and will thus bring to the surface the problem of excessive expectations.

The real problems of liberal democracy are not in the end about inflation. The spread of market relations itself tends, in ways explained by John Goldthorpe to undermine the status structure which provides capitalism with its legitimacy in the eyes of most people. One particularly serious problem arises from the contemporary belief that no constraints should stand in the way of an elected government, a belief sometimes given a traditionalist coat in Britain by expressions such as the 'sovereignty of Parliament' or 'the Queen in Parliament'. Another acute conflict, discussed by Dicey at the beginning of the twentieth century, is between the individual and the collective pursuit of self-interest. The two may not be compatible and the second may be explosive.

Whether these hypotheses are right or not, by disguising our problems as the semi-technical conundrum of inflation, we may be making them seem more tractable than they really are. Inflation may even have been a benign form of self-deception, a means of buying time. But we have come to the end of this period of grace.

Notes

1   Introductions to the economic theory of democracy can be found in the books by Barry and Tullock and Breton mentioned below.

2   There is now an immense literature on short- and long-term Phillips curves, the sustainable (or 'natural') rate of unemployment *et al*. An approach by the present writer can be found in *The Role and Limits of Government*.

References

Barry, Brian, *Economists, Sociologists and Democracy* (Collier-Macmillan, London, 1970).

Breton, A., *The Economic Theory of Representative Government* (Macmillan, London, 1974).

Brittan, Samuel, *Second Thoughts on Full Employment Policy* (Barry Rose, London, 1975).

Brittan, Samuel, 'The Economic Contradictions of Democracy', *British Journal of Political Sciences*, 5 (1975).

Brittan, Samuel and Lilley, Peter, *The Delusion of Incomes Policy* (Temple Smith, London, 1977).

Brunner, Karl, 'Comment' (on Gordon 1975), *Journal of Law and Economics*, 18 (1975).

Butler, D. and Stokes, D., *Political Change in Britain* (2nd edition) (Macmillan, London, 1949).

Cagan, Phillip, 'The Monetary Dynamics of Hyperinflation', in Milton Friedman (ed.), *Studies in the Quantity Theory of Money* (Chicago University Press, 1956).

Crouch, C.J., *Class Conflict and the Industrial Relations Crisis* (Heinemann, London, 1977).

Downs, A., *An Economic Theory of Democracy* (Harper and Row, New York, 1957).

Downs, A., *Inside Bureaucracy* (Little, Brown & Co., Boston, 1976).

Flemming, John, *Inflation* (Oxford University Press, London, 1976).

Friedman, Milton, 'The Role of Monetary Policy', *American Economic Review*, 58 (1968).

Friedman, Milton, 'Government Revenue from Inflation', *Journal of Political Economy*, 79.

Goldthorne, John H., 'Industrial Relations in Great Britain: a Critique of Reformism', *Politics and Society*, 4 (1974).

Goodhart C.A.E. and Bhansali, R.J., 'Political Economy', *Political Studies*, 18 (1970).

Gordon, Robert J., 'The Demand for and Supply of Inflation', *Journal of Law and Economics*, 18 (1975).

Hayek, F.A., *Choice in Currency* (Institute of Economic Affairs, London, 1976).

Hirsch, Fred, *Social Limits to Growth* (Routledge and Kegan Paul, London, 1977).

Jay, Peter, *Employment, Inflation and Politics* (Institute of Economic Affairs, London, 1976).

Laidler, D.E.W., Comment on 'Why Stable Inflations Fail', in Parkin and Zis (eds.), *Inflation in the World Economy* (Manchester University Press, 1976).

Niskanen, W.A., *Bureaucracy and Representative Government* (Aldine-Atherton, New York, 1971).

Nordhaus, William D., 'The Political Business Cycle', *Review of Economic Studies,* 42 (1975).

Schumpeter, J.A., *Capitalism, Socialism and Democracy* (Allen and Unwin, London, 1942).

25   Towards a New Political Settlement

Elective Dictatorship

The principal fallacy of an age is usually one that is taken for granted and not a subject of popular debate. In our own age this role is occupied by the principle of majority rule. This is endorsed just as much by conservative as by radical parties. Conservative parties are fond of objecting to innovations by saying that there is no majority for the particular proposal in the country; to which the reply usually is: 'Oh yes, there is; it is part of the *mandate* on which we were elected.' Neither side thinks of querying the divine right of the majority to impose its wish.

But is not an attack on majority rule an attack on democracy? No: only on a particular use or abuse of the term. If democracy is the opposite of dictatorship, it must be more than mere majority rule. Indeed, a system under which the ephemeral will of a majority either of voters or of their elected representatives must always and instantly prevail is itself a form of dictatorship, one that has been aptly labelled 'elective dictatorship' by Lord Hailsham.

The United Kingdom is almost unique in having a Parliament with unlimited and absolute powers. As Lord Hailsham has pointed out: 'Parliament can take away a man's liberty or his life without a trial, and in past centuries, it has actually done so. It can prolong its own life, and in our own time has done so twice, quite properly, in two world wars.' In any conflict between the rule of law and the sovereignty of Parliament, the sovereignty of Parliament is always paramount.

'Parliament' is of course a term of art. For practical purposes there is now only one chamber. The House of Lords is deliberately left with its hereditary element unreformed so that it can be more easily pushed aside. But it is not in fact even the House of Commons which exercises

303

power, but the Government acting through that House; and this generalisation is no more than frayed at the edges by the occasional well publicised defeat on an issue which the Government has been careful in advance to declare not to be one of confidence. The reality is, as Lord Hailsham points out, that the Government controls its party whips, the Civil Service and the party machine (always under the Conservatives; at least at election time under Labour). Talk about increasing the role of Parliament or reforming its procedure ignores the fact that individual Members are chosen as a by-product of electing a government, and that promising back-benchers are absorbed into the administration or the front benches. This is why the experiment in parliamentary committees has turned out disappointing, and why they can never hope to aspire to the role of their congressional counterparts in the United States. The powers of government are reinforced by the ability of the prime minister to choose his own election date – in many other countries the administration can try to manipulate the economy, but not the polling date; in Britain it can do both.

There is a further factor which imprisons rather than empowers government, but which nevertheless puts a steamroller over dissentients and vitiates reasoned discussion. These are the unheavenly twins of the mandate and the manifesto. Again, I cannot improve on Lord Hailsham's Dimbleby Lecture formulation:

> Before the election, the manifesto is written rather in the style of an advertisement for patent medicines; after the election it is treated as a pronouncement from Sinai, with every jot and tittle of that unreal, and often unreasonable document, reverenced as Holy Writ .... [The measures in it often include] the impossible, the irrelevant and the inappropriate. But however small the majority, the party activists, flushed with victory, insistently demand the redemption of all the pledges in the shortest possible time, and they are vociferously egged on by the various pressure groups whose collective support has been won by the making of the pledges.

The Government is then 'free to' (I would prefer to say 'feels forced to') impose a series of widely unpopular measures, not related to current needs.

That the Government is often unable to make its measures stick in the country, and engages in U-turns, does not detract from its potential oppressiveness – the only non-military forces it will respect are strike action and the movement of funds across the exchanges. Thus governments are simultaneously ineffective and dictatorial, desisting from their dictatorial pretensions only in the face of collectively organised superior forces – an unlovely spectacle.

The Social Contract Alternative

What has gone wrong can be simply stated. Majority voting is a convenient *decision rule*; but it has been wrongly elevated into a fundamental moral principle. Even if voters' views were well considered and could be translated into action with perfect efficiency by the government machine, there would be a prior difficulty in defining what we mean by the 'majority view'. This is an ambiguous concept if there are more than two alternative policies. It is well known that the decision a committee takes can depend on the accident of the order in which amendments are taken. The best chance of securing a clear-cut result would be to have series of votes on all possible alternatives considered in pairs. Even then a cyclical result – B is preferred to A, C is preferred to B, but A is preferred to C – is in fact possible and indeed quite likely with issues involving many voters and a variety of possible actions. These difficulties are greatly compounded by the complex policy bundles between which, according to democratic mythology, voters are supposed to choose at elections.

But this is merely the preliminary objection. For even if we could attach a simple meaning to a 'majority view', we would be up against a much more fundamental drawback. This is that unrestricted elective dictatorship allows a bare majority to impose costs on a minority which the latter has no means of escaping. An altogether bogus sanctity has been given in modern politics to the desirability of a 51 per cent majority prevailing over a 49 per cent minority. In fact, the only thing that can be said in its favour is that, other things being equal, it is very slightly less bad than 49 per cent prevailing over 51 per cent. But these need not be the only available options. It may be possible to modify a proposal so that the minority opposition is less intense in quantity and quality.

The opposite of dictatorship is not majority rule – miscalled democracy – but unanimous consent. Strict unanimity is an unattainable ideal in a community of any size, both because of the decision costs involved and because it would encourage people to conceal their true preferences for tactical reasons. But there is still a contrast between the principle of general consent and that of mere majority approval.

It is helpful to think of society as a set of individuals who have agreed to live with each other under certain rules, even though these rules often remain implicit. These rules can be called the *social contract*, in the correct sense of that much abused term. The social contract was originally used by seventeenth and eighteenth-century writers to refer to a mythical historical agreement under which men joined together to form a state. Modern American political philosophers have revived the notion to describe the understandings, whether implicit or explicit, that hold people together in a modern society.

This involves picking out a first or *constitutional* stage during which the main principles of association are agreed. These principles will determine how specific decisions are to be taken; which may be by appointed or by elected officials, by simple majority, weighted majority, plurality or any other procedure that may be suitable. But the constitutional decision about the rules to be used should in principle be taken unanimously if minorities are not to be coerced. During the second or *post-constitutional* stage, the agreed principles are applied in specific instances. During this stage people who have been outvoted or overruled cannot legitimately complain, as they have agreed to the decision rules at a time when they could not predict whether they would gain or lose. These two stages are of course a metaphor rather than an actual process. Even in a country such as the United States, which has a written constitution, its present citizens did not personally approve it. Nevertheless, the two-stage notion helps to make sense of the intuitive notion of political legitimacy.

The unanimity requirement has long been known to economists in terms of the Pareto principle. This states that a change is an improvement if, and only if, it makes some people better off and no one worse off. The Pareto principle is not of course scientifically demonstrable, but is an ethical and prudential starting point, and one that in my view economists need not feel ashamed to mention outside their textbooks. Practising cost–benefit analysts do not of course expect to find projects with no losers; but if they follow the Pareto principle, they will look to see if the gainers could compensate the losers and still benefit before they declare it a potential improvement. Compensation is not always likely or even practicable. But it is reasonable for any individual to expect to gain from at least a run of such decisions.

In the pure version of the contract theory, such as that of John Rawls, each individual has no idea of his station in life – or even of his own abilities or temperament – at the constitutional stage. Professor James Buchanan has an alternative version of the social contract designed to reflect existing power realities rather than feigned ignorance. His essential point is that, if the structure of rights is to continue to command adherence, it must respect the actual differences in the power of different individuals. It is thus not an ethical theory dealing with first-best states of affairs. The basic assertion is that everyone would gain from some constraint on the power of the majority of the moment to do what it likes, including those who for the moment belong to that majority. The gains would come from greater security and predictability. If elected governments claim to do exactly what they like, then not only is there no limit to attempted state actions, but there is no possibility of predicting how state action will affect us in the future. This is a step back towards the anarchistic jungle, to avoid which we put up with the many pains and restrictions of organised society. When the implicit social contract has broken down, but political competition still prevails, people are likely to feel that governments are simultaneously both oppressive and inadequate.

There is an important subsidiary point. If there are no constraints on state action, individuals have a much stronger incentive to invest resources in political activity and to try to use the state machine to supply them with goods (or contracts) on favoured terms. People work to obtain a government that will favour either council tenants or private home-owners; managers of enterprising firms divert their efforts into keeping on good terms with ministers and officials, sitting on time-wasting committees and keeping *au fait* with the latest governmental fads and fashions; and, at local level, it is wise to keep in with the authorities who dispose of the more desirable school places or subsidised homes.

One supposed objection to constitutional restraints on majority rule is that it increases the difficulty of reaching decisions on policy. This can appear a disadvantage in situations where the *status quo* is not an option. If an old building has been destroyed, living in it is no longer a possibility, and a choice of dwelling has to be made. The nightmare for those who believe in strong government (which includes most Conservatives) is that decisions would become too difficult if general support is required. But if doing something rather than nothing is in everyone's interests, a generally acceptable proposal should be forthcoming if sufficient imagination is exercised in framing it. If general agreement is not possible on one issue, it should be over a bargain on a linked series of issues, where those who lose on some will gain on others. (There is nothing wrong with logrolling, except the producer bias of most political systems and divorce between the interests of the bargainers and those whom they nominally represent.)

The most frequent objection to constitutional constraints on majority rule is that they tend to entrench the *status quo*. This is regarded as equivalent to obstructing social reform and protecting the wealthy from the inroads of democracy. But this is a misunderstanding of what a genuine social contract involves. So far from underwriting hereditary wealth, Buchanan argues that, if the structure of property rights is to continue to be respected, it needs to be redefined and renegotiated periodically to reflect the changing balance between people and groups. The lack of correspondence between, say, the possessions of the owners of hereditary wealth and what these same individuals could acquire or defend in a state of nature needs to be remedied by periodic changes in the rules of inheritance and its taxation.

The implicit bargain is a trade-off in which the affluent agree to a reduction in their property rights (in both their non-human capital and the earnings from their own talents) in return for a limit on state redistribution. The better-off make a sacrifice in previously held wealth in return for more certain enjoyment of the remainder. What would the worse-off gain from such a bargain? In return for a limit on the amount of redistribution that they could obtain via the ballot box, they would be secure of the redistribution they already have against a right-wing victory in the polls or against backsliding by a government of the Left. A constitutional brake on government might have seemed reactionary in 1900 or even 1964; but today it is at least as much in the interests of the beneficiaries of redistribution and state activity as it is of those who fear further intervention.

The argument is enormously strengthened by the fact that actual redistribution under the welfare state is far from being a clear-cut transfer to the less well-off, but is very haphazard and arbitrary. Much of it is wasteful, or self-cancelling, or diverted away from the poor to the middle-income groups or even the moderately well-off; and no one can be sure whether he will win or lose over the run of the next few Parliaments. Thus the interest in greater security and predictability is very widespread.

First Past the Post

So far, in order to concentrate on basic issues, I have been writing as if the Government were elected by 51 per cent of the electorate, or were supported by members of the House of Commons representing 51 per cent of the electorate. But the British political system does not even achieve this standard. As is well known, it works on the first-past-the-post system, which commonly returns parties to office with 40 per cent or less of the votes cast. Thus it is not even an elective dictatorship of the majority, but a dictatorship of a minority. It is true that, even under the existing system, we may in any case get a House of Commons where the leading party is well short of an absolute majority and is highly dependent on arrangements with other groups. But we cannot rely on this happening regularly, and if it does the leading party will be under a strong temptation to call an election at a favourable moment in an attempt to gain a majority of seats. The Lib-Lab Pact of 1977 reflected a very special situation, unlikely to last. In a deadlocked Parliament under the present system, the main gainers are likely to be fringe nationalists. Such a Parliament could be important mainly as an opportunity for electoral reform and not as a substitute.

There is an intimate connection between the excessive influence of party militants and the first-past-the-post constituency system. The latter tends to confine realistic choice to two parties; and this gives the party activists a role that they would not have in a free entry, vote-maximising system where political leaders were competing to offer the public the best buy. The role of the mass party is to foist on the country the views, neither of the wisest nor the most numerous, but of those who enjoy devoting their leisure to partisan activity. There have been times in the last fifty years when different people for different reasons have regarded it as imperative to remove the Conservative Party, or a particular Conservative prime minister, from office, but the only way to do so has been to bring in a Labour Government. Conversely, the only way of getting rid of Labour–TUC rule has been to bring back the Tories. In either case a revulsion against a particular government brings in a whole lot of partisan attitudes which it may not have been part of the intention of the voters to support. In a more open political system, where new parties could safely be supported without the risk of letting in the Conservatives or letting in Labour, the vote-maximising parties would have a chance of driving out the ideological ones.

The first-past-the-post system has had some of its worst effects on the main political parties – at the time of writing it has been on the Labour Party, but at other times it could be on the Conservatives. In the post-1974 Labour Government, many ministers did not attempt to justify their policies except on grounds of political necessity. If asked privately about indiscriminate and expensive housing policies, industrial subsidies or price and dividend control, the usual line was that changes of policy would split the Labour movement. In part, their attitude was determined by the desire to keep the TUC sweet for incomes policy; and there were a good many politicians and political observers of varying persuasions who believed that the only coalition that mattered was that between the Government (irrespective of party) and the TUC. If this were true, it would no longer be necessary to write pessimistic articles about the future of democracy, as democracy would be already dead and so, even more important, would be political freedom.

But this was not the only aspect. Ministers were also afraid of splitting the political side of the Labour movement; and both policies and ministerial appointments were often decided with an eye on Labour unity rather than on national unity. The attitude made a sort of weird sense under an unreformed electoral system. For any move that alienated a sizeable group of Labour MPs would have brought the Conservatives in, with no offsetting rewards for Labour moderates. Similarly, any Labour MPs who voted on, say, nationalisation or pay beds according to their private conscience would have risked being disowned by their local parties. But the socialist fundamentalists had just as much reason for dissatisfaction when they saw their leaders neither disavowing nor enacting a full-blooded socialist programme. Any of the widely canvassed electoral reform proposals would have allowed ministers and MPs to speak and vote according to their convictions without losing their seats, so long as they retained the support of a minimal body of voters.

As usual, there is a trade off between different systems. If there are more parties and individuals whom it is not 'a waste of a vote' to support, there will be a greater variety of choice; but election results will make less difference to the composition of governments. For the odds are that most governments will incorporate common elements to obtain a majority. In Germany in the 1960s and 1970s the government has included at least two of the three main parties – Christian Democrats, Social Democrats and Free Democrats – and all three possible combinations have been tried.

The adversary system is of course well entrenched in British and American life, going well beyond politics to the law courts, student debating societies and many other bodies. The threat of elective dictatorship comes not from the adversary system as such but from the extremely centralised form of that system which we have.

The British system is characterised by a fusion of the parliamentary and executive (and even parts of the judicial) leadership in the Cabinet

– which means increasingly the prime minister, the Cabinet secretary and the Number 10 Downing Street entourage. This, in combination with the two-party system and the British obsession with official secrecy and the confidentiality of Civil Service advice, leads to a centralisation unknown in any other major Western democracy. The evil is not that the Prime Minister can do what he likes – on the contrary, the constraints on his freedom of action are even greater than generally recognised – but the absence of competing centres of political patronage and authority. On top of all this is the extreme centralisation of the political conflict in a continuing election campaign. Where a consensus exists, it is hidden by the maximisation of trivial differences, while genuine differences not suitable to two-party conflict are not properly discussed. This matters because the preparation and discussion of policy in the Civil Service, in the press and among the interested public is geared to the political debate.

In the United States these influences are less important because of the greater separation of powers. There are several adversary contests, not one – the congressional as well as the presidential elections, the scrutiny of the Executive by congressional committees, and shifting alignments over issues where partisan loyalties do not predominate as the life of the presidency is not at stake. The presidential election is more clearly a Schumpeterian contest between personalities bidding for support, and less of a vote on issues. Congressmen have independent power bases; and open alliances on issues are possible across party lines without bringing down the government.

Electoral Reform not 'Fair'

Electoral reform is important mainly as a means of reducing the threat of elective dictatorship. There simply happens to be more chance of reforming the voting system than of substituting a series of American-style adversary contests based on the separation of powers. (Devolution of a few powers to subordinate authorities, also likely to be elective dictatorships, is not a serious mitigation of the system.)

But unlike some supporters of electoral reform my case is not that it would be 'fair'; for it is only slightly less unfair that a Commons majority representing (nominally) 51 per cent should impose its will on 49 per cent than that 39 per cent should do so. The justification for raising the threshold of votes necessary for rule to 51 per cent is the pragmatic one that a group standing for possibly 'irreversible' but certainly harmful changes would be unlikely to command a 51 per cent majority, especially if those against it had more than one alternative party for which to vote. A similar consideration could arise at the other end of the spectrum, if there were a move on the right to redistribute income away from the poor (as distinct from the beneficiaries of across-the-board subsidies) or to whip up support for some overseas adventure in the name of patriotism.

A related and vital question is the effect of electoral reform on the whipping up of expectations through competitive vote-bidding. Will a shifting or overlapping balance of parties, with periods of varying coalition rule, reduce the generation of excessive and incompatible expectations? If the leaders of the main parties shared responsibility, it would be difficult to pretend that all national difficulties sprang from the 'other side' being in power and that all would be well if there were a change of government. Those outside the coalition would be more likely to represent fundamentally different policies; and there would be no need for mainstream politicians to denigrate, as they do now, everything that goes on in the country for the half of the time that they are not in power.

The argument that there would be less outbidding under proportional representation is not foolproof. There would be marginal jostling for advantages among coalition partners, or parties trying to gain admission. More important would be the possibility of revolutionary or disruptive groups restarting the outbidding in a major way and exploiting disillusionment against all conventional politicians.

The argument is basically one of time and place. A 51 per cent threshold is no guarantee for a religious or racial minority in a country of sectarian politics such as Ulster. It is the unlimited right of elected governments to impose their wishes, hampered only by fears of physical resistance or a collapse of business confidence, that needs to be undermined. Electoral reform is but one aspect of the necessary attack; and it has to be carefully handled if it is not to be a diversion.

A Constitutional Approach

The stock of reformist ideas has changed little since I wrote *Left or Right*, published in 1968. It is still headed by one or other system of proportional representation (the main contenders being the single-transferable-vote and the additional-members system) and includes the German device of a 'constructive majority' to overturn governments (to reinforce the stability of coalition governments); House of Lords reform to restore the authority of the second chamber; fixed-term Parliaments with provision for emergency dissolution in rare cases; and explicit recognition for, and public accountability of, the Civil Service as a part of the state machine, with a life of its own not accountable to ministers.

The main change is a greater emphasis on some entrenchment of personal rights because of a growing feeling that these cannot simply be left to the good sense of the government majority of the day. A Bill of Rights – which in practice would have to be based on the European Convention – has therefore become a more prominent demand, together with a formal system of administrative law; and there has also been growing support for judicial review of constitutional matters, with a few signs of initiative by the judges in these directions. If we manage to go that far on both political reform and personal rights, we will have the elements of a written constitution; and there will be a good deal to be said for setting it out formally together with the agreed methods of constitutional change.

While the debate has been going on, some conventions have already begun to emerge limiting the absolute freedom of elected governments. The limitation of the House of Lords' veto required two general elections in 1910; and it is safe to predict that a temporary parliamentary majority would not be able to abolish the monarchy simply by invoking the Parliament Act. To take less fanciful examples: the doctrine has gradually emerged in the 1970s that changes such as membership of the EEC or the creation of regional assemblies require both parliamentary approval and the separate support of electors in a referendum. Thus a constitutional reformer has some wind blowing in his direction – which is one more reason for concentrating on this area rather than on the problem of collective acquisitiveness. The best way of tackling seemingly intractable problems is often to concentrate on more tractable ones rather than to go in for remedies born of desperation which might make matters worse.

A constitutional approach is a way of thinking that goes beyond those matters suitable for formal entrenchment. The emphasis needs to be placed not on any specific proposal or reform but on the principles (a) that voters – and MPs – need a wider range of choice than they are given by the two-party first-past-the-post system and (b) that some protection is needed of citizens' rights even against democratically elected governments. The current model of elective dictatorship needs to give way to the principle of more general consent. Majority rule is no longer, if it ever was, a sufficient guarantee of a tolerably stable, let alone free or efficient, society.

References

Buchanan, J. M., *The Limits of Liberty* (University of Chicago Press, 1975).

Buchanan, J., and Tullock, G., *The Calculus of Consent* (University of Michigan Press, Ann Arbor, 1962).

Hailsham, Lord, 'Elective Dictatorship', the Richard Dimbleby Lecture, *The Listener* (21 October 1976).

Hirsch, F., *Social Limits to Growth* (Routledge, 1975).

Rogaly, J., *Parliament for the People* (Maurice Temple Smith, 1976).

Scarman, Leslie, *English Law – the New Dimension* (Stevens, 1975).

Zweig, F., *The New Acquisitive Society* (Barry Rose, Chichester and London, 1976).

Index